ATTITUDE!

ALSO BY KATHARINE DAVIS FISHMAN

Behind the One-Way Mirror: Psychotherapy and Children
The Computer Establishment

ATTITUDE!

Eight Young Dancers
Come of Age at
The Ailey School

KATHARINE DAVIS FISHMAN

JEREMY P. TARCHER/PENGUIN

a member of Penguin Group (USA) Inc.

New York

Most Tarcher/Penguin books are available at special quantity discounts for bulk purchase for sales promotions, premiums, fundraising, and educational needs. Special books or book excerpts also can be created to fit specific needs. For details, write Penguin Group (USA) Inc. Special Markets, 375 Hudson Street, New York, NY 10014.

Jeremy P. Tarcher/Penguin
a member of
Penguin Group (USA) Inc.
375 Hudson Street
New York, NY 10014
www.penguin.com

Library of Congress Cataloging-in-Publication Data

Fishman, Katharine Davis.
Attitude!: eight young dancers come of age at The Ailey School
/ Katharine Davis Fishman.
p.   cm.
Includes bibliographical references and index.
ISBN 1-58542-355-6
1. Ailey School (New York, N.Y.)   2. Modern dance—Study
and teaching—New York (State)—New York.   3. Dancers—
New York (State)—New York.   I. Title.
GV1786.A35F57   2004   2004049847
792.8'09747'1—dc22

Printed in the United States of America
1   3   5   7   9   10   8   6   4   2

This book is printed on acid-free paper. ♾

BOOK DESIGN BY AMANDA DEWEY

For Amos and Vera

Contents

Introduction

Talent has always intrigued me. When I was a child, I had a friend named Genie who was a violinist: she was never available for playdates on ordinary afternoons, and twice a year my family and I would troop over to the Mannes School, one of New York's prime musical institutions, to see her onstage in a pink ruffled dress, playing a precious antique instrument donated by a famous performer. I grew up in New York in the area that became Lincoln Center, and there were artists everywhere: actors in my apartment building, singers down the block, painters and writers in duplex studios across the street. For much of my life, my neighbors have been people who came to the city—from the Far West, the Deep South, or the outer boroughs—to test their talent and get away from being different where they grew up.

Living here, I absorbed the New Yorker's respect for those who are different and have the courage to exploit that eccentricity in positive ways. And over the years I came to wonder exactly how talent reveals itself, and what is necessary to keep it alive. Is talent something that must be grabbed in early childhood, as my friend and her parents had done, for fear of losing it forever? Did different kinds of talent develop in different ways?

As an adult, I wrote magazine articles about education and a book about child psychology and eventually developed a professional interest in how talent emerges. I set out to learn what happens to children who choose—or have someone else choose for them—to build their lives around their talent. The conventional assumption is that these children sacrifice the pleasures of "normal" childhood and adolescence and are given over to the supervision of merciless, knuckle-rapping maestros.

I started my quest by reading about child prodigies, the most sensational type of talented people, but quickly discovered that prodigies don't often stick to their original bent. The more I learned about these young children with adult-sized talents, the less they seemed to tell me about the "normally" talented people in whom I was most interested: people whose skill and enthusiasm began to gather steam just before adolescence, until at some point shortly after they made a more mature—though still early—decision to invest their whole selves in one domain.

Then, as I was mulling over the sacrifices demanded by talent, events in the news brought in the idea that these days the standard teenage life of hanging out and mall-shopping was not necessarily an easier path. The school shootings at Columbine touched off what seemed like an epidemic of youth crime in hitherto placid settings. Magazines and newspapers began to run articles on the sociology of high school lunchrooms. Both the in-groups and the out-groups seemed directionless and cruel. And teenage society appeared especially rough on kids who were "different"—in anything from their clothes to their music to the way they spent their afternoons, evenings, and weekends. In this situation, how could a young artist wrapped up for hours in practice and rehearsal make friends, let alone keep them?

Around this time, as a writer who had expressed interest in talented teenagers, I was invited to a concert of classical music at the Professional Children's School, a private middle and high school for performers and athletes in New York City. The performance was sophisticated and ardent. To make music on this level, you had to give your youth to it—as had my friend Genie, who was, in fact, a PCS alumna. One performer, a countertenor—a male soprano—was, of all things, president of the student council. I talked to him at the post-concert reception, and he turned out to be just like every student council president I'd ever met, from the big wheels of my own high school days to the achievers trotted out for me when I was writing articles on education—relentlessly upbeat, outgoing, handshaking, room-working, vote-getting—except he happened to sing soprano. What was this environment in which a male soprano was considered not just acceptable but cool, and where—in between mastering measures of Rameau—he could polish his networking skills, rise through the political ranks, and become a student leader? Here was a kid who was different, and seemed to revel in it. So, apparently, did his classmates.

I began to make calls, and eventually arrived at the doorstep of The Ailey School, on Amsterdam Avenue and Alvin Ailey Place—actually Sixty-first Street, just south of Lincoln Center.

This is the official school of the Alvin Ailey American Dance Theater, arguably the most distinguished modern dance company in the world. Although the school does not feed directly into the First Company (as Ailey people call it), twenty-six of the thirty-one dancers in the company have spent at least some time studying there.

I did not come to Ailey as either a dancer *manquée* or an addicted spectator. As a child, I had been sent to classes in modern dance, but for me this was meant to be a remedial measure: my mother had hoped that a few years of skipping around with an elderly, tunic-clad disciple of Isadora Duncan would help my coordination and teach me left from right. No such luck. And while—over the years as a New Yorker—I had sometimes enjoyed watching dancers perform, it was the atmosphere of The Ailey School, and what I thought I might learn there about talent as a governing principle in life, that drew me in.

While musicians spend much of their time practicing alone, dancers have to come together daily with their peers, and those at Ailey, I saw, formed a community that began with five-year-olds and made a pyramid at whose summit was Judith Jamison. This was the company's artistic director, who no longer performs but has made an enviable life in dance. Everyone along that pyramid had once been where today's teenage dancers were now. Young students could see their progress colorfully displayed: for girls, pale pink leotards at Level I, white at Level II, light blue at Level III, navy at Level IV, maroon at Level V, lavender at Level VI, and black at Level VII and for the older female students. The boys were fixed eternally in white T-shirts and black tights: illustrating one unfortunate feature of the classical dance world (though, to be fair, less a characteristic of Ailey and other modern dance companies), they derive visual status only from the reflected glory of their female classmates.

I began to visit Ailey more often and at last decided to spend a year there, following a particular group of teenage students. I hoped to see, up close, the texture of the life they had chosen. I asked the school to introduce me to a diverse group of advanced high school students whose talent appeared promising, who weren't shy, and who had families who were likely to cooperate with me in interviews. Between September 2001 and June 2002, I went to Ailey two or three times a week, sat in on classes, and talked with students, faculty, and parents. This book is the result of that year.

I came in with a number of questions about the lives of teenagers in the dance world, and not surprisingly, more occurred as time went on. I wanted to see how these kids were both like and unlike "ordinary" kids. Would the Ailey environment affect individuals differently according to their temperament and background?

What makes a talented dancer, I wondered? What is physical, what is intellectual, and what is emotional, and is there a particular style of acquiring knowledge in this field? How—and how early—does dance talent show itself? How does an expert pick it up? Were the Ailey teachers, for example, capable of predicting which of the students I watched were likely to succeed?

I wanted to learn more about the role families play, both genetically and in terms of nurturing talent. What sacrifices did those families make to encourage their child's dancing career?

At a time when teenagers' bodies are changing and their self-confidence is low, these kids live in a world in which the nature—as well as the look—of the body governs the dancer's success. They face frequent injury and must make mature decisions about when to dance through it, when to sit it out, and when to seek treatment. Are they ground down by the tyranny of their bodies, I wondered? How do they spend eighteen and more hours a week dancing at Ailey and working for their scholarships while getting their schoolwork done and fitting in some sleep?

Finally, I was curious about how a life in dance—and indeed, deciding to be a dancer—differs for boys and girls. And how do these particular teenagers, who would be sensitive to adult scrutiny under ordinary circumstances, deal with being constantly corrected, evaluated, and rejected? Almost immediately, I was drawn to a word recurrent in the Ailey lexicon, a word with two specific meanings and multiple shades of meaning:

Attitude!

First, "attitude" is a ballet term that goes back several hundred years and is used in modern dance as well: in the dictionary definition, "One leg is bent either behind the dancer or in front. . . . The supporting leg is either bent or straight." A lovely *ah-titude,* requests Tatiana Litvinova, the school's Russian ballerina, of her students; "*Attitude, Attitude!*" shouts a modern choreographer as part of a difficult combination. But "attitude" also comes up fairly often in the sense we know better, as something you need a little bit of to survive but had better not have too much of to succeed. Very often among teenagers at The Ailey School, the attitude required titrating.

I began to focus on the eight students you will get to know in these pages: Brian Brown, Beatrice Capote, Afra Hines, Laurence Jacques, Travis Magee, Monique Massiah, Frajan Payne, and Shamel Pitts. During the year I met and talked with other students and many teachers—and they, too, appear in the story. I also visited some of the students' schools and homes. It was reassuring to discover that neither faculty nor students nor staff nor performers (except Jamison herself) seemed to have been prepped for me: I had to explain repeatedly who I was and what I was doing.

Indeed, in the several decades I have worked as a reporter, no institution has ever afforded me such freedom to roam the halls on my own and learn what I could. Cynic that I am, I suspect that some of this benign neglect was inadvertent, but it also seemed true that the Ailey people were proud of their school and curious what an outsider would make of it.

After my first few visits to Ailey, I began to read more about ballet instruction, which was given at every level in this modern-dance company's training school. It seemed that while there are three major ballet techniques—the French, the Russian, and the Italian—ballet classes have, overall, been more or less the same for two hundred years. As I watched these wholly contemporary teenagers, their Jansport backpacks piled in the corner, immersed day after day in a regime that would not seem strange to a seventeenth-century Frenchman, I wondered what keeps them doing it. Are there benefits we haven't thought of? Is there something this guild offers its apprentices that might be imported into the outside world?

PART ONE

SUMMER/EARLY FALL

One

The Ailey World

At ten minutes of ten on this first Saturday in August 2001, the front hall at The Ailey School is totally quiet, though not uninhabited. A few teenage girls wearing large numbers on their leotards walk silently in and out of the studios that abut the hall, talking to parents who wait outside. Inside Studio 3, some fifty more numbered teenage girls are stretching on the floor and at the barre, whispering to one another, sipping from water bottles, or sitting cross-legged beside their backpacks, meditating. Aside from their undisputable trimness, they vary in size and shape; their hair is short or pinned up in some sort of bun and occasionally cornrowed. About two-thirds appear African-American; the rest are everything else.

No one smiles. Though the heat hasn't quite kicked in yet, it is going to be a scorcher—one of those heavy, humid dog days that mark late summer in New York—and none of these studios is air-conditioned.

After twenty minutes, four godlike individuals glide in and the dancers come to attention. The apparent *première danseuse* steps forward, a tall glamorous-looking African-American woman in her middle fifties with long, curly, reddish hair, dressed for the weather in a sleeveless black blouse, white bermuda shorts, and flat sandals with big flowers on the toes. "We welcome you," she says. "I am Miss Jefferson, and the panelists here are Miss Person, Mr. Inman, and Mr. Benjamin. Our fellowship is the smallest and most selective for students, aged fifteen to twenty-one, with a lot of potential to be professional dancers—who pick up steps, who are strong and intelligent, and who work well in a group. All students work two or three hours a week in exchange for their fellowships. High school students' classes will begin on September 10. Be sure to leave the studio neat and clean."

Exit Miss Jefferson.

Miss Person divides the auditioners, all girls, by age—high school or beyond—and ushers the younger ones into the next studio where a Mr. Powell is warming up two self-assured dancers from Ailey II, the farm team that marks the next step on the ladder toward the First Company. Not much older than the auditioners, they are on a cloud just above them, getting paid today to demonstrate combinations.

While the Ailey is a modern company, it considers ballet the core of strong technique. The students at its official school will acquire proficiency in three different styles of modern dance as they move up, but ballet will be with them always. Thus fellowship auditions begin with a series of ever more challenging ballet combinations. The panel deliberates, the chaff is winnowed out, and the wheat, so to speak, tries its skill at another series of combinations in Horton, the company's primary modern technique, in which many first-time auditioners have no experience whatsoever.

A pianist is playing pretty, romantic old-fashioned music. French commands ring out: *plié, piqué, pas de bourrée, assemblé, entrechat!* Every opportunity is given: the demonstrators show the combinations twice, Person leads each small group of auditioners in practice a couple of times, and then it counts. "Ladies," Jefferson says at one point to the candidates, "we know you're nervous, but maybe you could relax and breathe a little. Demonstrators, do it again for a little more reassurance."

The auditioners range from elegant and confident to clunky, clueless, and progressively out of their depth. Occasionally, a good dancer stumbles, and one bursts into tears. It seems there are two classes of auditioners here: returning students—looked upon as Ailey family members—and newcomers, who may be decently trained or barely trained. Finally, all of them are asked to come forward and a sort of police lineup takes place: dancers standing awkward and still, panelists matching number to performance. And then the dancers are sent outside, and the panel is alone.

The girls they have taught before are the ones the panelists talk about. "This one is going through the motions," says one teacher. "She focuses, then it goes away," says another. "She doesn't appreciate what we're giving her." The teachers are offering different takes on each student: "This one is resistant at times." "She doesn't understand the techniques that well." "She is good, but complacent. Put the fear of God in her!" "It's almost like she has a complex about her breasts." "She's introverted, she has beautiful lines, she's serious, but there's no fire!"

"She doesn't work up to her capacity." "I agree, but I've seen her grow. I think she has more length of line than at the last class. Tell her, 'You did so well at the last audition—that's what we want to see.'"

All the talk before voting concerns the family members and how they are working in class, and that is the crucial factor that will govern whether or not their fellowships are renewed. If they have come this far, they are considered to have talent. For them, the audition itself, whether they happen to dance beautifully or mess up on this particular morning (though it injects a liberal dose of that "fear of God") might as well not exist, except as a sort of memory jog for the faculty. There is no preset number of dancers who will win fellowships; in this trial they are competing with themselves more than with one another.

Newcomers cannot be overweight. After that, the panelists look for good coordination, flexibility in the feet and legs, and the ability (or possibility) of the feet and legs to turn out from the hips. The dancers are given combinations that reveal how well endowed they are with these desirable qualities now, and how much, if at all, hard work might improve on nature. The clunky and clueless will of course be weeded out immediately after the ballet portion. The panel scores the dancers in points and half-points, and it is noteworthy to mention, at voting time, that the members agree almost perfectly on the newcomers without exchanging a word.

The no's look sad. "Take your ballet, take your modern, I would encourage you to study more," Jefferson tells them.

Mr. Powell, a recently retired Ailey star who is now the resident choreographer for Ailey II, leads the remaining auditioners in a similar series of Horton exercises accompanied by a drummer. "Really take your time, then explode!" he instructs them, and after the Horton section the dancers file out and the panel makes the final selection. "Out of the ones we rejected," Jefferson asks the panelists, "is there anyone to encourage?" The panel members come up with three borderline cases.

The outright rejects are the first to be summoned back and told the bad news: they pick up their water bottles and backpacks and go home. Next the borderlines are brought in. "You were close but didn't make the cut," Jefferson says. Their mouths are set and they tremble a bit. One is a family member, who, because the panel was unenthusiastic about her work over the past year, is asked to come back as a paying student. Another is a newcomer who was half a point off: "We hope you'll enroll as a paying student, get strong, and audition again in October," Jefferson tells her. She has never taken modern, the girl says.

By the afternoon, when the boys have their turn, it's so humid that even the spectators are dripping wet. Jefferson's speech is generally the same, but she talks more about discipline and the skills the students will acquire in working for their fellowships: office work, computers, finance. The school seeks dancers who have, as Jefferson puts it, "strong professional potential in concert dance or on Broadway, who are respectful of one another and the art form and the space. Our community," she says, "is a small, close one."

There are only six boys in the high school group, all family members, and the panel loves them all. In the Horton series they audition with the older boys, and Powell has them demonstrate for the senior group, which includes newcomers . There is more jumping in the boys' combinations than there was in the girls'. The drummer works furiously and the room is full of swirling boys. Some of the newcomers get it; some don't. "I want to see the sweat!" shouts Powell. "I want to see your numbers fall off! Each and every one of you has a heart and a spirit. That's what we're here for!" Nobody, of course, is perfect. To one family member he says, "Don't rush! You got a date?" The boy fights back tears.

The panel's discussion about the boys is not unlike that regarding the girls, but has its own character. "What a group!" says Jefferson about the high school boys. "They're so gifted!" The older boys have more problems. "How can we get this boy to stretch?" asks Jefferson. "I never met a person who couldn't stretch!" This boy needs to lose weight. That boy needs to gain weight. And then there is a newcomer in a very feminine-looking unitard, with a headband and a red shirt. "He's talented. Nobody knows him; maybe someone should talk to him. If we don't say something, he won't know," Jefferson points out. Won't know what? The panelists have worked together judging these auditions for so many years that they talk in oral shorthand. An observer, who hasn't yet learned to grasp the nuances of their communication, asks what the problem is. Powell and Inman are frankly gay. "He's too out there," Powell says. "If one of them gets here and starts, the others think it's okay. It gets around that the Ailey boys are really flamboyant."

Mr. Inman, the new codirector of the school's Junior Division, is elected to do the job. The boy is called in alone. "You are eighteen," says Inman. "This is going to be an issue when you go out to look for jobs. Take into consideration how you go into an audition. Your headband looked kind of feminine. We're not trying to tell you about your personal life, but don't bring it in here.

There are many talented male dancers, but not enough who look strong." Jefferson adds, "Think of moving with more power and weight in addition to your lovely lines. Come to open classes."

There are two levels of fellowships available to most Ailey high school students: a level II, in which they must pay $270 of the $2,000 tuition for the term and must work three hours a week; and a level I, in which they pay $185 and work two hours a week; in addition, everyone pays a $50 registration fee. By unanimous vote, the beloved high school boys are awarded the lesser fellowship. "Make them work for it!" Powell says. "A Level I has to be earned!"

When the successful dancers are called in, Jefferson's speech is rather tougher than her speech to the girls. "We're a very traditional school," she says. "We have a clear dress code: no shorts, no bandannas, no braids in the hair. Attendance is important. You conduct yourselves at the highest level, because you represent us and *Miss Jamison*."

In a day's nutshell, these are the values of The Ailey School— a guild of master craftsmen who are such spiritual kinfolk that they talk to one another—and their apprentices—in shorthand. The rules are clear: the faculty's first names are almost a diplomatic secret, and no women teachers are addressed, in the contemporary idiom, as "Ms." (The etiquette, as Jefferson had told me when we met, is that of the European dance culture.) It is professional, it is highly visual, it is tough and demanding but not without compassion, and it is just a tad quaint.

Two photographs of Alvin Ailey in middle age—beard, muscular shoulders, air of command—look down on the anteroom in the office suite where callers wait to see Ailey administrators; in one photo he is posed right behind his designated successor, the dancer Judith Jamison, who appears equally commanding, her head turned away in profile. They are icons, their separate images presumably joined at some central spot beneath the picture plane, he looking out, she looking sideways in her own direction. Below the pictures the atmosphere is bustling and informal, and just about everybody who enters and leaves this room, carrying bags of lunch or papers for the copier, hugging friends hello and good-bye, looks to have done an enormous number of *relevés* at some time in life.

The Administrative Office is the air-conditioned section of Ailey. Outside, where the studios are, it gets, in summer and early fall, quite steamy. A sign in the corridor reads AILEY STUDENTS: PLEASE, NO STRETCHING IN FRONT OF THE ADMINISTRATIVE OFFICE AND BEYOND STUDIO 1 ON THE LEFT. Out in the corridor the dancers are draped over every surface—benches, floor, desk, one another—swigging water, spooning Chinese chicken out of foil pans, reading magazines, doing homework, snoozing, gossiping, and peering into the studios. On any given day, a visitor looking into Studio 1 might see rows of navy blue leotards bobbing up and down to precise piano music; in Studio 2, an equally precise drumbeat keeping the count while a floorful of black leotards is improbably perched on their coccyx, arms and legs stretched forward by an invisible lasso; in Studio 3, a small group of maroon leotards huddling to work out a combination; and in Studio 4, a thundering horde in batik, leaping across the room to insistent bongos. At twilight on midweek evenings and on Saturday mornings, when the younger students take class, scampering small brothers and sisters and harried-looking mothers and fathers mingle with the dancers in the corridor.

Ailey culture is a distinctive hybrid of the European and American, ballet and modern, traditional and contemporary dance worlds. This blending pervades the organization from the first company down to the three-year-olds.

The most familiar dancing school to laypeople—that is, the prototype of the one seen in films and read about in books for the past forty-odd years—is the European-style ballet academy like the School of American Ballet (familiarly known as SAB), which feeds directly into the New York City Ballet. Students enter through competitive audition at age eight and pursue an eight-year training regime which, if they are lucky, leads them right into the corps de ballet. If they are even luckier, they will then move up to become soloists and finally principals. With less good fortune they may be weeded out at any year during their training. Many SAB students also go to the Professional Children's School. They hope to (and are encouraged to) start professional dance careers immediately after high school.

Ailey's way of weeding out students is gentler than that of the SAB prototype. Since Alvin Ailey's most famous dictum was "Dance is for everybody," the audition is supposed to determine placement—a necessity for children who grow at different rates—rather than acceptance or admission. Among students fifteen and over, the semiannual audition is also used to award fellowships. At Level II—the white leotards, who are aged eight through eleven—a tracking system begins, whereby Level II A takes three classes a week and Level II B (plus several coeval tracks below that as the school has grown) takes only two. At every level the time commitment is raised, and when students reach the age of twelve, the A track is required to take seven classes a week. Level IV students must be pretty serious. Dance has begun to take priority status next to—and with some children, over—academic work. At this level a student's parents are willing to put in the time to support their child psychologically, logistically, and financially. Students who aren't serious actually begin dropping out when they're ten or eleven.

The Alvin Ailey American Dance Theater is structured like a modern dance company, and thus a bit more democratic than ballet companies. At least in theory, dancers in a modern company are equal, though of course some are more equal than others because of their technical prowess and stage charisma. Stratification, which is important in the school's preprofessional programs, vanishes in Ailey II. Ailey students go to a variety of high schools, but most attend public conservatory schools: Professional Performing Arts School (an academic high school with a dance-major program run by Ailey in Ailey's studios) and Fiorello H. LaGuardia High School of Music and Art and Performing Arts (which has its own dance department) account for most of them. Others attend private and public schools around the city and in the suburbs. Lately, Ailey students have tended to go to college or a conservatory before becoming full-time professionals, and then—depending on what happens in their lives over the next four years—they may come back and audition for the Ailey company. They have been told by their families and by some faculty members, including Denise Jefferson herself, that it would be wise for them to prepare for more than one career.

It is not news that dancers don't make much money, and the students know it. Those who aspire to professional careers assume there are other compensations, which they hear about when they spend time with company members. Company salaries for performers are pegged to length of service. The national contracts administrator at the American Guild of Musical Artists, which signed a new three-year contract with the Alvin Ailey American Dance Theater in June 2002, calls Ailey, which is one of the few companies to guarantee its members a job for fifty weeks out of the year plus a week of paid vacation, "among the best in a difficult field." In 2002 a new dancer in the First Company made $675 a week and a seventh-year dancer $1,000, and a twenty-first-year dancer—presumably the legendary Renee Robinson—made $1,475 a week. Every dancer (as well as the stage managers and production assistants, who are also covered by the union contract) was scheduled to get a raise in 2003 and 2004.

It's important to remember that modern dance began in the early twentieth century as a rebellion against ballet. While the Ailey company, at age forty-five, is by now part of the dance establishment itself, some of that old rebellious spirit remains. It was evident, for example, one day when the choreographer Kevin Wynn, demonstrating a combination at his student workshop, shouted, "I want your weight *down*! I want your pelvis *down*! If you do it *up,* this way, you should be in pink tights!" And on a spring day in 2002, a year later, the boys' ballet class heard it straight from the instructor Franco De Vita (of all people)—born in Italy, raised in Belgium, and steeped in the classical tradition. He called for two double pirouettes from his agile young gentlemen, explaining in a heavy French accent, "At the New York City Ballet the *girls* pirouette. *We are The Ailey School!*"

When Ailey and the modern dancer Pearl Lang founded the school in 1970, they made ballet the connective tissue in the curriculum. This approach has continued into the present day: after all, both Jefferson (who teaches Graham) and Jamison herself had begun their training with ballet. Students learn one modern technique at a time, and may also be taking jazz, West African, or flamenco, but they are in ballet class every day they're at Ailey. At the same time, when the school participates in the gala benefit for big donors that it has in the spring, it is a modern piece the students will dance. When high school seniors enter the prestigious Arts Recognition and Talent Search competition, it is almost always in the modern dance category.

There is, of course, a certain irony here, a sense of the pendulum swinging. The founders of modern dance in America— Isadora Duncan, Ruth St. Denis, and Ted Shawn—sought to free dancers from the strict postures and fairy-tale plots of European classical ballet. But lately, American audiences have again become smitten with the ballet aesthetic. As the ballet instructor Robert Atwood observes (with a certain competitive pleasure), they are "more interested in seeing people who stretch their legs, point their feet, jump high, and have the ability to turn. They find that more exciting. And the only way you get to do that is by learning the physiologic principles and body uses that are taught in ballet."

The Ailey organization is an institution carrying on after the death of its founder (Ailey died in 1989), and periodically it is criticized from within or without for veering into slickness or identity politics. Ailey people may point out—as do most heirs— that no one knows how the founder's ideas would have evolved had he lived. But the question of what-did-Ailey-mean-and-how-has-Jamison-changed-it? is complicated by the fact that Ailey himself was far more eclectic than people seem to remember. The center of the Ailey repertory—both Ailey's masterpiece

and the company's ubiquitous crowd-pleaser—is *Revelations,* a dis-
tillation of the choreographer's childhood experiences in black
churches in Texas, built around a series of spirituals. But as Jamison observed to me, "Alvin was always talking about his 'blood
memories,' but he also created ballets that had nothing to do with
his blood memories." Unlike Martha Graham and other company directors, Ailey felt a charge to develop new choreographers: ballets by Louis Falco and Ulysses Dove, for example,
signed up long ago by Ailey himself, were in the repertory for
the 2001 season, and Jamison herself has continued Alvin Ailey's
tradition, commissioning work by Ronald K. Brown, Dwight
Rhoden, Jawole Willa Jo Zollar, and Ailey's old friend Carmen
de Lavallade.

Jamison is an imposing, authoritative woman, with hair dramatically caught up in a crown of many thin silver braids. Her idiom is down-home, but acquaintances had better not presume.
Much of today's repertory, she says, describing the choreography
that has emerged during her regime, reflects the dancers of today: the challenges they give their bodies are very different from
those that performers took on when she herself was onstage.

Jamison's middle-class upbringing included a reverence for
the arts. Although the school predates her regime, its atmosphere
seems to evoke that of the first dance classes she attended in
Philadelphia, which she describes in her autobiography:

> "In Marion's classes you behaved and you acknowledged
> the fact that you were in a 'holy' place. When you came
> into her studio you knew you were there to work and you
> came in wanting knowledge; you came in there wanting
> to be a sponge. You did not 'mess around'; you did not

drape your belongings across the barre. You entered ready to dance and you danced every class as if it were a performance. You danced to an imaginary audience."

The Ailey School seeks to produce dancers of professional caliber, versatility, and broad technical skills, who look, in Denise Jefferson's words, "like racehorses." Its curriculum is designed to meet the company's needs: Jamison likes to say she hires performers who "have practiced their scales and know how to play their Strads." As prospective teenage applicants are often told, this is neither a recreational sport nor a course in art appreciation. On the other hand, the First Company takes only a couple of dancers every year—in 2002, it hired one college-age dancer straight out of the school's Professional Division—and so the average high school student's prospects of ultimately dancing with Ailey are not, in actuarial terms, highly favorable. But that year's Ailey graduates found jobs in twenty other companies, including troupes as varied as Cirque du Soleil, Martha Graham, Philadanco, and the Toronto cast of *The Lion King.*

The jagged energy, athleticism, and tricky balancing that mark an Ailey performance mostly reflect the technique of Lester Horton, the late California-based dance choreographer whom Alvin Ailey called the greatest influence in his career; Horton also shaped the careers of the dancers Carmen de Lavallade, Joyce Trisler, and Bella Lewitzky. Horton exercises work toward strengthening the body and exploring the range of movement, and look nothing like ballet exercises. A basic Horton warm-up, more or less similar at every level, as laid out in a book written by Ailey instructor Ana Marie Forsythe and two collaborators, would include, for example, "flat backs," in which the dancers stand with feet parallel, the torso tilted forward at a ninety-degree angle, the arms extended vertically upward with palms facing each other; and "primitive squats," in which the feet are parallel, the torso erect, both knees fully bent and aligned over the toes, the heels flat on the floor, the buttocks as close to the floor as possible, and the arms stretched horizontally forward, palms facing each other. A characteristic arm position is called "opened Egyptian" and resembles what you might see on a tomb frieze, with the arms raised to the side, elbows at shoulder level, and forearms at a ninety-degree angle, palms facing each other. But the most dramatic-looking position of all is the coccyx balance, which is just that.

Horton classes work to give the "racehorses" long, flexible backs and hamstrings and a sophisticated sense of dynamics bred by varied musical accompaniment. Dancers say Horton technique feels good; to the lay observer, it looks devastating. It reflects an aesthetic as rigorous as ballet but less contained and formal, and young dancers trained in it may thus see the world, and the way one moves through it, rather differently from those whose apprenticeship was based on ballet alone. Ballet and Horton represent, one might say, two different states of mind.

Modern dance at Ailey follows a sequence based on what the school feels is the difficulty of the technique for still developing bodies and minds: thus the students start with Horton, move up to José Limón when they are thirteen to fifteen, and begin Graham at Level VI, for ages fourteen to sixteen (the ages at each level overlap one another, because individual students mature at different rates). The basic Graham movements involve contraction and release of the pelvis and a spiraling of the torso, with a lot of movement based on the floor. The themes of Graham dances tend to be mythical or psychological, and thus, some instructors believe, are rather complex for dancers to comprehend until they have had some worldly experience. Beyond that, there is considerable variety in the spirit of the technique, because Martha Graham lived well into her nineties and the approach an instructor brings to it has much to do with the time when the instructor danced with Martha.

At increasingly sophisticated levels in the curriculum, Ailey students study West African dance—that is, dances that come from Senegal, Ghana, Guinea, Dahomey, Nigeria, the Ivory Coast, and Mali. All African dance is regional, but the different versions have certain common characteristics: for the spectator accustomed to ballet and modern dance, it looks devilishly complex. It is polyrhythmic and polycentric: that is, instruments play several different rhythms at once to accompany the movements of different parts of the dancer's body, so the hands move to one rhythm, the torso to another, and the feet to a third. The jumps, falls, and runs are precisely choreographed, but they are passed along as part of an oral narrative tradition, and because each dancer is considered a conduit for the divine creator, there are no Balanchines or Grahams taking credit for the choreography.

Preschool children at Ailey get West African as a balance to ballet, to release the energy they have controlled for the previous hour: a familiar Saturday morning sight is a bevy of tiny girls in leotards and lappa skirts (short, colorfully printed sarongs that most laypeople know by the Pacific term, "lavalava"). At the higher levels, African dance broadens the dancers' range, showing them, for example, higher jumps, undulating movement, and deeper *pliés.* There are, of course, African movements in the Ailey company's repertory and those of modern choreographers.

Finally, there is a substantial jazz dance department at Ailey, and jazz is important in both the company repertory and the repertory workshops that prepare students for school performances. Jazz is the only technique that is taught to recorded, not live, accompaniment, but a spectator at a jazz class will not hear Miles Davis. Jazz dance is pegged to the social dance of every era, and looks like what you see on Broadway and television; of all the techniques it is the one that most reflects popular culture, and as the jazz instructor Sharon Wong points out, "These dances evolve from the political climate."

This was the curriculum, by now familiar, that awaited the advanced students due to report back to The Ailey School during the second week of September 2001. None of these students was new to the school, and as the month began they were quite ready to get back to the customary routines that would move them further along toward the professional caliber of performance they hoped they would soon achieve. But this year, school did not begin in the customary way.

On the second day of the school year, Steven Brown got to work at 8:30 in the morning. Brown is the first official face an outsider sees after climbing three flights of stairs (or if less fit, stepping off the elevator) to the Ailey studios. He is a stocky, fairly dark-skinned man in his middle forties with glasses and hair in short braids. A graduate of The Ailey School's Certificate Program (which has a two- to three-year conservatory syllabus for students of college age and just beyond), he still performs with a small modern company, and has college training in music and graphics; his Ailey job, of nine years' standing, helps support a full life in the arts. One way or another, his story is fairly typical for Ailey staff.

Brown sits in what is called the money booth, a windowed room from which tickets are dispensed, information is dispersed, and class fees are accepted. His first duty is to get everything ready for the nine-o'clock classes, making sure the teachers' roll books are ready and directing students who are taking open classes to the proper studios.

Sometimes Brown turns on the radio when he's opening up, and he did that day. A few faculty and staff members were in the offices by then and heard the announcement and subsequent bulletins on their radios, describing the terrorist attacks on the World Trade Center and the Pentagon. They soon gathered to decide what to do.

The Ailey School had an enrollment of 1,000 students for the year 2001–2002. But the Junior Division, composed of elementary and high school students, which will be our focus here, accounted for just over half that enrollment. The other half of the school, aged 18 to 23, embraced the Professional Division, which offered classes to even more advanced students from all over the world: it included the Certificate Program from which Brown had graduated, a less intense Independent Study Program, and a new BFA Program set up in collaboration with Fordham University, which would graduate its first class that year. There were also a few smaller collaborative programs outside the Professional Division, including the high school group from Professional Performing Arts School.

The Junior Division students—except one boy who will be part of our story—all lived at home with their families in New

York City, many in the outer boroughs or in the suburbs. The immediate worry of Denise Jefferson, who presided over all the school's programs, was more for the Professional Division with its roster of 234 students from all over the country and the world. The Ailey School stood in loco parentis for these students, and thus Jefferson kept it open, with classes cancelled and a small complement of faculty and staff on the scene, through mid-afternoon, to help these students reach their families. Brown called his, in Atlanta.

The year began with a cataclysm, and it is surely necessary, before continuing with our story, to discuss what apparent effects that cataclysm had on The Ailey School in the months that followed. In practical terms, the school lost more than a week of classes and two weeks of rehearsal time for an upcoming performance, and didn't quite settle down until early October. It had made a ragged start in the first days after the attack with a few Manhattan students in attendance, but the following week— because the extent of the immediate threat to New York was still uncertain—Jefferson simply closed the school down. While classes resumed the week after that, confusion over subway and train routes, and the fears of some parents about letting their children travel, gave the first month of school the same tentative air that existed throughout the city.

In spirit, the school, in its own style, was no different from the rest of New York. Among the young adults, in particular, there was what Linda Hamilton, the school psychologist (who, at Jefferson's request, gave two special workshops), described later as "a crisis in meaning." What these older students kept asking was variations of the question, "How can I be concentrating on steps in class when the world is in this situation?" For most of the students this lasted about a month, reflecting the general state of mind around them. Then things seemed to quiet down. At Jefferson's suggestion Steven Brown set up a bulletin board on which he posted useful and inspiring articles that people sent him; even at the end of the year he continued to receive submissions.

The teenagers, as far as I could see, seemed ready to get back to work even sooner. Perhaps the tendency of adolescents to focus on their own problems saved them from the posttraumatic stress disorder and agoraphobia which, according to one local study, had gripped many younger children in the New York public schools.[1] Perhaps the older students were showing the stoicism that dancers and other performers are always encouraged to display, concealing their personal emotions unless there is a way to put them to use artistically. One day during the winter, when I was watching a Graham class at LaGuardia High School, where some of the students were enrolled, the accompanist came up to me later to say that he was sure the kids were "more muted" this year. But I could not see it. Whether they will develop into a "post 9/11 generation" that is marked by some particular characteristics will take, most probably, another decade for us to discover. Meanwhile, like all New Yorkers and with that particular urgency that comes from focusing on a goal, they wanted to get back to their version of a normal life.

PART TWO

FALL

Two

Starting the Year

E ven in ordinary years The Ailey School, mini-empire that it is, does not have an official first day on which all one thousand of its students troop in. Rather, they dribble in according to their class levels over a period of ten days. To an outside observer, therefore, the first day of school, at least for this advanced group, looks no different from any other day: this afternoon in September might just as well be November 15.

At 1:30 the dance majors from Professional Performing Arts School, finished for the day with history and math, pile into a bus that deposits them at the Ailey studio. PPAS, in an old building on West Forty-eighth Street in the theater district, provides the academic classes for a group of students who then pursue majors at several New York City performing arts institutions, one of them The Ailey School. They take separate classes at Ailey until 4:30, when most of them go home. The more serious ones, however, stay on to join other students in the Junior Division, in which they are also enrolled, taking more classes until early evening, doing the office work required by their fellowships, and rehearsing for workshop performances.

At around four o'clock the students who aren't from PPAS arrive for the 4:30 class, hang out a bit in the student lounge (which features beat-up sofas, snack machines, and bulletin boards with notices of auditions, masseurs, and apartments for the Professional Division students) and finally duck into the locker room to change quickly. They drop their enormous backpacks—which, besides schoolbooks, water bottles, and the usual high school belongings, contain street clothes and additional dancewear, which is often not stored in the lockers—at one end of the studio.

Most of these students have been together for at least a year, and are well primed on each other's strengths and weaknesses. Still, a summer has gone by, and all of them have spent at least part of it studying dance somewhere, either at Ailey's summer-intensive program, the Dance Theatre of Harlem, or the Joffrey School, or at a local dance program in some otherwise peaceful spot where, perhaps, their relatives live.

So there is a certain tension among the students as they look in the mirror today, darting sidelong glances to see if someone they know has put on weight or taken a giant leap—so to speak— in facility over the summer. But what is even more important to these students—as it is to every dancer from the time he or she first gets serious at age eight to fourteen until the time he or she retires at age thirty to forty—is *how do I look to the others? Have I put on a few extra pounds that they will notice? Will I get that leg up high enough?* The others, of course, are not really noticing quite that carefully, because they are all focused on themselves.

For example Beatrice Capote, Travis Magee, and Afra Hines, seventeen-year-old PPAS seniors in Level VII, have all arrived here by different paths, and illustrate three variations on the theme of dance talent. While all of them are applying to Juilliard for college next year, and all are hoping that Ailey will sponsor them in the Arts Recognition and Talent Search—the prestigious national competition for high school seniors which is the artistic counterpart to the Intel talent competition in science—each has a personal agenda as well.

Beatrice—a dark, round, pretty girl with hair in innumerable skinny braids which she ties back or pins up for class in obedience to the Ailey dress code—wants to increase the number of pirouettes she can do, lose weight, and keep life's punches from knocking her down. All three goals are more connected than one might think.

Beatrice has been at The Ailey School since she was ten, longer than any of her classmates, and since her sophomore year has held the Edward and Sally Van Lier Fellowship of the New York Community Trust, the most lavish fellowship the school offers. Awarded to minority students and held by three of them at a time, it covers a student's tuition for three school years and the summers in between and adds a stipend sufficient to pay for incidentals like toe shoes, leotards, and transportation. It is a gamble that the inchoate adolescent to whom it is awarded will continue to dance well, work hard, and behave respectfully for what, to any adolescent, may seem an eternity. Like the winners of more modest awards, Van Lier fellows have to work in the school's office or help in the younger children's classes to maintain their fellowships.

Since Beatrice's early childhood, her talent has been fueled by recognition, both at school and at home. As a two-year-old she would copy any adult she saw dancing, from her mother moving to the radio in the kitchen to the chorus gypsies on a television show. It was obvious to her mother, Barbara Santiago, that she should have lessons, so Barbara signed Beatrice up at a local school in her suburban town of West New York, New Jersey, as soon as she turned five. In the past couple of decades, state and national dance competitions have become a snowballing phenomenon for neighborhood and suburban schools. When Beatrice, at age nine, was picked to dance a solo representing the school at a ballet competition in New York City, Barbara was sufficiently impressed to ask her daughter whether she would like to dance more seriously. Beatrice—at this point more suggestible than ambitious—said, "Yeah, why not?"

Barbara had just heard about Ailey Camp, a summer program at which all the children are on scholarship, and she decided to send Beatrice there every morning as well as to the local dance school two afternoons a week. Once she had a standard of comparison, Beatrice agreed she had outgrown the local school, and wanted to try her skills in New York. She auditioned for the Junior Division at The Ailey School and was put in Level III.

Barbara Santiago is a medical assistant; Julio Santiago, Beatrice's stepfather, is a computer tech support man at Coopers and Lybrand, the accounting firm. Tuition at The Ailey School was a heavy burden for the Santiago family to pay, and Beatrice was far too young for a fellowship. But officials at Ailey Camp saw something in her that merited nurturing and they prevailed on one of their board members to foot the bill for her first year. The next summer, Barbara took advantage of her union's benefit fund,

Beatrice as a seven-year-old dancer at Amaryllis
Academy in West New York, New Jersey
(COURTESY THE SANTIAGO FAMILY)

which provided summer camp money for the children of hospital employees. The union fund covered two summers for Beatrice at The Ailey School's eight-week summer-intensive program. Barbara was becoming savvy at grantsmanship and the Ailey world was drawing Beatrice in: during her early years at the school, her tuition was almost completely funded by Ailey Camp. The Ailey people had enough confidence in Beatrice's potential to keep footing the bills, as they sometimes do when there is a child they don't want to lose.

In 1995, when Beatrice, now ten years old, started classes at Ailey, she felt she was behind her classmates: she was coming from a small-town school and was surrounded by New Yorkers. She was a quiet girl, not a showy performer, as one teacher remembers, but she had, the same teacher says, "good facility, a malleable body," and she worked hard. She shot up one level every year—which meant that each year she was equal to a stiffer set of challenges—and when she was twelve and in Level V, wearing the burgundy leotard, she learned that Judith Jamison was planning to use some Junior Division children in the First Company's December performance of *Streams* at City Center. Beatrice was asked to audition and—to her own great surprise—she won a coveted role. She had felt nervous and intimidated, surrounded by older students and company members, but she also experienced, for the very first time, the thrill of performing with a professional company for a New York audience in a famous hall. There was no turning back.

So Beatrice entered PPAS for high school, and began to live the committed life: academic classes from eight in the morning until 1:15 in the afternoon, on to the Ailey bus, dance classes until six o'clock, an hour and a half of office work, a fifty-minute bus trip back to New Jersey, and on Saturdays, work and classes at Ailey from 9:30 A.M. until 4:30 P.M. A routine with almost no time for a social life—although Ailey kids often go out together for pizza and a movie after Saturday classes.

Especially for little girls, dance is a bit of a time bomb. By the time they reach adolescence, they are already hooked on it, and then they discover what kind of body nature is giving them. Body is all important to a dancer. As Beatrice's body matured, she began to put on weight, which affected her speed and agility. Diet is an obvious solution to weight gain, and agility problems can be solved by exercise and training. But in her sophomore year, when Beatrice was learning a new swing dance in which her partner had to flip her over, she fell on her left side. The fall brought on tendinitis in her left shoulder. An orthopedist told her to restrict her dancing to ballet until the tendinitis abated. This took a year and a half and kept her out of a repertory performance of Judith Jamison's ballet *Divining,* which the school put on for the spring gala.

Injury and weight gain were not all the strains on Beatrice during her sophomore and junior years. After a long day at Ailey, she often went to visit her beloved grandmother, who had taken ill with Lou Gehrig's disease, and ultimately, she and her family felt the sadness of her grandmother's death. Both Beatrice's grades and her Ailey evaluations went down. Not surprisingly, all of this together began to depress her and gave her dancing what Ailey teachers call a "muted" quality. Beatrice would get to thinking, gloomily, that when she was eleven, she had been skinny in the behind, and now she was broad and muscular. She loved to dance, but in class, when the shoulder, then the neck, and finally the whole upper back felt all knotted up, she would start to wonder if she had a future in dance.

But Beatrice continued to work hard and eventually pulled through, so she is up to the challenges of Level VII as the year begins. Why has she persevered despite two years of justifiable melancholy? First, it is fun and rewarding to be part of the select group that stays together at Ailey to dance more—often until 8:00 in the evening—after fulfilling the ordinary requirements of

PPAS or LaGuardia. Not having time for a social life is almost a mark of honor: ordinary PPAS students are "not the same as me," according to Beatrice. "I'm serious about dancing." Feeling herself part of a family in which everyone is sharing the same tough experiences is rewarding. It is a group in which Beatrice, not a conventional extrovert, is popular, because once she gets to know people, she is a good friend who likes to talk on the phone and who listens to people's problems.

The confidence bred by ensemble spirit amplifies the pure pleasure Beatrice feels in dancing. And when she despairs, not only her friends but the adults in her life sustain her. "There was a time," she says, "when I was tired of dancing, and my mom kept pushing me and saying, 'Oh, no, you have to, you have to.' And now, I'm like, 'Yes, I have to,' because this is my talent and I want to succeed in it. I was told—here at Ailey—that I'm going to make it and be up there, that I should keep going."

So Beatrice has begun to show a doggedness that will serve her well when she suffers reverses—both injury and personal troubles—that are part of every dancer's life. What has she got going for her that counteracts her weight problems and the depression that comes from them? Earl Mosley, a Horton teacher who knows her well, says "Beatrice has a lot of passion. She's a wide mover, but at the same time she has long legs and arms so she can look very lyrical but also do a percussive movement. Her technique is clean in modern and ballet." She is also known to be a quick study: Sharon Wong of the Jazz Department says that when some other group of students is working on their part of a repertory, "Beatrice will stay in the corner and I can guarantee that everything that was done in the studio today with all those different sections, she knows it all."

Beatrice and Travis Magee are good friends, but they are almost opposites in terms of personality. Travis is a slightly built boy who wears his light brown hair in a proper crew cut to conform with Ailey regulations: in the summers, he allows himself flights of funkiness like bleached blond hair (the summer before last, when he attended Ann Reinking's Broadway Theatre Project in Florida) and a beard (this past summer, when he stayed at Ailey, which is more permissive during the summer months).

Travis has been at PPAS and Ailey since the ninth grade. He is starting this year, his second at Level VII, with many plans: senior year, he says, is going to be "getting ready to move on to the next step where I can start to develop myself and put myself into the dance world—to get myself known and eventually be considered a reckoning force." If Beatrice is diligent, Travis is entrepreneurial. Like some of the other boys at Ailey—but like no girl I spoke to—he dreams of someday having his own company, his own school. Right now he has a germ of a choreography idea, which would involve Beatrice's dancing to Desdemona's prayer in Verdi's *Otello.* At the same time, he has signed up to take an advanced course at the International Center for Photography two evenings a week. Since he had not taken a class at ICP before, he was admitted after school officials reviewed his portfolio and decided he could handle it.

Travis has been interested in photography—especially in photographing dancers—for the past couple of years, but until now he has been entirely self-taught. At PPAS he built a darkroom and ran workshops for the students. He wrote a grant proposal, sent it to Nikon, and got two cameras donated to the school. He is hoping to line up some jobs taking publicity photographs for dancers who work in Ailey's back office and have their own small

Travis by Travis
(TRAVIS MAGEE)

companies: he would do this at cost, with an eye toward beginning a professional photography career that might tie in with dance.

Last March, Travis discovered politics and the law when he was nominated by PPAS to represent the school at a student law forum in Washington, D.C., where the kids staged mock trials, toured the city, and met judges, senators, congressmen, and members of the American Civil Liberties Union. He started to think about how to, as he says, make a difference. So this year he is carrying a book about the First Amendment in his backpack. Admittedly, law might make a good fallback career in case he gets injured, but for Travis it does not seem to be a case of choosing which field he wants to make a difference *in:* at the age of seventeen, he wants to be in all of them. Pursuing his interests in photography and even law, he believes, will somehow make him a better dancer.

At PPAS, Kim Bruno, the assistant principal for performing arts, calls Travis the Renaissance man. "He's made it his business to come into my office and propose fifty different suggestions at a time," she says. Meanwhile, Travis has finished up his math and science credits and thus can walk up to Ailey by noon, take a Professional Division class before his PPAS class, and be out at 4:30. He has Saturdays free for SAT prep.

But despite the undeniable enthusiasm and optimism with which Travis embraces everything, during the summer he felt his dancing was in something of a rut. Ailey evaluations confirmed this belief. "A lot of the teachers said that I have to start finding myself," Travis reflects. "I have the technique, but now I need to figure out what's going on within my spirit." It is not an unusual criticism for students beginning their senior year, but Travis's problem—being both cerebral in his dancing and diverse in his passions—is at least to some extent peculiar to Travis.

Afra Hines, a third Level VII student, who came to PPAS and Ailey last year when she was in the eleventh grade, had moved to New York from the Boston suburbs in order to dance. She is a tall, strapping girl with long, curly, light brown hair and very fair skin, which she gets from her English mother, and African features which come from her African-American father. She is considered a charismatic dancer, the one among the group onstage that draws the audience's gaze, and she is said to have a flexible body, which means she doesn't have to work quite as hard as many others—

both boys and girls—to look wonderful. She has lost some weight this summer, which Ailey teachers have told her is all to the good, although she didn't have a real weight problem to begin with.

Like Travis's, Afra's interests are diverse, but hers are all squarely within the fields of music and dance. She finds Ailey, compared to other places where she's studied, to be "more professional, more big-time." Success, for Afra, would be to actually earn a living as a dancer. Thus, one of her goals in coming to New York was to get a talent agent (achieved), and she is just as interested in performing in commercials, films, and music videos as she is in getting into a contemporary dance company like Ailey, whose varied repertory Afra also finds congenial. On the walls of her bedroom in the small apartment in an Upper East Side high-rise where she lives with her mother are pictures of the performers she admires: a host of rap stars and Judith Jamison dancing *Cry*. But while she displays these not-surprising icons, Afra is also a particular fan of Tatiana Litvinova, the most classical woman teacher at Ailey.

Afra is going to be auditioning for outside gigs this fall—a practice LaGuardia's dance department would not permit but PPAS mostly smiles upon (provided a student keeps up with grades). It is one toward which Ailey, however, shows ambivalence, because it can affect attendance, divert students from concentration on dance class work (thus diluting technique), and cut into fellowship work time.

The students received their fall schedules at the end of the previous term, with their evaluation sheets. That is how they learn whether they have been promoted to the next level. In general, because children's bodies develop at different rates, it is not a disgrace for advanced students to remain on the same level for more than one or even two years: it is, in fact, inevitable for

those who have been around for a long time and moved up rapidly to slow down at the higher levels, but school officials often
find themselves explaining this to angry or distraught parents, who
feel their children have been left back. The students in Level VI,
for example—the lavender leotards, just below Beatrice, Travis,
and Afra—range from thirteen-year-old Charlotte Kaufman, an
eighth grader at the Brearley School in Manhattan, to seventeen-
year-old Joi Favor, a twelfth grader at Nyack High School in suburban Rockland County.

This year there are forty-four students in Levels V, VI and VII.
The most significant group of them, even larger than that from
PPAS, has walked over from LaGuardia a few blocks north.

LaGuardia is the descendant of the high school depicted in
the movie *Fame*. The LaGuardia kids are a coterie of driven devotees (soulmates of the PPAS trio we have just met) within their
school, which has its own studios and a distinguished dance department with a conservatory curriculum; they have been dancing there for three hours before coming over to Ailey to dance
some more. Then there are a few singletons from the suburbs,
like Joi (new this year), who has traveled for an hour or more after school to get here, and the New York City private schools,
like Charlotte (in her second year at Ailey after four years at SAB).

Once all of these students have checked one another out, the
next thing that concerns them is any teacher they haven't had before. They will need to please that teacher, so first they must learn
to "read" that teacher. Each has a different set of idiosyncrasies.

The ballet instructor who will see the Level VI girls five times
a week and the Level VIIs twice (the VIIs take some of their
ballet in the Professional Division) is Tatiana Litvinova, once a
prima ballerina with the Bolshoi and Kirov ballets, and now Ai-

ley's link to the old world. Litvinova is a tall woman with short blond hair; today she is wearing brown bell-bottom leotard pants, a white T-shirt, an apricot-colored sweater, and black jazz oxfords. She is a handsome and youthful fifty-one, but of course the students have no clue about how old any of their teachers are. The arches of her feet are extraordinarily well developed, the mark of a ballerina and a beautiful singularity—like Litvinova herself—in this modern-dance environment. She speaks in a heavy accent, with no articles preceding the nouns and a presumably Russian sentence structure which the students must unsnarl. When I ask her one day how it is to start with a new class, she says, "It is very difficult. The students have different idea, not bad idea but different idea. And also they're testing—can they just enjoy to have private lives, but, no, we won't have private life over here. We will work and it will be very serious, and it will be joyful, but we are not talking—we are talking with our body."

Before Litvinova gives a combination, she works it out silently for herself, deeply lost in thought, with an occasional flutter of hand or foot: her concern here is to give clear instructions. Students regard her with mixed emotions: she is intimidating for who she is, what she can teach, and how she raises the possibility of Russo-American cultural differences. For most, she turns out to be more approachable than she seems, counseling fourteen-year-old Monique Massiah, who has taken a big growth spurt over the summer that seems to have given her pain in the joints and hamstrings, to be patient; Litvinova tells Monique she herself has had this kind of pain, and it takes a long time to heal.

A ballet class is a coordinated series of exercises,[1] each of which becomes more refined and difficult as levels advance; in addition, each teacher puts his or her own spin on the basics, which also vary slightly according to whether the teacher uses the Russian, French, or Italian method. The class starts at the barre, warming the dancers up with deep, slow *pliés* that bend the knees while the back is straight and the behind pulled in. Next come *battements tendus,* in which the dancer slides one leg out along the floor until the foot is fully pointed, strengthening the turnout of legs and feet. Third are the *ronds de jambes,* turnout exercises for the legs, in which one foot describes a semicircle on the ground or in the air, with the supporting leg either straight or bent. A variety of *battements* and *ronds de jambes* at the barre work the hip, knee, and ankle joints and muscles. At the same time, the dancers will be refining arm and head positions that coordinate the upper and lower body and add expressiveness. Litvinova, like other instructors of the classical Russian school, emphasizes the development of the upper body, a weak link, she believes, for American dancers.

After the barre exercises there is often a break, which the dancers may spend limbering up by doing splits on the floor or, in effect, while standing up, grabbing one foot and pulling that leg as high in the air as it will go. Then they do another series of exercises in the center of the floor, without the support of the barre, to improve balance and coordination. The last and most exciting part of the class, the *allegro,* consists of various fast jumping and turning combinations.

The boys in Level VI and Level VII are taking a similar class with Franco De Vita, a trim, precise man about Litvinova's age, who performed in ballet companies all over Europe and had his own school in Florence for fifteen years before coming to the United States. De Vita also has a heavy accent, which means he pronounces the French names of the dance steps perfectly—a new linguistic experience for the class—and the American names of the students oddly. When he says "*ills* down!" it takes several repetitions before the boys, smiling with relief, figure out they should put their feet flat on the floor. De Vita sings the combinations to emphasize musicality and uses his voice to demonstrate the strength or lightness of an exercise; whatever mood the students may be in, they are expected to smile a lot when dancing because he believes it makes for a relaxed class atmosphere and will help them present themselves to best advantage in auditions. De Vita smiles almost all the time, but he expects crisp footwork, well-coordinated arms, and disciplined memory of combinations and corrections.

What qualities have moved these particular students up to the advanced level at a school as rigorous as Ailey? What Beatrice, Travis, and Afra—all of whom have been pronounced "talented" early in life—have in common is the desire to make dance the center of their lives and the willingness to work hard to improve their skill. Beyond that, they—and all their Ailey classmates— look different and move differently in class and onstage, and want different things in their dance careers. Throughout my year at Ailey—and indeed from the moment I arrived there, some time before that year—I asked teachers to predict which students were bound for stardom and which for failure, and which had the most talent. What, in fact, does "talent" consist of, I wondered?

It is a logical layman's question: I never got a direct answer, but I never let go of it. It is easier, I discovered, to pick out raw talent in untrained dancers—little children or late-starting preteens, for example—than it is to predict which Level VIIs will end up in the First Company. Once a dancer has had several years of training, the nature-nurture questions kick in, as do those of the spirit and the flesh. One child has a "hard body" but works incessantly to overcome it; another has an "easy body" but gets distracted. Some teachers use the terms "hard body" and "easy body"; other teachers flinch at them, because they negate the role of diligence and training.

Probably no one at Ailey has thought more about all this than the aptly named Elena Comendador, Tracy Inman's predecessor, a petite, crisp, no-nonsense Filipino woman of forty-two who was codirector of the Junior Division for eight years; this year, Comendador still teaches some ballet classes and has opened a costume studio which dresses most of the school's performances. She has performed with both ballet and Horton-based companies. While Denise Jefferson is The Ailey School to the adult world, Comendador has been the school to the kids since they began here, the one who commanded them to stay on track and commended them when they acted professional, the one they didn't dare disappoint, the one who interpreted kids to families and families to kids, the one that students will tell misty-eyed stories about when they're fifty.

Comendador says you can pick up talent from the very beginning, from the time a student is eight to ten years old, at Level I or Level II. "You can pretty much tell whether a child is very focused, clear in the mind, clear in spirit," she says. "You can tell who's distracted and who's not, who takes in information, and how developed is the mind-body connection: for some kids it happens earlier and for others it takes a little longer." Comendador describes learning to dance as a complex intellectual effort. "The children are absorbing information about their muscles, about directions—front, side, and back," she says. "They're accumulating movement sense in different parts of the body, they're traveling through space, and they have to bring all these things together: moving forward and moving a part of the body and listening to what happens in the music. It's a lot to take in."

The day I arrived at Ailey, Comendador took me into her Level II class, where eighteen prepubescent girls in white leotards and tights and two small boys in black tights and white T-shirts were facing the barre, doing *piqués* (in which the dancer steps sharply onto one toe without bending the same knee[2]). "Get taller! Strong legs!" she called out. "Which leg is stronger—front or back?" "Both!" the kids shouted. "Strong first position, squeeze those muscles around your popo and get taller!" shouted back Comendador, as the pianist played a lusty interpretation of "Meadowlands." "This exercise is about learning to move the leg only," she told them. "What does it mean? Nothing else moves! I want to see you don't forget these things."

Comendador whispered to me, "The third and fourth girls from the end, I can tell you right now, they'll be something. Look at that line! That one looks like a princess." She had one of the talented girls demonstrate first position, while the pianist switched to an equally lively "Charade." Beaming at the demonstrator, Comendador said, "That leg looks endless!" Everyone applauded the girl, and Comendador added, "If you do this position and the squeezing, you should have no problem standing on one leg at all."

The adults at Ailey can quickly identify which small children have a natural endowment that others don't. Recalling one student, Denise Jefferson says, "There was a little girl ten or twelve years ago, I think her name was Annick. Her teacher came into my office and said, 'Denise, I want you to see this little girl in Level One.' I thought, 'What am I gonna see some seven-year-old do that is so extraordinary?' So I went in and the teacher was

choreographing a little piece for the end-of-the-year performance. And this little girl was in the center . . . very musical, so focused, so concentrated the other kids would kind of fall down
and laugh. Annick was really doing this step and took it very,
very seriously. That musicality is one thing you see. A focus, a determination, the ability to block everything out but what you're
doing that moment.

"The girl did an extension and her leg was over her head in
second position, and she had it! I said, 'Oh, my God!' We were
talking about focus, determination, and musicality, but also physical capability. It's a gift! We saw that in Level One with her. She
stayed with us through, perhaps, Level Four or Five, and then unfortunately her mother decided she wanted her to have a more
normal life, and not to do so much dancing, and she pulled her
out. We were really sorry."

Evidence of an inclination to dance, as we saw in Beatrice's
case, shows up very early in life. Travis's parents tell a charming
story of their little boy on a family vacation at a Catskill resort,
running up onstage when the band started playing and dancing
all by himself. When Travis was seven, he asked to take formal
classes. His mother, Deborah Magee, remembers, "You could
just see how whenever he had an audience, he would light up—
it was remarkable to watch. At home he would put on a pretend
show, and if he had a couple of people sitting there watching
him, he was really happy."

As a preschool child, Afra Hines showed both desire and ability. Her mother, Mary Anne Holliday, had been a dancer, so it
was quite natural to take her two-and-a-half-year-old child to a
dance class before she had displayed any talent. Her daughter's
first class was what Mary Anne describes as "creative dance, run-

ning around the room with scarves and that sort of thing" but when Afra saw a tap-dance performance by children, she said, "I want to do *that*!" So Mary Anne found a good school that taught tap, and carried three-year-old Afra in on her hip.

"They took one look at me," Mary Anne says, "and they thought, 'Oh, here's another pushy mom, trying to make her daughter something she's not!' I said, 'She wants to do tap,' and they said, 'She's really too young, but if you insist, we'll test her out.' And within two years she had gone up so many age levels it was just extraordinary."

These sorts of stories abound in the early history of Ailey students and performers. How, then, does this early response evolve as the children get older? What are the elements of innate pure talent that are visible to adults in the dance world, both from their own dance experience and from observation of their students?

Ana Marie Forsythe, who heads both the Horton department and the BFA program Ailey runs with Fordham University, has been teaching at Ailey since 1973. She began her career as a ballerina and later switched to Horton and danced with Joyce Trisler; these days she is teaching the college-age students in the Professional Division. When Forsythe talks about talent, she has mature dancers in mind, and she stresses the intellectual aspect of their ability. "There are people who have a different kind of memory ability from other people," she says, "and it has to do with how their brain thinks about how their body moves, and remembering those things. Some of it is that they've learned patterns, some of it is the ability to duplicate something they see and turn it into a physical action on their own bodies.

"I can remember dances I did when I was fourteen years old," she continues. "It's a ridiculous thing to keep in my mind. If I hear the music played, I can get up and do most of it, not all of it, but we're talking forty-something years of not having done it since and still remembering. Practically all of the counts in my Horton book[3] are in my head. I rarely have to refer to them.

"The highest compliment that was ever paid to me," Forsythe remembers, "was by Joyce Trisler. I was working on a solo I had seen her dance so many times, and we had a rehearsal and then I came back the next day and rehearsed again, and she said, 'That's why I love working with you, Ana. You always come back the next day and it's better!' I hadn't worked between the rehearsals, I just had the ability to retain all the information she'd given me. And was able to incorporate all the corrections, all the nuances, the musicality, so that the next day we were able to build on that, so it would be better and better. Anyone who tells you dancers are dumb just doesn't have it right."

At the same time, Forsythe mentions a personal quality that is quickly evident but hard to name. "You can usually tell from the first ten minutes in a class who's got the spark, the artistry," she says. "It's not just a technical thing—it really is something that comes from inside people. It's like they open up—they suddenly feel something they hadn't felt before—and that draws you in to them."

"Hunger? Ambition? Charisma?" I ask her.

"It could be all of those things," Forsythe says. "It could be none of those things. It's a kind of magic that happens inside a real dancer, a real performer. You could have a dancer with absolutely perfect facility, wonderful turnout, beautiful feet and legs, and nothing is communicated between that person and you as an audience. And there's another dancer who may be short and fat and doesn't have a great body, doesn't have that terrific turnout, but she steps out onstage and something happens." Forsythe admits that sometimes it's the dull technician who gets the job and the plump artist who doesn't. "But there's always the gray area," she says, "where, maybe you don't have the perfect body, where you can be as thin as you're able to be, and work on doing certain kinds of therapeutic work that will make your feet better, that will make your legs go higher, that will improve your technical capacity."

Like Forsythe, Franco De Vita, the boys' ballet instructor, talks of a particular kind of intelligence that dancers must have, but also illustrates the difficulty of predicting who will succeed. "You can be very intelligent and understand corrections straightaway with your brain," De Vita says, "but in our job you need body memory as well. Some people can understand and translate everything straightaway with their body. When your coordination is good, your body understands movements more quickly. But I had a student in Italy and after each class I saw him in a corner, this little boy writing. One day I said, 'What are you writing?' He was writing every single correction I gave him during class. This boy had very difficult coordination." Then De Vita, still the performer, pauses.

"This boy," he says, "is with the Royal Ballet now." Foretelling a student's future, then, is not as easy as it might seem.

The teacher whose predictive skills are most regularly on the line is not at Ailey. She is Michelle Mathesius, who heads the dance department at LaGuardia High School. Every year some 1,500 eighth graders from around New York audition for sixty-six places in LaGuardia's freshman class. An applicant auditions by participating in a small group that takes a short class in ballet and another in modern dance, while Mathesius and her colleagues observe. Those applicants who look talented to the panelists return to take a second, more advanced series and perform a one-minute audition piece in any dance style. From this the teachers decide who really has talent.

"We sometimes admit children who have never danced and reject children who have studied for seven to ten years," Mathesius told me. "Some children who have never danced have an ability to coordinate their movements, and they can move in space as if they're wild people. That's what we're looking for. We've had kids who've had many years of experience with wonderful teachers, and they're just not children we want because they don't have that ability to move with wild abandon—and with some kind of coordination."

So what the future holds for Beatrice, Travis, and Afra is unclear, since it will engage not only the broad, familiar questions of nature and nurture but will also depend, within these categories, on various overlapping traits of temperament and development. Ailey teachers change their assessment of students from year to year and sometimes from month to month—and, of course, besides the children's developmental arcs, teachers have their own moods and favorites. "Did something happen in class today?" is a question that sometimes would occur to me as I listened to a teacher bubble or fizzle about some student.

Tracy Inman, co-director of the Junior Division, has, from personal experience, a good sense of the twists and turns of a young artist's life. Inman himself was first judged to have talent as a teenage violinist at Duke Ellington School for the Arts, the counterpart of LaGuardia in his hometown of Washington, D.C. He played and traveled all over the world with a youth orchestra, and didn't even begin to dance until he was in college. Once he discovered dance, he gave up the violin, came to New York, won a scholarship to The Ailey School, and danced in both the Second and First companies as well as in the small company that Judith Jamison ran for a while. Now, at forty, he no longer performs. He says that once a dancer has been training for a long time, that raw talent—presumably what Mathesius means by "moving with wild abandon"—is just gone. What takes over, he says, is "discipline, muscle memory, all of the things you acquire during your training."

Through years of professional experience, dance instructors have developed their own opinions on talent and how it shows itself. The same questions have piqued the interest of a number of scholarly researchers who look at talent within the framework of intellectual development. They study dancers in company with artists, musicians, and chess whizzes to discover what is similar and different among talented people in every area.

Howard Gardner, a professor at the Harvard Graduate School of Education who is also in the neurology department at the Boston University School of Medicine, has labored for some thirty years to dispel the notion widely held by lay people that, as he writes in his best-known book, *Frames of Mind,* "intelligence is a single, general capacity that every human being possesses to a greater or lesser extent," a capacity that is measurable by standardized tests.[4] This idea of one single factor called intelligence is now less widely held among other researchers in the field as well, although they may have different ways of parsing out the mind.

Gardner—who received a MacArthur Prize Fellowship in 1981—characterizes intelligence as the ability to solve the problems that are valued in a particular culture. As primary examples of intelligent behavior that is specific to a culture and can't be measured by an IQ test, he has offered the sophisticated navigational skills of a Puluwat Islander in the South Pacific, the linguistic ability of an Iranian youth who has mastered enough Arabic to memorize the Koran, and the proficiency of a teenager who has programmed a computer to compose music with a synthesizer. For Gardner, all intelligence differs according to what we are learning, and he measures intelligence using every kind of evidence but those overrated standard IQ tests. Neurological evidence tells us which abilities are lost and which survive when different parts of the brain are damaged. Anthropological evidence describes, for example, the successes and limitations of Suzuki violin instruction, which turns out, for cultural reasons, to be more effective in Japan than in the United States.

In *Frames of Mind* Gardner arrived at seven different "intelligences": linguistic, musical, logical-mathematical, spatial, bodily kinesthetic, interpersonal, and intrapersonal. Most individuals are well-endowed with several of these and shortchanged on others. What the Ailey students are exhibiting are bodily kinesthetic, musical, and spatial intelligence: they need to convert De Vita's verbal instructions into *glissades* and *pirouettes,* translate both the counts and the dynamics of the accompanist into dance combinations, and estimate how many pirouettes will get them from point A to point B. And they must do it on the spot. People who haven't read the detailed and rigorous discussions in Gardner's books might call the abilities to do these things "talents." Gardner, too, has no trouble calling these abilities talents, he writes, "so long as one calls language or logic talents as well."[5]

Gardner illustrates bodily kinesthetic intelligence by describing the mime Marcel Marceau, who uses his body in both agile and expressive ways (as indeed the Ailey students must develop their intelligence by learning to do). Dancers and swimmers exemplify one component of bodily kinesthetic intelligence; the other component is working well with objects large and small, as illustrated by artisans, ballplayers, instrumentalists, and surgeons. Elena Comendador's second career as a costumer and Tracy Inman's original bent as a violinist suggest a generous endowment of this kind of intelligence.

Both Gardner and other scholars in this area draw a distinction between "intelligences" or "talents," the innate abilities that may equip individuals to follow one or another particular specialty—as the combination of musical and bodily kinesthetic intelligence helped Inman to become both a violinist and a dancer—and what they call "domains." These are disciplines like musical performance and concert dance which people can choose to study and in which teachers and audiences can evaluate their competence. Once a student enters one of these domains, he or she must reckon with a third element called the "field." That is the cultural component. For our students it consists of Ailey teachers who write reports on each one of them at the end of the term, choreographers like Judith Jamison who choose dancers from auditions, panels that award prizes like the ARTS fellowship, and reviewers who tell us which dancers to watch. Thus young dancers like Beatrice, Travis, and Afra start out with a "talent," must develop it by studying a domain (like dance or the violin), and finally have to meet the standards of a group of adults who may judge differently in 2002 from those who judged in 1985.

What goes on in the mind and body of dancers like Beatrice—who has, according to Sharon Wong of Ailey's jazz department, a mind like a steel trap—and her fellow students when they learn new combinations, intrigues researchers, as do other examples of the bodily kinesthetic learning process. While I was working on this book, I encountered Trevor Marchand, a lecturer at the School of Oriental and African Studies at the University of London. Marchand is a Canadian architect and anthropologist with an interest in nonverbal learning. Between September 1996 and August 1997, Marchand—whose sister runs a ballet school in Montreal—joined a team of minaret builders in Sanaa, Yemen, working as a building laborer to learn how expert builders passed on their skills in a world in which there is no formal training or drawn architectural plans. Construction workers, of course, are artisans, who also employ bodily kinesthetic intelligence as Gardner has described it.

Marchand wrote a book about his experiences called *Minaret Building and Apprenticeship in Yemen.* Like the minaret builders, Ailey students undergo a process of apprenticeship, learning basic steps, putting them together in ever more difficult combinations, dancing in repertory workshops, and ultimately, if all goes well, joining a company. In Yemen, the young building apprentices had gone to schools that taught the Koran by rote, an experience which Marchand suggests had primed them to learn basic tasks without any explanation. Promising students would then be chosen to work closely with a master builder, watching him, copying what he did, and eventually coming to a detailed understanding of his skills. Finally, the apprentice would become a master in his own right, at which point, according to Marchand, "His thoughts and actions are absorbed with the drive to reproduce the 'beauty' of the craft over which he has acquired mastery."[6]

These three stages in the young Yemeni builder's education harmonized with the style of Islamic education as Marchand had observed it, and contrasted strongly with Marchand's own architectural training in Canada—a product of Western culture—in which students were given a lot of broad knowledge and abstract spatial concepts before zeroing in on the particulars of building construction. In addition, Marchand found disparities between the Yemeni builders' training and that of carpenters in Quebec, which were similarly tied to cultural differences. While the Ailey students' instruction—which also reflects their culture—involves a fair amount of verbal explanation and less rigidity from stage to stage, it, too, is hierarchical.

Just as demonstration and mimicry are an important part of dance education, Marchand found them to be key to the Yemeni apprentices. As a new laborer doing somewhat risky work, he was assigned tasks by gesture, not name, and without explanation of the processes the builders used. To accomplish his tasks, he watched the others work and drew on a lifetime of experiences in childhood, in athletic activities, on architectural sites, and in school. Whatever prior knowledge guided him, he points out, was "*not thought about through language. . . .* The bulk of the concepts that I relied upon to situate myself and coordinate my actions were primarily sensorimotor or image-related."[7] When at last he was allowed to carve bricks, Marchand learned entirely through copying a demonstration and having his mistakes corrected. The final stage of training evoked what Ailey teachers had told me about the quest for artistry, the last piece in a dancer's evolution from the Junior Division to, say, a performer like Inman or Powell. Foundations were technical but artistry could not be taught. It depends on, as Marchand puts it, "*aptitudes, motivations* and *aspirations. . . .*"[8]

Marchand bristles a bit at Ana Marie Forsythe's comment that talent in dance partly involves "how the mind thinks about what the body does." It suggests, he says, a mind-body dualism right out of Descartes. "If we did have to reflect on our actions before 'our bodies' performed them," he says, "chances are we wouldn't have survived long as a species."

Rather, Marchand suggests that the body itself is intelligent. This is not the sort of intelligence that is usually associated with logic, reason, and conscious thought, but it is, he says, "a form of knowledge nevertheless." Sounding rather like Franco De Vita, he observes, "These are two very different ways of knowing something, and a process of translation must occur at the interface between them." Dancers, he says, may start by reflecting on what they've been told, but the words must be converted into body-knowledge, which happens with training and practice—exactly what Inman pointed out. If the verbal knowledge didn't disappear, it would get in the way of the dancing—which, perhaps, is why Litvinova's brow gets furrowed when she tries to give her students clear instructions on new combinations.

There is a subtext to the musings of Gardner, Marchand, and the Ailey teachers on what constitutes talent and how bodily learning goes on. It is that talent in any field is tied to motivation and is at least to some extent in the eye of the beholder. A few years after *Frames of Mind* was published, Gardner and Joseph Walters, an educational researcher at Harvard, interviewed master teachers in mathematics, music, and the visual arts,[9] posing the same question I asked the Ailey teachers: how do you spot talent? The teachers in the Gardner-Walters study equivocated. On the one hand, they said there were differences among their students that could be ascribed to talent; and on the other hand, they reaffirmed the comments of one distinguished number theorist that "'*anything* can be taught!'"[10]

Gardner and Walters attribute this seeming contradiction to

feelings of ambivalence, not conflict: "The two views were not stated as contending points of view," the researchers suggest. "Instead, they constituted an inconsistency within a single point of view." They explain the ambivalence by pointing out that good teachers are obliged to believe that teaching makes a big difference in how far a student develops, and at the same time, all teachers feel the need to invest their personal efforts where they are likely to pay off.

The tension between what is called "talent" and motivation dog my efforts to figure out, during my year at Ailey, which students are destined to succeed and why. As Gardner and Walters point out, good teachers feel it is their skill and duty to motivate students, but on the other hand, they criticize students who lack motivation. Gardner's "multiple intelligences" approach—"MI theory" as it's known in the education world—resolves this question quite logically. We like to do what we do well. And because we do it often, we come to do it better. Beatrice and her friends are serious about dancing, so they're at Ailey some twenty hours a week. They got into this art because they were good at it, and every year they're improving. As this year begins, it seems that talent and motivation are inseparable.

Three

Families

It is a truth universally acknowledged (to invoke Jane Austen) that high school students live in the dominion of their families. Pupils of college age, in The Ailey School's Professional Division, have left home—which may be halfway around the world—and are, for the first time, managing their own domestic, economic, and professional lives. As the school discovers every now and then, they are not fully fledged: a psychologist and, this year, a nutritionist are on tap to help young adults overwhelmed by the life of insolvent arts students in a large, unfamiliar city. After September 11, the administration felt comfortable focusing its attention on the older students, worrying less about the teenagers who went home to their parents every night. Thus in a time of real crisis, Junior Division parents take a large burden off the school's shoulders. At other times, however, they can be a mixed blessing.

Like it or not, when the Junior Division or the PPAS Program takes on a student, it has bought a family package. In the moment, the parents' attitude directly affects a child's school career: ideally their enthusiasm rubs off on their child, who becomes upbeat, energetic, and cooperative, eager to learn new steps and consistently present in class. Such parents' children tend to get chosen for workshops and repertories, because the choreographers, like all of us, want things to go easily.

It is worth the school's while to engage the parents, and perilous to alienate them. That is why, on September 14, Tracy Inman and Melanie Person, the codirectors of the Junior Division, sent a two-page letter to parents whose children had been chosen to perform in a concert for children at Carnegie Hall in November, describing the performance, and identifying the coordinator and choreographer. They also stated that each student would get one free ticket and offered additional tickets at $5 each. The letter noted that the presentation—while "an opportunity for your child to learn and gain valuable performance skills"—was not part of the scheduled curriculum and did not replace technique classes. Thus the school had made every effort to plan rehearsals for days when the children—who were at different levels—would be around anyway. Page two of the letter was a commitment sheet for all rehearsals and run-throughs, which student and parent had to sign and return (and if, of course, a student defaulted on this written commitment, the school had a paper trail for whatever it might decide to do next).

At worst, parents can, also in the moment, be very unpleasant for the school to deal with: they can furiously demand to know why their child was not chosen or promoted, and some have angrily insisted on extensions of the deadlines to pay fees. Rich parents can project a disagreeable air of entitlement; poor parents can project a chip on their shoulder. Some parents are unalterably opposed to their children's dancing. But for the most part, once students have reached the upper levels, the parents are more or less on board.

Still the family, as a culture, continues to shape the child in idiosyncratic ways. One family prizes academic work above all and sees dance as a detrimental diversion; another thinks dance is a great recreation that keeps the child off the streets but doesn't take it seriously; another dreams of the child as a star; another sees the child as too independent or assertive and wants the school to remake the child through discipline, or sees the child as not independent or assertive enough and wants the school to push the child forward into the front row. The school, up to a point, may try to be cooperative by encouraging the child to audition for repertory workshops, but if a student hangs back or fails to show enthusiasm, it cannot resculpture that student's character. The school is in the business of training dancers, and needs to do so efficiently. Finally, the family may be in some sort of crisis and the school, out of sympathy and affection, may cut the child some slack or offer whatever guidance or resources (such as the psychologist's help, within reason) seem pertinent. How much of all this it provides, however, may depend on how promising a dancer the child appears to be.

Since Ailey School families are so varied, the relations between school and family, family and dancer, and dancer and school are, I discovered, triangular and highly nuanced. As the year begins, I see three striking examples of how these nuances color individual students' school lives.

Even this early in the fall, Travis Magee has taken two body blows. It is his second year at Level VII, the highest in the Junior Division. Generally, Level VIIs take most of their classes with the college-age students in the Professional Division, and Travis was on track to do that. But he wanted to leap ahead of the usual progression and try his skill at still more advanced classes in that division. When he asked Denise Jefferson for permission, she gave him an unequivocal "no."

Then, Travis hoped Ailey would sponsor his entry in this year's Arts Recognition and Talent Search. Ailey sponsorship means that rehearsal space and choreography and coaching by Ailey teachers are available to a student without charge, while students without sponsorship must make their own arrangements to enter ARTS. This year, Ailey chose to sponsor Beatrice and Afra, but not Travis.

How Travis came to experience the first two disappointments of his Ailey School career tells much about two cultures—that of the Ailey world and that of the Magee family—and how they missed understanding each other. It tells about the adjacent values of commitment, drive, and hard work—and how Ailey and the Magees defined them differently. And it tells about what needs to happen in the internal climate of a seventeen-year-old boy before he is ready to move up and out into the dance world, something which neither the school nor the family nor probably even the boy can control.

Like every family's core beliefs, the Magees' have evolved historically over more than two decades together. Travis spent his childhood in Warwick, New York, a small upstate rural community which received an influx of artistic types during the seventies. His parents, Fred and Deborah, had grown up in Brooklyn and were, when they got married, "two hippies," as Deborah remembers. For the first ten years of their marriage, Fred played guitar and piano professionally; Deborah, an educational administrator, had danced as a hobby since she was in college.

Now Fred and Deborah are in their early fifties, and Josh, Travis's older brother, is beginning his senior year at Stanford. All the Magees are slightly built. Fred, now an independent management consultant, has light brown hair, a beard and glasses; Deborah, who runs the lecture program at New York's renowned 92nd Street Y, is red haired, and favors ethnic styles and jewelry. Josh and Travis, four years apart, could be mistaken for fraternal twins.

The Magee family culture is what one might call "hands-on." When Travis was seven, he was smitten with Fred Astaire, Ginger Rogers, and Gene Kelly, and asked for tap dance lessons. Not only did he get them, but the other three Magees joined in for a whole year. Moreover, they are a family that reveres the performing arts and are somewhat savvy about the world of artistic performance. Travis came to Ailey with what Howard Gardner, the Harvard professor, and other researchers who study talent call "cultural capital." The Magees feel comfortable in the dance world, and when Travis got into it they didn't need to learn its workings from scratch.

For Travis's first lessons, the family chose a school run by an elderly lady in a town near Warwick where Deborah had taken exercise classes. The elderly lady eventually got Travis out of tap and into ballet, and he took to it. He was the only boy in the class.

A variety of other performing talents began to enhance his life even before grade school. In early childhood, Travis had a collection of puppets, and he used to put on puppet shows for family and friends, presenting the dialogue of lively, invented characters in a range of different voices. When the Magee brothers were six and two respectively, Fred gave them an electronic keyboard. Josh pounded. Travis, four years younger, picked out little melodies with two fingers. So Travis then studied piano and a bit of Suzuki violin, sang, went with Josh to a performing arts camp, and starred in many school productions.

But as he got into middle school, it became apparent that dance was his performing art of choice. At the same time, he began to get hassled. "In rural schools," he says, "there's no acceptance of anything that's outrageously different. I couldn't really be open about being a dancer because it would have brought a lot of ridicule, which—when it finally got out—it did. And it was difficult because I was doing something I really loved to do, and it wasn't socially acceptable."

While there was a good dance school in Warwick, Travis insisted on staying with the elderly lady. Her world, in a different town, was safe for him, but at home in middle school, Deborah remembers, "you could really see this happy-go-lucky sparkling kid becoming very quiet, very insecure."

Defending Travis and helping him defend himself became the job of all the Magees. Fred taught him to fight: he was trying to take it lightly when the other kids made fun of his dancing, and it took a year to instill a tougher response. Deborah told him to stand up to people, to get in their faces and let them know they can't mess with you. The former hippies were amending their values in response to their son's needs. At last Deborah got a call from the principal because Travis had got into a fight in the school yard and ripped a kid's jacket. To her own great sur-

Travis, age ten, ready to sing and tap "Thank Heaven for Little Girls" at Marya Kennett Dance Studio in Goshen, New York
(COURTESY THE MAGEE FAMILY)

prise, she sat in the principal's office, behind closed doors, and said, "I'm glad this happened." Meanwhile, Josh put the word out that you didn't want to mess with Travis because he was Joshua Magee's brother, and if you bothered Travis, Josh's best friend, known in school as a martial-arts expert, would take care of you.

Around this time, the family also realized that the elderly lady had taken Travis as far as she could. Two male counselors at the performing arts camp he attended had said that from the way

Travis was dancing, he was obviously being taught by a woman, and he was now at the stage where he needed to be dancing with men. He was in the seventh grade, and he told his parents he wanted to study dance in New York. In their usual style, the Magees talked over in detail the commitment that three out of four of them would be required to make (Josh would be going off to college by the time the family moved to New York). They said of course they would move if Travis still wanted to a year from now, provided he kept his grades up and got into a good dance program. When he talks of this now, he expresses a debt he feels he owes his parents, saying, "I think they really understood that I would be much happier if I could just be in a place where I could be myself. I think in some ways they were looking at it like they had to save me."

So the Magees encouraged Travis, now an eighth grader, to sniff out the New York dance world, look at schools, and go to auditions. He ended up at Professional Performing Arts School and Alvin Ailey. Until he got into Ailey, he didn't know that at age nineteen, Deborah, sitting in the $2 seats, had worshiped Judith Jamison, and had begun to take dancing lessons after seeing her in *Revelations*. The Magees stepped back, but not too far: while Travis auditioned at Ailey, Deborah sat downstairs in the car, trying to contain her excitement.

Like most young dancers and their families, the Magees had made some sacrifices in the past. Thanksgiving holidays had always been cut short for dance rehearsals. When Travis's best friend had a birthday party, Travis was always performing. Now, however, on Travis's behalf the family turned itself upside down. Deborah got a good job at the 92nd Street Y, so she became the New York parent, while Fred continued to work out of War-

Travis as the prince in The Nutcracker *at the
Marya Kennett Dance Studio in Goshen, New
York, with his costar Rebecca Nodturf*
(COURTESY THE MAGEE FAMILY)

wick, coming in to New York a couple of days a week. They
found a minimal apartment with a pass-through kitchen, in a
high-rise in the theater district. They supplied it with just
enough basic furniture to sit on and hold the computer and an
enormous number of CDs and videos which became the main
item of decor. Home was still Warwick, and a second house the
family has on Cape Cod. The Magees are on the phone with
each other several times a day.

Here, then, is a family that, by its perception, has done back-flips to support Travis's commitment to dance, and has toughened up a vulnerable child, teaching him to protect himself and advance his interests in the cold, cruel world. In Fred's view, coming to Ailey demanded much more energy and commitment from Travis than what was required for weekly classes at the local dance school. "That was a hurdle he had to jump over," Fred says, "and he did."

As Travis moved up to the top level, he jumped over whatever further hurdles the school presented him with, but the Magees knew there was an open question at Ailey about the nature of his commitment. Did he want to be a concert dancer like those in Ailey or a song-and-dance man—he'd spent a summer at Ann Reinking's Broadway Theatre Project, an intensive three-week program in Florida—or a choreographer or a photographer or what? He had expressed all those interests. And as Fred further admitted, everybody knew that if Travis suddenly did an about-face and said, "I want to be a marine biologist," in a minute the whole Magee family would wheel around and be standing right behind him in the aquatic world. Travis, in his way, was as passionately driven to make his mark as any student in the school. But his passion was diffused, and the Magees understood that. As Fred put it, the Ailey people wanted to see Travis "be more singularly devoted to becoming a great dancer." The Magees, with a viewpoint more natural to parents, were quite content to wait a few years for Travis to choose a career.

When I hear the news of Travis's setbacks, it seems clear to me that there is something about this student and his family that is striking a sour note at Ailey this year, and I think I will understand the school's values better if I track down what it is. To an outsider, the Magees seem to be an intelligent, cooperative, charming family devoted to their son and to the arts. I ask Denise Jefferson and some other Ailey teachers how they view Travis, and how they define commitment. Jefferson feels that Travis has not worked as hard as he should to "change his body" and thereby sharpen his technique. Changing one's body, overcoming the obstacles it presents, is particularly important in a school like Ailey which doesn't screen out students according to physical criteria. "The school has been preparing ARTS candidates for twenty years," she says. "The students who were in it have worked like dogs to change their bodies, after class, between classes, in extra classes. I've never seen that drive in Travis." Moreover, to Travis, his request to leap ahead into more advanced classes was itself evidence of the desire to challenge himself: it was the dance equivalent of signing up for an AP math course. To Jefferson, though, it suggests a lack of artistic humility.

The ballet instructor Robert Atwood, who coordinates the PPAS program and is thus responsible for Travis, sizes things up this way: "Travis has had a relatively easy life up to now. He has a lot of family support, a lot of encouragement from everyone. He's a boy [a member of the much smaller and therefore more desirable demographic group], he was picking up well, he's bright, he's receptive, he works hard. And so he got a lot of positive reinforcement off the bat. This year has been his first experience with disappointment and he's having a hard time taking it."

Last spring, in a progress report given by Atwood and Comendador to the Magees, Atwood told Fred that Travis needed to break through a boundary. "Travis had come four-fifths of the way there," Fred remembers being told, "but there's a sheer wall in front of him that he has to scale, and he could walk along that wall for years or he could put the energy into scaling." Travis's problem, according to Atwood and Comendador, is one of both attitude and soul.

The attitude part is a tendency to negotiate everything—a lighter class schedule when he was in a repertory workshop, for example. But the soul part was something else again. "There's a point of fluidity where you become the dance," Atwood says to me. "It doesn't look like you're working, it doesn't look like you're thinking. That's a hard place to get to. It's intangible. As a teacher you try to nudge him in that direction, to give him ideas, images, thoughts, encouragement, sometimes discouragement to kick his butt."

One of Travis's faculty mentors, the jazz teacher Sharon Wong, feels this is a matter of maturity, that Travis has the talent and needs another year to start developing into an artist. He is too cautious and thus too cerebral, she believes. "Sometimes we get in the way of our bodies because we're so busy analyzing everything down to the nth degree," she says.

When Atwood and Comendador spoke with Fred and Deborah in the spring, they suggested Travis attend Ailey's summer intensive program, in hopes of progressing more rapidly to the next stage of artistic accomplishment. Travis followed their advice. He and his parents believed that was an illustration of his commitment, and in some way they expected a reward to follow. But at the beginning of the fall, the teachers thought Travis still hadn't scaled the wall and was not ready for either the advanced classes or Ailey sponsorship in ARTS. Nobody sits down with him and tries to cushion the blow. So Travis and his family feel betrayed, and the Ailey people feel he has only had a taste of reality in the dance world, and should bite his lip and soldier on.

At the same time, Shamel Pitts, a sixteen-year-old junior at LaGuardia, feels called upon to show a different sort of stoicism, and displays a single-mindedness that is quite in the Ailey mold. The forces that drive him are far different from Travis's, and family is—once again, in a nuanced way—at the root of them.

The first two things that happened to Shamel in this, his second year at Ailey, were absolutely wonderful. A slim, tallish boy with big, bright eyes and a frequent smile, he is one of those students who had no formal training before high school, outside of a dance class given by a gym instructor at his local junior high. Still, as an eighth grader, he showed something to the audition panel at LaGuardia that got him into that school. In tenth grade, he added Ailey to his dance program, and displayed enough potential throughout that first year to be rewarded this fall with a Van Lier Fellowship, the same substantial long-term stipend that Beatrice Capote has: it usually covers tuition and expenses for up to three years. More often, Van Liers go to students beginning tenth grade who can enjoy their benefits for a full three-year term, but Shamel, now an eleventh grader and in Level VI, was worth making an exception for.

The second wonderful thing that happened to Shamel is that in November he is going to star in a production at Carnegie Hall. Right away, as soon as school started, he won the title role in *Anansi,* a ballet based on the African folktale of a curious spider, which The Ailey School will put on as part of a children's performance. Shamel makes a good spider—he moves lightly—and there is something about him that fits the adventurous character who wants to gather all the wisdom of the world.

Underneath this careful lightness, Shamel is as driven as any young dancer. At LaGuardia, his Graham teacher, Penny Frank, likens him to her old student Troy Powell, the newly retired Ailey star who has just become a resident choreographer. Neither Powell nor Shamel, however musical each may be, has what dancers call "an easy body." Both started with an innate lack of flexibility, always an obstacle to overcome. But Powell, who enjoyed a glittering career in the First Company and who all the kids think is really cool, was, Frank remembers, focused, bright, and determined, knew what he wanted and went after it. Shamel, hoping to overcome the tightness in his feet and legs, is working as hard as Powell did.

But something must fuel that drive. At Ailey, Elena Comendador thinks Shamel "lives and breathes dance. He dances as if he could just close his eyes and dance away." This is important because the third thing that happened to Shamel this year, right after he won the part of Anansi, was about the most terrible thing that can happen to a sixteen-year-old. His mother died. She was thirty-six years old. When asked, he says she was his best friend.

Besides that, he doesn't say much. Right after she died, he missed a day of rehearsal and classes, later telling De Vita only that there was "a death in the family." Briefly, he went to a support group at LaGuardia. He has talked at length to only one of his Ailey-LaGuardia friends. Gradually, the news filters out. The adults at Ailey are watching, afraid something might snap. But he looks like the same Shamel, coming off the elevator in a cap and dark glasses, sort of like Troy's. Kwame Ross, the *Anansi* choreographer, calls him "the Warrior." He smiles a lot, and not just because De Vita says you're supposed to. Nothing shows. Not a trace. He might as well be onstage every single minute. Perhaps he is even performing for himself.

When I see Shamel, he tells me it hasn't really hit him, that he

doesn't believe it and that he tries to keep busy. They are Jeho-
vah's Witnesses, his family, and he believes in resurrection, that
he will see his mother again.

Shamel's rehearsals for *Anansi* overlap practice for the First
Company's production of *Memoria,* Alvin Ailey's elegy for Joyce
Trisler, which the company will perform at City Center in December together with a group of students from the Professional
and Junior Divisions. As another way to stay busy, he auditioned
for this performance and got in. Besides rehearsing through early
evening for the two presentations, he takes the usual dance classes
at LaGuardia and Ailey and keeps up with his academic work.

By late November, Penny Frank and Shamel have developed
a particular bond. Frank has been teaching at LaGuardia for thirty
years and has also taught at both Ailey and the Graham School.
Last spring, David, one of her three grown sons, died, and teaching young dancers at LaGuardia is what has kept her going this
terrible year. She and Shamel don't discuss it much, but there is,
she says, an unspoken connection between them because of their
mutual loss. She sees that he is doing his best to persevere through
sorrow, and she says, "School is a place where he can lose himself and get into a different world, not pretend it didn't happen,
but for a moment push it aside." Still, most of the talking is done
by Frank. "How was your Thanksgiving?" Shamel asks her. "Not
as bad as I was expecting, since there were many times David
wasn't with us," Frank answers. Long silence. "How was yours?"
she asks him. "It was okay," he replies.

Most dancers, even offstage, whether or not they are carrying
a heavy emotional burden, are more physically than verbally expressive. Movement is what they are used to and what they do
well. They spend most of their time in a regime that expects

them to move immediately as they have been directed. Hardly anybody ever asks for their opinion, or expects them to hunt for the right words to describe their feelings. They communicate with others through touch: they hug and kiss and stand with their hands on one another's shoulders and sit with their heads in each other's laps. Ailey and LaGuardia boys have the style of greeting older women with a hug and a kiss, which is equal to a wave or a handshake or what, in olden days, might have been a bow or a curtsy. Frank finds Shamel genuinely affectionate in this dancers' language: she does not feel, somehow, that he is denied affection at home.

Home. Shamel is considered by his teachers to be a hungry dancer—that is, someone who almost never sits still, never misses an opportunity to stretch, bend, jump or turn; someone who spends off-hours practicing in an empty studio. Though we are born with a set of talents, not all creative people have this drive. It is by no means inevitable that a child or teenager with a talent for dance will develop that talent, an interest which demands much from students. Someone or something must induce that child to spend his life honing his inborn skills. It is far from certain that the child's family will direct him toward a career which demands much from them as well, and leads at best to a few years of ill-remunerated glory, with maybe a life in the dance world later that might seem, on the outside, a bit shabby. One of the reasons I have come to Ailey is my own curiosity about what impels kids like Shamel to dance seriously. Do they keep on because their families push them, or because they need to escape their families, or because they want to defy their families, or is the story more varied and complicated?

This year dance is Shamel's chosen refuge from tragedy, but

the truth is that he was a driven dancer long before his mother's death. Several months before, Shamel had sent a fan letter to Elena Comendador, who was stepping down as codirector of The Ailey School, even though she would continue to teach there. "Dance is not just an art form to me—it's a way of living," he wrote.

Shamel and his family live on a quiet street in the Bushwick section of Brooklyn. Though the neighborhood is generally considered "inner-city," the house itself, bright and pleasant, seems to belie that phrase. Linda Taylor, his mother, married her high-school sweetheart and they had four children, of whom Shamel is the second. His parents separated amicably a few years ago, but his father remained, at least to some extent, part of the children's life.

Linda came from a large, lively extended family, and sports and performing were what they did for fun. Two uncles, four aunts and both grandparents played basketball—the grandfather and one of the aunts coached it—and one cousin is a fencer. And when the whole family got together, which was often, they would give talent shows, to which everyone had to bring a "gift"—which might be words of encouragement or a joke. The shows were full of laughter, but not necessarily very good: the point was to enjoy one another without judging. Like Travis, Afra, and Beatrice, Shamel began dancing to music when he was very small. He and his older sister made up dances that they did together. He was brought up to feel that movement was something you pursued with skill and competitive zeal (in sports) but which also brought you pleasure and relaxation (in dancing).

Before moving to Brooklyn, Shamel's family lived in Queens. When he was in the seventh grade, Shamel started to feel as though he had nothing in common with his friends. They were getting into a lot of street fights, and Shamel didn't like it. His friends turned cold to him. "People thought I felt I was too good for them," he says. "But I didn't." Throughout that year, Shamel stayed in the house and focused on his schoolwork. He was rewarded with a 94 average, his best ever, and the next year he took up with a whole new group of friends who were much more supportive of his interests.

What Shamel doesn't mention, but his aunt Zanthea, now his guardian, does, is that this was the year Linda first fell seriously ill and was in and out of the hospital ever afterward. That, Zanthea says, is when Shamel got more intensely involved with dance: "He had danced in the sixth grade," she remembers, "but in seventh grade it was different. It took him away from his mother's situation." The gym instructor taught hip-hop, and the class gave performances. First, Shamel wanted to be a hip-hop choreographer. Then, when it came time to apply for high school, he heard about LaGuardia and other kinds of dance.

While escape—both from his mother's illness and from the wrong friends—figures prominently in Shamel's passion for dance, it is not the whole story. For the past five years, he has been raised by both Linda and Zanthea. Zanthea took the children on school breaks and when their mother was in the hospital. Both women had strong personalities and encouraged Shamel to do what he wanted in life as long as he committed to doing it well. Linda, an optimistic, humorous woman even in illness, had never expected this interest to go as deep as it did, and was bemused by it; moreover, she hadn't the energy to do much more than attend one of his performances. She didn't see the need to go to school conferences, because all her children were doing well: the teachers at Ailey and LaGuardia had not met her. But she made herself felt, and she thought seriously about Shamel's new interest. She believed, for example, that he was strong enough to deal with the pressures of both school and dance; she worried, on the other hand, about his traveling out of town to dance, but knew she couldn't stand in his way.

When Shamel had his callback audition for LaGuardia, Linda was in the hospital and Zanthea was on duty. At the very last minute, when Shamel was without music for the audition, she produced her favorite Willie Nelson tape and told him, "Whether you get in or not doesn't really matter. Just be glad you got an opportunity to shoot for the moon." Zanthea, a tall, fit-looking woman in her forties who teaches biology, health, and phys ed at a small high school in downtown Brooklyn, sometimes runs sports camps in Brooklyn during the school breaks. She often asks Shamel to help out by teaching dance to the younger kids, because she knows it's fun to be an expert.

As a biology teacher, Zanthea knows that exercise relieves stress, and sees that it's helping Shamel to be embraced by Ailey and LaGuardia. But beyond these things, what impresses her most is that while, say, a basketball player has a bit of downtime in every game, a dancer must be performing every minute. "You can't fake it," she says. "If you're not present, people will know."

Being at Ailey has enabled Shamel to deal with his family crisis; being in the Magee family has governed the way Travis deals with his Ailey crisis. Day by day, life in the dance world makes constant, minute logistical demands on dancers and their families even in the absence of crisis, and the way they handle these both derives from and affects family life. Afra Hines, a seventeen-year-old Level VII Ailey student, relies enormously on her mother,

Mary Anne Holliday, in order to manage her various responsibilities for schoolwork and dance studies without (so to speak) falling down, while the logistics of Mary Anne 's work, added on to those of meeting Afra's needs, create a tricky balancing act for both of them.

Afra and her mother live in a high-rise building on Ninety-third Street and First Avenue. On a typical morning in early November, Mary Anne awakened Afra, as usual, at 6:15. After a healthy breakfast she dropped her daughter at PPAS, on West Forty-eighth Street, for Afra's 8:05 class. From there, Mary Anne drove uptown to her job as art teacher at St. Hilda's and St. Hugh's School, on 114th Street and Broadway. This is not an unusual run for Ailey parents, many of whom chauffeur their children into Manhattan from around the five boroughs before going to work. A school bus takes dance majors from PPAS to the Ailey studios early in the afternoon, and Afra carries a two-way pager through which Mary Anne lets her know whether she will be able to drive her home at the end of the day; if not, Afra will take two buses back to Ninety-third Street.

At six P.M. Mary Anne collects Afra, and they pick up hero sandwiches for dinner. Upstairs, Afra takes down her ballet bun and puts her hair in a ponytail, changes into a black bare-midriff T-shirt with sparkly red lips on it, black sweats, and sneakers, gobbles down her sandwich, and does a bit of homework. At 7:30 Mary Anne is waiting downstairs to drive her to the Broadway Dance Center on Fifty-seventh Street to rehearse for a performance this coming Saturday: Afra has landed a part in a show given by a small dance company unrelated to Ailey.

In the car, mother and daughter discuss how Afra is going to handle dance rehearsals, Ailey classes, schoolwork, and sleep. Afra is thrilled to be the only seventeen-year-old in the show, and she says, "I don't *know* how, but I will do it." They go into the weekend's logistics in greater detail. Afra needs to get a pair of baggy jeans to wear in the performance. She is going to have to rehearse till two A.M. Saturday, then get up and go to Ailey from 9:30 to 4:30, and be in the performance at 5:00. First, Mary Anne volunteers to lighten Afra's load by buying her the jeans, but that really isn't enough. Something has to give, and they finally agree she has to skip Ailey on Saturday. They arrive on Fifty-seventh Street and while Afra rehearses, Mary Anne sits downstairs, reading in the parked car. At 11:15 P.M. Afra comes down and they drive home.

It has been a long day for both Afra and Mary Anne. While many of the other Ailey students are surrounded by large families (either nuclear, like Travis's, or extended, like Shamel's), Mary Anne is a single parent and the energy, the nurturance, and the financial support that Afra needs are solely her responsibility. She has taken a second job, working at home as an independent associate with a company that sells prepaid legal services.

Afra and Mary Anne live in a one-bedroom apartment with a small kitchen and a living room where Mary Anne sleeps on a foldout bed and works at the computer. There are files and big art books all around, and the living room walls are hung with Mary Anne's paintings. At present, Afra is sharing her room with the daughter of family friends who were called away for some sort of emergency. Besides including some fairly typical teenage paraphernalia—old trophies, stuffed animals, balloons, books, lots of clothes, a kindergarten diploma—the room reflects its owner's particular interests, featuring dance posters, playbills, and a wall montage of Afra's favorite rap stars. In the hallway is a poster from a performance of *The Nutcracker* put on by the Miami City

Ballet, Edward Villella's company, in which Afra at age six danced an angel. More than the other girls at Ailey, Afra enjoys fashion, and during the day at PPAS she had spruced up her jeans by wearing a red "I Luv New York" shirt with a gold-flecked suede heart on it and sleeves separated from the shoulders, big hoop earrings, and high-heeled boots.

Perhaps none of the Ailey students I followed presents as complex a picture of environmental and biological influences as Afra. Afra's parents have given her a significant genetic and cultural endowment in the arts. Her father is a jazz trumpeter, and Mary Anne, who is half British and half Austrian, toured Europe with a performance art group before coming to the United States. Afra's parents met when both were working at a supper club in Miami.

When Afra was eight, she and Mary Anne moved from Miami to Framingham, Massachusetts, so that Afra could go to the Sudbury Valley School, an American exemplar of the ultraprogressive British Summerhill theory, which Mary Anne was smitten by when she was getting a master's degree. Sudbury Valley operates on the premise that students who are completely free to choose the way they spend their time will spend it satisfying their intellectual curiosity and learning more profoundly than they would if directed by adults. The school puts teachers and educational materials at the students' disposal, without any specified curriculum.

Despite the artistic rapport between Afra's parents, their marriage has been off and on since their daughter was little. At first Afra's father, who was getting a law degree at the University of Miami, visited Framingham on holidays, but over several years the parents' relationship deteriorated and the two separated formally. After a year, they decided to get together again, for Afra's

Afra, in classical mode
(MARY ANNE HOLLIDAY)

sake. But the reconciliation proved disastrous, and ultimately they separated once more.

For ten years, Afra studied dance at a variety of good schools that taught ballet or jazz in Miami and the Boston area. At one of the Boston area schools she also took gymnastics: all this was not only time-consuming but punishing on the body. Mary Anne says "she was pretty good at gymnastics, but she'd come home, hobbling, and she would have aches, and I really started to dislike it. But at the same time, it was her choice." Leaving Afra free to make as many choices as possible is the central belief for Mary Anne as a parent. Afra says she was better at dance than at gymnastics, so when the time came to focus, dance is what she finally chose, and she came to love it.

At the start of high school, Afra decided to leave Sudbury Valley. The school was about 99 percent white and she wanted more of a racial mix. In addition to attending the local public high, Afra was also dancing at the Boston Ballet School, a forty-five-minute daily train ride from home. It was hard to find time for homework, and since her friends weren't dancers, the friendships suffered because Afra was often too busy to hang out. Attending a performing arts school would solve both her logistical and her social problems. Afra also wanted to be part of the New York dance scene, so she could work with an agent and go to auditions.

Just before Afra began her eleventh grade year, she and Mary Anne came to New York. It is difficult to get into public high schools that late in a student's career. Neither LaGuardia nor PPAS wanted Afra at first. Academically, Mary Anne says, because of her belief in the self-educational philosophy of Sudbury Valley, she did not care what school her daughter went to. "You find information and you teach yourself," Mary Anne believes, "and that Afra does very well." But after officials of the Board of Education offered her schools that featured subjects like marine science and cosmetology, Mary Anne finally persuaded them to send Afra over to PPAS. As soon as the teachers saw her dance, Mary Anne says, they accepted her into the school's joint program with Ailey.

Once Afra was settled at PPAS, a teacher suggested she enter a citywide essay contest. "The Woman I Most Admire," her winning entry, was about her paternal grandmother, Beatrice Hines. Ms. Hines was the first black woman journalist on the *Miami Her-*

ald. Her pioneering spirit and dauntless ambition, along with some traditional, church-related African-American values, are among the varied familial influences that have shaped Afra's behavior. "She has always been the stronghold in our family, and her house has always been the family meeting place," Afra wrote, describing also how Ms. Hines took her to church, made dresses for her and cooked soul food, and came to Afra's first ballet and gymnastics performances in Miami. This makes an unusual combination with her mother's progressive philosophy and the type of education that resulted from it. Finally, Mary Anne's own personal warmth and Afra's genetic background and heritage in the performing arts have produced a talent and love for dance that may serve as an anchor in difficult times. Thus almost any theory of hardiness or child-rearing could offer Afra as Exhibit A should she succeed, or provide the "aha!" should she fall down: strong family support, strict religious values, freedom of choice, encouragement of artistic development, and single parenting after a stressful separation are all part of the picture.

In her first months at Ailey, Afra had some adjusting to do. The Sudbury philosophy with which she'd grown up is quite the opposite of the strict, traditional Ailey regime. A teacher would give Afra a correction and she'd make a face. The teacher—not surprisingly—would interpret that as an example of attitude, while by Afra's lights she was trying to improve and listening to corrections, even though her facial expression didn't reflect those feelings. Afra felt she was dancing for herself, not for her teachers. "Even if I don't agree with what other people think of my dancing," she says, "I'm still going to dance, you know?"

In the middle of her first year at Ailey, relations between Afra's parents and between Afra and her father took a sharp downward turn. Afra became—in Mary Anne's words—"so depressed she was catatonic." Mary Anne thought of seeking professional help for her daughter. Finally one day she lost her patience and said, "Look, we came to New York so you could dance. You chose to go to this high school, you chose to dance here." Then Mary Anne went out to put money in the parking meter. By the time she came back in, she had cooled down and said, "I just want to help you, so tell me what it is going to take. You could leave school, you could stop dancing, whatever you want." Afra began to pull out of her depression. "She became so much more serious about her dance," says Mary Anne. "Everybody at Ailey noticed it." Mary Anne believes that by expressing support, instead of irritation—by staying true, in the end, to her philosophy—she turned Afra around.

The family stories of both Afra and Travis reflect the heavy load placed on the parents of young dancers. They are just two samples of the Ailey families whose lives are configured around the need to support talent. There are some Ailey students who are dancing despite resistance from one or both parents, but most of those who are doing well in this world have parents who take on extra tasks, from chauffeuring to checking the tights for runs to pondering a host of decisions more complicated than those that confront the ordinary parent. Are these teenagers with their impressive technique outrageous prodigies or normal kids with above-normal ability in music and movement, who have reached Level VI or VII partly because the adults in their lives have worked especially hard to maintain their climb? Might there be other equally talented children whose talent we'll never see, since they've dropped out or failed to start because they lacked family support? And does it take special kinds of families to produce distinguished violinists, tennis players, and mathematicians as well as dancers?

The classic study of talent development, published in 1985,[1] was done at the University of Chicago by a team of researchers under the direction of the late Benjamin S. Bloom, an educational scholar of worldwide distinction, whose previous cognitive research ultimately guided the federal government's Headstart Program. This later work is a retrospective study of 120 Americans who by the age of thirty-five had achieved international renown for their accomplishments in some branch of sports, the arts, or mathematics and science. Subsequent research on talent development tends to cite Bloom, particularly on the role of the family.

The family life of Bloom's distinguished subjects took place during the fifties and sixties, and there have been important cultural changes since then. But the families he followed and many of the Ailey families—particularly those mentioned here—still resemble each other. The parents of talented achievers all seem to set an example of active leisure and hard work, and expect the same of their children. Shamel, Travis, and Afra all get good grades, and have family models of industrious effort. If Shamel comes home late, he gets a talk on time management from Zanthea, an expert at balancing domestic and professional tasks, who is out coaching in her spare time. Mary Anne Holliday, an artist herself, works two jobs, and Beatrice Hines's professional courage is part of Afra's family legend.

At leisure, most of the Chicago families were enthusiastic amateurs in the domains their children ultimately entered. Sports parents were the type who pushed their children to go out to play ball, and sporting events were family entertainment. The cultural parents, on the other hand, played musical instruments and took the family to concerts. It was parents and relatives in the Chicago study who first introduced the children to their talent field, usually in the context of informal family activities. They did not do this with some particular career goal: it was just something the family did together, or a way for the child to have fun. The children took to it, so the parents got them lessons. There are echoes of this in the stories of Shamel, Travis, and Afra: the shows that Shamel's family put on, the keyboard instrument Fred Magee gave Travis and the way the whole family studied tap, the early preschool dancing lessons Mary Anne offered Afra.

When Bloom's subjects were growing up, most mothers did not have jobs outside their homes, but shepherding their children's nascent careers required a sacrifice just the same. The work of being an arts or sports parent involved vetting prospective teachers and coaches, reading books and subscribing to magazines in the field, and arranging the family's routine to conform to their child's schedule. All of the Ailey children I got to know had working parents, and yet the way many of those parents reconfigured their lives to accommodate their children's talent was not much different from that of Bloom's group.

As the children in Bloom's study grew older, their parents' roles altered somewhat, but talent was still at the center of their lives. The parents had generally been strict and demanding about schoolwork in the lower grades, but they gradually began to make concessions. Given the demands on their children's time, they realized that something had to give, and parents were content with average grades. Similarly, while Shamel, Travis, and Afra do well in school, academic excellence is clearly not their first order of business, nor that of their families. As long as the kids don't develop problems, their parents seem to accept a slightly lower standard than that child might otherwise have achieved. Still, as Fred Magee notes," Travis is one broken leg away from not being a dancer, as all of them are." Most Ailey parents don't forget that, recognizing their child's need to have something else to do should misfortune strike.

While the parents of Ailey teenagers, like the Chicago parents, are beginning to defer to their children's expertise in their chosen field, dance is still the main topic of family discussion, and families' lives are built around Ailey. The Chicago parents quite naturally grew close to other families with similar pressures, and so do some Ailey families.

During my year at Ailey, I also encountered dancers whose parents did not support them, and who seemed to continue dancing as a refuge from who knows what grief at home. We will be meeting a few of those. But the dancers who become successful in spite of overwhelming personal obstacles are, by my observation, in the minority at Ailey. For the most part, my experience bears out Bloom's conclusion of "strong evidence that no matter what the initial characteristics (or gifts) of the individuals, unless there is a long and intensive process of encouragement, nurturance, education, and training, the individuals will not attain extreme levels of capability. . . . "[2] Most of the stars at The Ailey School, the dependable students whose performance is consistent and improves over time, have a claque of family devotees behind them.

Atwood and Comendador have urged Travis to compete for ARTS on his own. One of Ailey's Horton teachers has agreed to do his choreography without charge, even though Travis will be an entrant to ARTS without official Ailey sponsorship. Travis himself is trying to deal with disappointment maturely. Maybe, he says, his expectations were considered arrogant, and he doesn't want to give that impression. He must learn to just let it go, because pushing would make everything worse. He has learned to exhibit the stoicism of the dancer, and in this respect Travis's style, which fits both the situation and his personality, is one of positive reframing. He says he is working on college applications, doing photo shoots, and taking class, and he is sure this year will be "amazing."

All the Magees have talked it over, and in essence they have told Travis just what the Ailey people told him: to bite his lip and soldier on.

Shamel, bolstered by relatives and focused on dance, seems to be controlling himself remarkably well. For the past five years, with his family's support, he has used dance as a haven and an outlet; this year, because of events in Shamel's life, the value of this solution is being tested most seriously. Zanthea Taylor, his guardian, still waits for her nephew to break out with an attitude, but she hasn't seen it. He never seems to raise his voice, even when he is challenged or frustrated. He doesn't act like a typical adolescent. Perhaps, she says, he might be a late bloomer.

And Mary Anne Holliday looks forward to hearing Afra's plans for what she will do after graduation, whether she will apply to colleges or just plunge into the professional dance world. What matters, she believes, is that Afra pursue her dream wherever it may lead.

Four

Building an Ensemble

While October is the month in which students have begun to settle into their classwork, it is also a month of rehearsing for the school's first performance in early November. There are four rehearsal studios that are scattered around the floor above the main Ailey complex, and it is in these studios that both the First Company and Ailey II rehearse when they are in New York. Their lounge and dressing rooms are here, and so is the physical therapy room. Some Ailey School classes are also held in these rooms, and part of the floor belongs to the Trisha Brown Company, another dance troupe. During a rehearsal, the sound of, say, a pianist tinkling away at a lively Gershwin tune or a drummer intensely hammering out competing African rhythms may travel into the studio, distracting the young performers' con-

Shamel practices.
(TRACY INMAN)

centration and jangling the nerves of the teachers and the choreographer. There is never enough space in the building, which
keeps the hallways humming with activity and sprinkled with
dancers doing homework and practicing splits. Only staff at the
highest level in Ailey have anything resembling privacy.

Tonight, at six on a dark Monday evening late in the month,
Studio 7 and the hall outside it are abuzz. Shamel is in the hallway, pirouetting. Three other Level VI boys, Serge, Ryan, and
Jerome, are stretching and turning with him. Beatrice arrives,
along with the three Level VI girls who will dance in this performance, Monique Massiah, Frajan Payne, and Laurence Jacques.

They are LaGuardia students who are best friends, known to Ailey teachers as the Supremes and to their classmates as the Three Musketeers. They go into the studio and dump their bags in the corner.

Inside, Melanie Person is working with a group of preteen girls in navy leotards and lappa skirts. "Let's do the Indian dance while we're waiting," she says, and the girls go into head isolations and square, Hortonish movements. A round man with glasses is telling the girls that the arms here should be "almost like an ostrich," which seems to mean the hands are flexed. He is Kwame Ross, the choreographer, and a minute later he calls into the hallway, "Gentlemen, come inside! We've gotta create magic in an hour and a half!"

Rehearsal is not like ordinary class. There is electricity in the air. Instead of one focused group in the center of the room, there are knots of people doing different steps in corners. While the adults bustle and confer between segments of drilling the dancers, the boys and girls are bantering and flirting and cutting up ("Gentlemen," shouts Ross. "This is called rehearsal, right?").

Dancing in performances teaches students to work with the resources at hand—that is, the time allotted for rehearsals and the space where the presentation will be held—and to cope instantly with stressful circumstances that may happen onstage. When students perform together, it strengthens their bond, a truism captured in the phrase *esprit de corps,* and group performances improve as dancers (or actors or musicians) get to know one another. Accordingly, The Ailey School offers its advanced students a balance of concerts and classwork. Students perform both in school repertory workshops and, on occasion, with the First Company. From the school's point of view, of course, there is an additional benefit: showing off its student performers is a good way to raise money and increase the status of the institution.

While the school gives two regular studio performances during the school year and an end-of-the-year show in the auditorium of John Jay College nearby, opportunities to perform for the outside world vary from season to season. This fall a group of students reaching down to Level IV will dance in *How Anansi Learned His Greatest Lesson. Anansi* is a new half-hour ballet which the school will present for an audience of children aged five to twelve at Carnegie Hall on Saturday afternoon, November 10. The other half of the program will be Ailey II dancing an excerpt from *Revelations.*

Surprisingly enough, The Ailey School has never actually put on a show for children, although it has an arts-in-education program that sends out performers and "teaching artists" into the schools. When Carnegie Hall invited the school to participate in its matinee series, Nasha Thomas-Schmitt, the retired Ailey dancer who runs the program, was delighted. Most particularly, she wanted to give the boys a chance to play leading roles in a performance, because they were complaining that the girls got all the "good stuff." To hold a young audience's attention the ballet would have to be based on some children's story, so Thomas-Schmitt began mulling over Dr. Seuss and talking to librettists, composers, and choreographers. One of them suggested that an African folktale would be more unusual and interesting.

The one that leaped out at her was *Anansi,* the story of a spider who wants to gather all the wisdom of the world, builds a boat, and sets off from his African village, and is buffeted about from France to India to China and back home, where, like the heroes of folktales the world over, he finally learns that much wisdom resides. This would work, Thomas-Schmitt thought. It had parts for younger Ailey School dancers: the older children in the audience could relate to them. There were a couple of lead parts for boys, and this served a double purpose: some of the boys in the audience, Thomas-Schmitt knew, would have to be dragged to a dance performance, and this would grab their interest. Shamel, the boy chosen to play Anansi, was limber and spiderlike and "very personable," she told me, describing an appeal that would be as evident onstage as it is off.

The planning had begun in June, at the end of the previous term. One of the teaching artists in Thomas-Schmitt's program was Kwame Ross, who is both a percussionist and a choreographer, and is the rehearsal director for Urban Bush Women, a small, socially conscious modern troupe with studios in Brooklyn. When Ross teaches, he uses a movement style which Thomas-Schmitt calls "African mix"—that is, it has elements of West African and Caribbean style, but also some ballet and some Hortonesque modern. It is his own creation, she says, and very exciting. Thomas-Schmitt had Ross give an open evening workshop which drew about thirty kids, and their responses to his movement looked promising. No one was able to assign parts at that time because it wasn't certain which kids would be back in the fall.

So Thomas-Schmitt and Ross had to cast the production at the very beginning of the fall term, when they held an audition, placed everyone who came to it somewhere in the ballet, and found themselves with a troupe of twenty-six kids, some new to Ailey and some veterans. The rehearsal schedule was complicated by the closing of the school for about a week following the September 11 attack, and the fact that things did not really settle down into business as usual at The Ailey School until October. Some kids registered late. Two scheduled rehearsals were canceled. Shamel, the star, missed a rehearsal after his mother died. The other lead character, an energetic LaGuardia boy who played the Wind, dropped out of both *Anansi* and The Ailey School, finding it too stressful to fulfill his dance commitments and keep up with his schoolwork. The logical replacement was another LaGuardia boy, a dynamic tenth grader named Serge Desroches, who had started at Ailey over the summer. Both lead dancers now had choreography to catch up with.

In the hall outside tonight, Elena Comendador is measuring the Supremes, Beatrice, and three Level VI boys for their costumes for the balletic French Court Dance: white and gold brocade vests and skirts for the girls, the same fabric in tunics for the boys. Thomas-Schmitt and Ross have bought baskets for the African villagers and raffia skirts for Desroches and the boys who will dance with him in the village and boat scenes and then change into their brocade court costumes. As Anansi, Shamel will wear knee-length tights and a fishnet shirt. A prop shop has supplied a papier-mâché dragon for the Chinese New Year piece, which features the younger girls dancing with parasols.

Melanie Person, drilling the blue leotards for the Indian dance, says "Exaggerate your gestures—onstage is not like a studio! Really do it big, so I can see you!" Tracy Inman tells the village girls, "Do something with your basket—put it on your shoulder or your hip." Some of the girls try it on their heads. Person says, "Look like you're listening: a little more energy! React to what Anansi is saying!" This is not the daily *plié* and *relevé*: it is acting, and the kids are not used to it. There is a point in the script where the villagers have to sing a few lines: nobody seems particularly troubled about how well the dancers sing. They have fresh, young voices, and they will be fine. While the steps must be perfect, the clarity of vowels and consonants is apparently not a priority.

Kwame Ross does not do the daily *plié* and *relevé,* either. He uses only a minimum amount of the basic dance vocabulary so the kids will feel comfortable, but mostly choreographs by demonstrating and working with the dancers until the dance looks right. Only Kwame knows what's in Kwame's head, which makes Thomas-Schmitt, Inman, and Person nervous because Kwame tends to arrive late for rehearsals, and precious time gets lost. Studio space is at a premium. Rehearsals are tightly scheduled to take place after the regular dance classes, but with the knowledge that children have to get home, have dinner, and do their homework. Ross feels the rehearsal time is not adequate, especially since there are so many costume changes, and consoles himself by saying he is more about process than product, but the Ailey people, understandably, are about product.

Throughout the rehearsals, the adults are clearly tense while the kids are cool. On Thursday afternoon before the Saturday performance, there is a run-through at Carnegie Hall. I ask Thomas-Schmitt what worries her the most: "Nothing worries me—they're going to be fabulous," she says evenly, and right afterward sharply yells, "Everybody has to do this a bit faster; it's a big stage!"

Off to one side in the orchestra, Inman is working with Beatrice, who will be playing the Queen of France. "Walk out there like you're the queen," he says. He reads a line from the script: "I'll show you my gardens with flowers!" Beatrice swishes a bit. "No, not like a Valley girl!" he pleads. "Look at your body—this is what you look like! Use your arm like it's a flower. Use your neck and your head. Use your back. How long have you been dancing? Practice this walk. You're looking up—you're proud this is your kingdom. 'This is what I have!' you're thinking."

When Beatrice finally gets the movement to Inman's liking, she looks credibly regal but very embarrassed. Whatever fantasies this down-to-earth teenage girl might have, being the Queen of France is not one of them. "You're so shy," he says. "How can you be a dancer if you're inhibited about what you're doing?" When Inman leaves her, Beatrice tells me, "Ailey is very technical. You have to be taught to act."

A large bag of raffia skirts has been emptied out on the stage. "You guys have to learn to take care of your props," Nasha says. "When you finish, fold all that up. Singers, do that again! Show me that dancers can sing!"

In the first rows of the orchestra, some parents sit watching while a few little brothers scamper up and down the aisles. The Supremes, who have a break, are sitting a few rows back, checking out the leotards in the new issue of *Dance Discount* magazine. I ask them if they're excited to be here. "No," they all answer at once.

It is Saturday, November 10, backstage at Carnegie two hours before the performance, Elena Comendador is doing some last-minute stitching on the boys' court costumes; bright Indian silks are hanging on a rack nearby. "Sew the elastic on your shoes," Comendador says to the boys. "I don't want any lazy-man knotted elastics. Don't cheat. Cheat once and your whole life is cheating! If you want to be dancers, you have to sew your shoes! Sewing shoes is good luck."

In the big dressing room where boys and girls can mingle,

everybody is eating pizza. Serge Desroches plays quiet jazz on the piano. Walkmans are everywhere. Some dancers are rehearsing their parts; some are praying or meditating; some are putting their hair in buns and sticking sparkles on their eyelids; a boy and girl are entangled on a stool, making out, and nobody pays them any mind.

I realize that for the kids these performances, whether in repertories, in school shows, or with the First Company during the season, are why they come to Ailey twenty hours a week, year after year. Without regular performances, they might have given up. Yes, they are disciplined, but the discipline is *for* something. One day, Laurence Jacques tells me she feels different when she's performing: "I feel like all my emotions are just coming out of me," she says. "You take deep breaths and all the pain and agony comes out of your body and these feelings take over." Laurence became aware of her emotions back in Level IV when she was thirteen and first performed with the company. The music for the ballet she was in made her happy, and she smiled and danced with it. She responds personally to the music and mood of the ballet: sad music makes her think of the time her parents were getting separated, and she dances with a sad face. "If you were feeling some kind of emotion on an ordinary Wednesday afternoon in class," I ask her, "would that come out?" "No," she says. Class, of course, focuses on technique, and it is essential to subordinate the emotions and concentrate on getting each movement right.

I get the same answer from three of the boys, who are surprisingly matter-of-fact in front of each other in describing dance as a release of feelings. Serge, at fifteen, thinks of dancing—into which he puts depression, sadness, and happiness as well—as "a way of getting rid of waste." He appears to grasp the idea of emotional discharge on a highly sophisticated level. He, Kyllian Franklin (who is fourteen), and Ryan Rankine (sixteen) all agree they dance better when they're sad. "There should be a connection between your real life and the steps," says Ryan, who already understands that a dancer's experiences in the world improve his art.

For an hour before the concert, there is a preconcert session in which Ailey II dancers, a storyteller, and the musicians are available to chat with the audience. The Junior Division students are not part of this because Thomas-Schmitt wants them to be perfectly relaxed before the performance. She herself tells the audience a bit about the school and the company, and introduces the narrator and the musicians. Backstage, the Supremes are putting on their elaborate court costumes. There is a video monitor near which Shamel, now in costume, lurks, stretching, pirouetting, watching the introduction, and waiting for his cue. Shamel has resolved to be calm, relax, and have fun.

Thomas-Schmitt is finished and walks offstage. Shamel says, "Miss Thomas, when am I supposed to go on?" "Not now, I'll come and tell you," she says, walking off. Shamel relaxes a bit, and suddenly he hears the music. He had better get out there, take charge, and just do it. It does not feel the same as rehearsal. It is dark and there are millions of people in the audience.

The dancers have not rehearsed much with the real musicians, and more important, the real musicians have not rehearsed much with the dancers. So whatever happens, the musicians keep on going. To one audience member who has watched a lot of piecemeal rehearsals, something looks strange with the performance. Shamel seems to be improvising a bit. The villagers come out and

things are as they should be. But when it is time for the French
Court Dance, the entrances are late and from the wrong place,
Laurence's partner has not arrived , and the musicians keep playing. There is more improvisation. Though most of the audience
wouldn't notice, the performance lacks crispness. It seems as if
there are two separate Level VI and VII ensembles, one for the
girls and one for the boys.

Afterward, the girls are upset and angry at the boys, but
pleased with their own work. "I loved those costumes," Beatrice
says sadly, wishing that every detail of the performance had been
as perfect as the white-and-gold vests and skirts. Laurence says
she gets a headache every time she thinks of the missed entrance.
Monique feels satisfaction that she looked the audience in the
eye and improvised. All the girls say in an ironic tone that their
parents liked it.

When I track down Thomas-Schmitt for a debriefing, she appears to be, in general, very pleased. She says she wished all the
girls had come out when the music started instead of waiting for
the boys. "That kind of thing comes through learning," she tells
me. "It could be fifteen years from now when they're dancing
professionally and they will know how to work through a situation." She had talked with the kids about what to do if part of a
costume falls off (just leave it, pick it up if possible during your
exit but don't make a big thing of it), and what to do if a dancer
falls down (it doesn't matter—people fall all the time—it's how
you recover that's important: keep your composure and stay in
character). But no one, of course, imagined the problematic entrance. *Anansi* was not, she pointed out, a finished work like *Cry*
that can be taught: it was being made on student dancers during

these scant rehearsals. The younger dancers had never been in a major performance before, and Thomas-Schmitt thought they were amazing.

Shamel and the rest of the cast had indeed gained a vivid lesson about the surprises of performing, which perhaps might turn out to be more useful than if everything had gone perfectly. When Thomas-Schmitt forgot to come back and give Shamel his cue, he saw that adults make mistakes, and everyone learned that knowing the choreography and dancing artistically are not enough, that you have to keep your wits about you and be ready to improvise, that "escape" and "emotional release" are imperfect benefits. Just as Kwame Ross had insisted a couple of days earlier, they were learning that training to be a performer is about process, not product.

Part of that process was what the young dancers experienced as a group: the girls, together, were disappointed in the boys and happy with themselves and one another: they had a common memory of *Anansi* which they would bring as an ensemble to future performances. Perhaps this time the boys' memory—the uncomfortable feeling of not quite measuring up—was a bit more private. Still, they had other opportunities to build a sense of ensemble, which is equally a by-product of the less exciting hours spent in class.

Even while the students were rehearsing for *Anansi,* they have had to keep up with their ordinary dance class work. By adult standards, this is even more important than the transitory highs of dancing onstage. A serious student may dream of performing explosively, moving with artistry, and standing out in the crowd, but to bring all this off well requires the slow development of strength, balance, and coordination. Besides the urgency, passion, and excitement that hold an audience's attention, the student must have both the patience and the discipline to spend day after day polishing difficult, unglamorous steps.

Therefore, at the advanced levels of the Junior Division the kids must learn not only to do big jumps and turns but to keep control in the landings, to shift the weight between legs easily, to polish the little connecting steps, to hold the upper body still but not stiff, and then to make the same upper body absolutely fluid. To cultivate this ability requires that students postpone gratification, a skill which, of course, adolescents must learn in life as well as in dance. In the context of dance, it means getting the hard stuff right before you reach the fun stuff.

Pacing these two types of learning is a challenge for the school as well as the students. Tatiana Litvinova tells me that "in Russia we are not afraid, oh, they will be bored and they will leave, because we are choosing ten or fifteen kids from one thousand. Here we are a bit concerned. . . ." And Litvinova is also contrasting American dance training with that of a culture that prizes perfection in the art of ballet and lavishes admiration on its principals. As Robert Atwood describes a continuing problem, in Ailey and in some other American dance schools, a child has talent, beauty, charm. The child gets picked for performances, at Lincoln Center, at Kennedy Center, at City Center: he or she looks good in the front row. And what happens? "The kids start thinking they're pretty good," Atwood says. "And they stop working." The children who are really going to go someplace, Atwood says, are the ones who bite the bullet and work on, for example, strong *fondus*—bending the knee, going down slowly on one leg, and holding it, no wobbling—and not just what's faster and fancier. But of course, without something faster and

Elena Comendador, in turtleneck, second row, and her Level Vs, Spring 2001—
who became Level VIs that fall. In the rear: Shamel, Monique, and Roger
form a "center" trio; to the left of Comendador: Frajan.
Front row: Laurence, left; at far right, Charlotte.
(MARBETH, 2001)

fancier, without some pot of gold, why work on the strong *fon-dus?* Finally, how hard one works is to some extent affected by how hard others in the studio are working, and by the constant consideration of where one stands in relation to a roomful of other people doing exactly the same steps. To thrive in a school and later in a company, dancers must learn to manage relations with other dancers for their own profit.

It is an especially mild and beautiful fall this year, and the autumn leaves are still visible from the studio windows through November.

This afternoon the lavender leotards—Level VI—are in Litvinova's ballet class. The Supremes stand next to one another at the barre as usual. At the break, between the barre part and the center part, they help one another get a leg up, then go over a combination. Other girls in the class are either trying to join their conversation or sitting on the floor, looking up at them. Before class they were sitting in the lounge, sharing french fries and reviewing the day. It is not that they are very exclusive—different people join them from time to time—but if one is there, the others are not far away. And they take care of one another: if one can't find her leotard, the others will help her look for it and they will all be late together. If one of them (always the same one) gets to fooling around with someone not in the group when she should be paying attention, another one (always the same one) will tell her to stop, and thus the two girls will get in trouble for talking together.

The quietest one, Frajan Payne, who is African-American, is composed and ladylike. The bubbly, mischievous one, kept in line by Frajan, is Laurence Jacques (Laurence is a common French girl's name), who is Haitian-American. And Monique Massiah, whose mother was born in Haiti and whose father is African-American, is the willowy girl with high cheekbones and fragile beauty, the one who looks most like a ballerina. Each girl has a different aura, a quality which some teachers hope will ultimately keep them from competing for the same roles.

Relative to the others in their group, they are cool and self-confident: clearly less so than twelfth graders like Afra and Beatrice, but they are at ease around The Ailey School: they own the place. They are the stars at their level.

Films about young dancers tend to focus on either the first audition or the moment of stardom, finding it convenient to gloss over the years of patient, repetitive polishing, working, and marking time in between. Frajan, Laurence, and Monique, tenth graders at LaGuardia, are in that middle period, as if they were in a sailboat becalmed on a big lake, waiting for a strong breeze to come and blow them to shore. Of course, it is not one sailboat that they are in together; it is three separate sailboats, which may reach shore at different rates. Frajan has won the third Van Lier this year. Chalk one up for her. Shamel and Beatrice have the other two. Monique has just got a photo shoot, modeling leotards for *Pointe* magazine: chalk one up for her, although Monique, being several months younger than the other two, will not be eligible for a fellowship until the spring term. Probably for that reason, she was put one class below the others in Graham, an Ailey decision she finds very irritating, because she knows she is on the same plane as the others. Laurence, like most of the lavenders who are old enough, has a Level II fellowship. She has very good feet and terrific energy, and when she focuses that energy in the right place, she will be splendid.

For these three, the high point of their time at Ailey—so far—came a year and a half ago, when they were part of a group of nine girls from the Junior Division who went down to Washington, D.C., to dance *Cry* with a company member, Dwana Adiaha Smallwood, on the occasion of Judith Jamison's winning the Kennedy Center Honor for Lifetime Achievement. *Cry* is the exultant and demanding solo dance that Alvin Ailey made on Jamison in 1971 in tribute to his mother: it had established Jamison's fame, and after her retirement she taught it to a series of women dancers who thus became the anointed, the *Cry* girls, acquiring a special luster in a supposedly egalitarian company. The little girls dancing the last section in vivid white dresses just like

Monique models a leotard for Pointe *magazine.*
(PHOTO BY ELLEN CRANE FOR
POINTE MAGAZINE, 2001)

Smallwood's were an affecting surprise for Jamison, and a perfect commercial for The Ailey School.

The Kennedy Center performance turned out to be an intense day in an intense year. The Supremes and the other student dancers had got on the bus at seven in the morning to ride down with Smallwood and the rest of the First Company, spending hours hanging out with them, and then had stood in the wings *this close* to Bill Cosby with celebrities all around. The whole presentation, girls included, was on nationwide television. Before they went on, they were of course extremely nervous and had held hands and prayed together, but the performance was so captivating the kids got to repeat it at City Center with another *Cry* girl, Linda-Denise Evans, and finally again at the school's spring show.

Something very special happened after the spring show. Dwana Smallwood herself had invited the girls to her apartment for a sleepover. Smallwood—who was at that time twenty-six—believed she had a responsibility to reach out to teenage girls, to bridge the gap between people her age and theirs. She had a workshop she had developed for girls in public schools to help them see "the hero in themselves." So right after the show Smallwood rented a limo and picked up the Supremes and another of the student dancers. On each girl's seat was a journal that Smallwood had made for them. The limo took them to an Indian restaurant, then to Blockbusters to rent a movie, and then to get ice cream. When they returned to Smallwood's apartment, they sat up till 3:30 in the morning talking about, as Laurence remembers, "girl things." The next morning, Smallwood cooked breakfast, after which everybody sat on her bed and drank tea and gave themselves facials with hot towels and did their nails. Later, they put on their best clothes and went to the Brooklyn Academy of Music, the borough's leading cultural center, to see a documentary about girls their age, and finally they stopped off at Smallwood's favorite restaurant, an African place across the street from BAM.

But after that glittering year, the Supremes had four years of

The Supremes and others dance Cry, *2000.*
Front row: left, Monique; center, Frajan
(MARBETH)

high school and Junior Division ahead of them, a limitless stretch of *pliés* and *relevés* on dark February afternoons, and how they would weather it was anybody's guess. At fifteen, they are, as Laurence wistfully points out, too old to dance *Cry,* but too young to have formed a personal style.

Laurence and Monique met as ten- and eleven-year-olds in Level II. They were youngest in the class, surrounded by older girls, but didn't exchange phone numbers and become close until the next year in Level III. That was when Frajan came to Ailey, and the manner in which she joined the group foreshadowed the way all three girls would relate to one another: Frajan plopped down on a bench in the hall, right next to Laurence's mother, and started doing her homework. When Laurence came out, her mother said, as Laurence remembers it, "This is a nice little girl named Frajan—she's doing her homework. You would never do that." That would seem to be a surefire friendship killer, but apparently it wasn't, and the twosome became a trio right away.

The differences between quiet, conscientious Frajan and effervescent, distractable Laurence have been a running joke among the girls and their mothers ever since. One day I am sitting in Ailey's reception room with the two girls. "How much are your parents on your case?" I ask them. Laurence rolls her eyes upward. "My mother is on my case too much," she says. "'Why aren't you more like Frajan? If I was Frajan, I wouldn't be your friend!' I'm just like, 'Mom, all right!'"

"What's so great about Frajan?" I ask.

"She's more responsible than I am," Laurence says. Frajan adds, "I think her mom tells her to be more like me because Laurence is really crazy and can get off track very quickly. People can persuade her to go somewhere she's not supposed to go. So her mom is letting me lead her—that's the message."

Besides having danced together for the past four years, the Supremes and their families have much in common, as indeed, there is a certain sociological common ground within many of the small groups of friends at Ailey. All three girls have older sisters, and Monique and Frajan have brothers in middle school who go out for sports, pulling their parents in two different directions. Laurence's mother and Monique's mother are registered nurses at different hospitals. Frajan's father and Laurence's father are both bus drivers. Monique's father is deputy director of human resources at the Port Authority of New York and New Jersey, which was headquartered in the World Trade Center, where Frajan's mother, a clerical worker now at SONY, was once employed. On September 11, Yvonne Payne knew the Massiahs well enough to scoop up Monique along with Frajan and take her back to Brooklyn where they waited together at the Paynes' until they heard, after many hours, that Michael Massiah was safe.

Perhaps, when their enthusiasm flags and they look with just a bit of envy at LaGuardia classmates who get to go home or just hang out when the school day ends, it is friendship, community, and defined identity that keep the Supremes here. Like Beatrice, Afra, and Travis at PPAS, they are part of the special select group that walks over from LaGuardia to Ailey, that gossips about the others, that talks on the phone and instant-messages one another when they finally do get home. For all these years neither Monique nor Frajan nor Laurence has had to be the new girl, the oddball, the interloper. It is the Supremes who choose to befriend others.

It is, of course, most unlikely that all three of the girls will cut loose and become mature artists at the very same moment. Each of the Supremes admits that there are some things so personal that she wouldn't tell the other two; that is testimony to an inner life—a set of feelings to express or not express in dancing—that will affect their progress to the next step on the ladder. I ask Kevin Predmore, who teaches Graham to Frajan and Laurence, to size up those two girls, and what I know about their differences—Frajan's caution and Laurence's cheekiness—seems to emerge clearly in his observations about his class. "Frajan stays in the front and observes very well, but doesn't put herself into the fire right away," Predmore tells me. He senses a reserve in her dancing and feels she needs to "move the body in the space and the space with the body." Using Graham-esque terminology, he comments, "Right now, the body stops almost even before the fingers do."

Laurence, on the other hand, is, in Predmore's perception, more willing to take risks. "She puts herself right into the fire," he tells me. But he thinks she is feigning nonchalance, trying to look as if she's not paying attention when, out of the corner of her eye, she is. "Laurence fidgets quite a bit, but she's listening, " he says. The third person in this freighted equation is Monique, slightly younger, with some need for physical strengthening, and more inclined toward ballet than modern.

In one way, Monique, Frajan, and Laurence are typical teenage best friends. But teenage best friendship, and Supremacy, are a special, complex thing among dancers. At the end of a good class or a particularly skillful demonstration by one of their peers (who is also a competitor), dance students applaud. When one dancer feels depressed or insecure, another dancer, exhibiting no schadenfreude, must tell her it's just a bad day and tomorrow will be better. Those who attend the performing arts schools know that as students they are special for having passed a selective audition, and at minimum their classmates, who passed the same audition, are special, too.

The adults at Ailey, LaGuardia, and PPAS, not surprisingly, celebrate the intensity of friendship in the dance world and in the artistic world in general. Paul Saronson, principal of LaGuardia for fifteen years, points out that many of his students travel for up to two hours each way to get to school: they have made a commitment to leave neighborhoods where they feel comfortable and undertake a tedious journey to develop their talent among strangers. (Another view of the students' commuting might be that they are leaving neighborhoods where they feel uncomfortable and taking on a tedious journey to develop their talent among kindred souls.) Either way, as Saronson notes, "You're starting off with a population that is different. Being in the school tends to solidify this." Difference from the neighborhood kids is a point of pride.

Within LaGuardia or PPAS, students, not surprisingly, feel a strong bond with those in their discipline. When I join the Supremes at lunch in the LaGuardia cafeteria, they tell me that the tables break down by major: the actors are here, the musicians are there, the artists are the ones over there with the purple hair. The dancers in the upper grades don't come to the lunchroom, preferring to hang out around the Dance Department office. There are always a few practicing in the studios. It is, of course, natural that students should want to talk over the day's experiences with others who have shared them. But more affinities exist than these: some temperamental similarity among students within each major is apparent to those faculty members who teach everyone.

Like Saronson, Kim Bruno, as assistant principal for performing arts at PPAS, has a chance to compare dancers with other performers. She finds a strong contrast between the dancers and, in particular, the musical theater students, and her observations reinforce the notion of dance as an ensemble activity. As Bruno notes, the success of a dance performance depends on everybody being good and in phase with each other, while musical theater students get up one at a time and present. "Look at someone like Nathan Lane. How do you think he would fare in a dance class at Alvin Ailey?" Bruno asks me. "Kids gravitate toward the kind of discipline they feel comfortable with." It is true that the sum-

mer at Ann Reinking's workshop cured Travis Magee forever of
his desire to be a song-and-dance man because he didn't like, as
Deborah Magee remembers, "the pushing to the front of the
line, the in-your-faceness of musical theater."

Thus dancers relax best with other dancers, but still feel comfortable and friendly with the artists, actors, and musicians at the
performing arts schools. Not all students at Ailey go to these
schools, however, and those who commute from the suburbs or
attend ordinary New York private schools feel a definite distance
from their civilian peers. Joi Favor, a classmate of the Supremes
in Level VI, is in the twelfth grade at Nyack High School, and
says she feels she lives two separate lives. Part of her suburban life
is her boyfriend who, she feels, like most people "from the outside," doesn't understand that you have to spend time and live
with pressure to get anywhere in dance. "If you really want
something, it's not going to come to you," Joi says. Speaking to
the same point of separateness from the mainstream, Charlotte
Kaufman, another Level VI and an eighth grader at the challenging Brearley School, says she, too, feels divided. The combination of dance and a heavy load of schoolwork has kept her away
from her schoolfriends and caused a rift with them, which was
only healed when she invited them to see her dance in an Ailey
School performance. After they saw how much she loved the
dance part of her life, they began to understand what she was
willing to give up for it.

Among fellow students within the dance world, then, spiritual connection and community membership are clearly one side
of the coin. What is the other?

The answer is brought home to me one night when Level VIs
and VIIs are rehearsing for a repertory workshop with Fred Ben-

jamin of the Jazz Department. A tape of the music—an infectious piece dominated by flutes and drums—is playing while Beatrice, Travis, and Serge Desroches are leaping and swooping across the room like great birds. Some other kids, temporarily unoccupied, are flirting, clowning, and gossiping at the side of the studio. Benjamin, who is fifty-seven years old and has thinning hair and a little silver hoop earring in each ear, turns toward them, glaring. "You're so perfect, you can chitchat?" he thunders. "When someone's working, he or she might have some information useful to me! When I was first in a company, I had very little to do and so I learned everybody's part, and then the lead dancer fell and broke his kneecap and *guess who went on?*"

"Did you *make* him fall and break his kneecap?" says one of the boys.

He is joking, but not entirely. If ensemble spirit is the avowed value, competition is the elephant in the living room, a great gray looming thing that's part of daily life but about which it is not polite to talk. Wanting to know more about how competition affects friendship, I seek out Linda Hamilton, The Ailey School's psychologist, who graduated from SAB and danced with the New York City Ballet before launching her second career. Hamilton, a tall, blond woman in her early forties, runs workshops for the college-age students at Ailey, consults at SAB, writes an advice column for *Dance Magazine,* and devotes her private practice to treating performers. The insularity of the dance world definitely colors relationships, she feels. "You eat, sleep, and think dance, how you're doing, who got attention in class today. What dancers do a lot is compare themselves to others," she tells me. "That judgment can be very hard on self-esteem."

When I talk to Ailey kids about competitive feelings, their

answers sometimes sound too good to be true, or at least unrealistic. "So here are the three of you, all doing the same stuff. Are you in competition perhaps?" I say to Laurence one day. "What happens if one of you gets ahead?"

"We're very happy for the other person," she replies. "We try our best to catch up. If Monique gets a little bit ahead of us, then Frajan and I would work hard to get to where Monique is, so we would all be together."

"But you would not resent Monique?" I ask.

"Of course not," Laurence says.

"What if someone drops behind?" I continue.

Laurence stops to think a minute. "Well," she says, "we'd tell that person to pick it up a little bit. We'd be there for her, too."

Laurence does admit to me that she sometimes does feel competition in the way students treat one another. "Sometimes people will have an attitude toward another person, a slight attitude that someone who's watching them could notice," she says. "They'll roll their eyes or they'll smack their teeth or they'll have a sarcastic comment. I thought they were friends with that person but now they're talking about them like that."

"About the way they dance or the way they act?" I ask.

"About the way they dance," Laurence says. "They'd say, 'Oh, she's not pointing her feet properly, her *attitude* is turned in, her legs are turned in'—something that's not even necessary for them to say." (Laurence is using the word "attitude" with facility, switching from one vernacular—the contemporary slang in the first two uses—to another, the dance terminology, in the last example.)

The girls—and the boys—are not unduly virtuous: in the student lounge one day, the LaGuardia group is gossiping about who looks in the mirror too often and who is egotistical. The chitchat tends to be about other people's motives, not about each other's clothes or hairstyles. It is, in a manner of speaking, office gossip.

One afternoon a few days later, I am sitting in the office with Melanie Person, codirector of the Junior Division. Person, thirty-nine, studied ballet at a small school in Columbia, South Carolina. When she was twelve, her teacher brought a group of students to New York to audition for the SAB summer session, and all of them were accepted and enrolled. The following year, Person won a scholarship to the summer session at Dance Theatre of Harlem, and was invited to stay on as an apprentice to the company. She joined as a full-fledged member on graduation from the Professional Children's School. She has been where the Supremes are now, down to the small core group of girls in the school in South Carolina, several of whom became professional dancers.

"There were six of us who were very close and also coming along together," Person remembers. "And then at one point three excelled and three got left behind. It changed the social structure. So we three started staying together and the other three started staying together. And what happened in time was that I became a professional before the others, and then I separated from the other two."

I tell Person the rosy things the Supremes said about what would happen if one of them got ahead or fell behind. She laughs. "Ideally, what they're saying is what they mean, and what they hope will happen. You never really know how you're going to handle a situation when one is progressing or two are progressing until you're there."

Person wonders whether friendship may, perhaps, be holding them back. "I think for them it may be that to keep the situation as it is, they may not push themselves as much as they could," she says. "At this age it's important to be part of a group."

But for Monique, Frajan, and Laurence and any of their classmates who ultimately choose a life in dance, managing the competition between friends will be an important and endless task. So covering up one's jealous, inadequate, or superior feelings with rosy, optimistic words provides a way of dealing with a difficult reality.

Serge Desroches, one of the swooping birds in Benjamin's repertory, is new at Ailey this year, but he has learned to put competition in perspective. Auditions are one thing, but in class he tries to be philosophical about other people's strengths and his own weaknesses. "Some people have feet, some people have turnout, some people can turn," Serge says. "All I have is stretch and turnout, but I can't turn, and other people can. There is that jealousy, like, damn! You always say that. But you're good with what you've got."

All the Ailey kids confess to feeling competitive, and have learned to say something sensible and consoling—to themselves and to others—about it. To get a better understanding of how deep competitive attitudes go, to see through this self-protective shield, it is perhaps more enlightening to ask which other students they admire. Everyone in Level VI freely admits to admiring Beatrice, who is two years older than most of them and in Level VII. "She's *fierce*," Serge says, using the dancer's word of highest praise. "You give her a step and she gets it like that! And she has a lot of attitude—she looks very happy when she performs." Beatrice is, of course, sitting right next to Serge at the time, and Serge absolutely will not mention any other classmate he thinks is fierce. But even when Beatrice is not in the room,

Frajan admires both her technique and her artistry. "If I was in the audience," she says, "my eyes would be glued to her because she doesn't just do the movements—she adds something to make it more."

Then I ask Frajan who she admires in her own class. "Nobody in my class," she says. "I don't admire anybody in my class." Admitting high esteem for a dancer who is one's peer seems to be quite a different story.

Last year, the acknowledged boy star of the Junior Division was Randy, who won Honorable Mention in ARTS and got into Juilliard. Travis says he never felt competitive with Randy because Randy was older, and Travis knew that by the time he reached Randy's age, he would be just as good. Coevals were more of a problem, but this year Travis is one of only two boys in Level VII, which in general happens to be a very small group.

Thus it is safe to admire a student who is not your own age. Charlotte, the eighth grader, admires not only Beatrice and Afra but also Monique; Monique returns the favor, graciously complimenting the skills of a girl who will always be two years younger and is, of course, *amazing*.

Does the competition that underlies (or coexists with) the friendship ever get vicious? This year the media have discovered a psychological phenomenon called "relational aggression" characteristic of teenage girls, as delineated in several current books.[1] I look hard for signs of it—a sort of all-consuming manipulative nastiness among girls that seems to surpass the ordinary cliquishness most of us remember from our own school days—at Ailey, and can't find it, at least not to the degree I have been hearing about in current magazine and television parlance. I watch the girls' behavior before and after class and during the breaks, and while classmates focus their attention on the Supremes, there is a fair amount of mixing; no girls are conspicuously out of things.

Ailey girls tell me they are nicer than their counterparts at SAB, some of whom go to LaGuardia. The SAB girls, according to Laurence, "don't initiate conversation; they stick to themselves. They all socialize together in this little group at lunch, on the floor while stretching, eating their vegetables. That's all they do."

What do the Ailey girls do?

"The kids from Ailey and DTH [Dance Theatre of Harlem], we sit together because we spent our summer together," Laurence replies. "We all sit together at one table and we talk. We enjoy ourselves, we laugh, we make jokes, we have fun."

So Ailey people, apparently, also have a sense of ensemble in competing with SAB people, whom they perceive as rivals, while relations are more fluid with DTH.

Charlotte Kaufman came to Ailey after a few years at SAB, which she found more competitive than Ailey, because, she says, everyone there wants to become a professional dancer, while some Ailey students don't have this kind of ambition. At SAB, she felt, the teachers would focus their attention on students with professional potential, whereas Ailey teachers pay attention to everybody. Linda Hamilton, the psychologist, deals with a slightly older population at Ailey, but she herself was a teenager at SAB and says competition there can be pretty intense: scapegoating by cliques sometimes got nasty. "How it would exist from my experience," she says, "is they wouldn't say hello to you—they'd ostracize you socially, they would laugh at you when you went across the room." In her private practice, Hamilton says, she counseled a few SAB girls who were going through this.

Neither Joi nor Charlotte seems terribly disturbed that the Supremes are an obvious clique: Joi says groups at Ailey organize, inevitably, according to where members go to school, but are friendly enough to others. Charlotte agrees. There is a dance pecking order, she says—"It's definitely visible who's favored—the Three Musketeers, because they always get picked to do shows"—but this ranking doesn't poison the social scene. The LaGuardia girls are close to one another, but not snooty, she says.

Almost all the Ailey boys attend the performing arts schools, and, like the girls, tend to organize in groups according to which one they go to. They are chums with the girls, they talk with them regularly on the phone and IM them on the computer. Friendship between boys and girls often involves giving each other pointers on how to dance better, which is not perceived, at least outwardly, as condescension. A lively and vocal member of the LaGuardia group is a boy named Nigel Campbell, a tenth grader who is a bit younger than the others and has entered Ailey this year at Level V. He is an explosive dancer and tries to get Frajan to break out of her shell. Frajan is making an effort to follow his suggestions and improve her performance. "He wants me to be all I can be, not to hold back," she says. "He's a very good friend."

"So you feel you can criticize each other's dancing," I say to Frajan. "What suggestions would you give to Nigel about his dancing?"

Frajan says she would tell Nigel not to give up when he sees a combination he thinks he can't do: he needs to be more persistent, she thinks. And she says to him, "'How are you telling me to do something when you're not applying it yourself?' I'll be a better dancer the way he wants me to be," she continues, "and he has to be up to par by doing what I want him to do." To some extent, the kids really do help one another; and insofar as they are jockeying for position, the girls and boys have clearly learned to give as good as they get.

Inevitably, as an outsider trying to understand how both friendship and competition play out at The Ailey School, I start wondering about racial factors. Ailey is thought of in the outside world as an African-American dance company, and much of its repertory, by both Ailey himself and by other choreographers, delineates the African-American experience. Official attitudes toward race—like all cultural values at Ailey—filter down from the top. When I ask Judith Jamison about the racial composition of the company, her eyes flash fire. "I don't talk about stuff like that," she says. "People don't say to Peter Martins, 'You've got this European-based company.' It's not called Alvin Ailey African-American Dance Theater because everyone isn't African-American and the people you might think are European are not, and we don't discuss that because that's not what the company is about. The company is about the celebration of the art form."

There appear to be two Caucasian dancers in the First Company, and during the academic year by my informal count the Junior Division looks to be about two-thirds students "of color" and one-third Caucasian or European or whatever one chooses to call the others. It is worth noting, however, that the borders are murky: a student who looks "black" may be Latino or Caribbean-American, and some who can look either Caucasian or African-American are interracial. A few students are Asian and there is disagreement as to what category they fit into. If Jamison sounds disingenuous, to some extent she is right.

The sharp racial separations any passerby can see among students pouring out of most New York public schools are not visible at Ailey, PPAS, or LaGuardia: mixed groups are always in evidence. Paul Saronson, LaGuardia's principal, points out that his school's demographics—40 percent white, 25 percent African-American, 22 percent Hispanic, and the rest Asian—resemble that of the city, rather than that of the public school system, in which Caucasians represent only 15 percent of the students.[2]

Students differ about racial divisions at LaGuardia. Laurence, speaking about the Supremes, says, "We mix with a bunch of people: Hispanics, whites, Russians. We like to mix," although Monique feels some divide exists at LaGuardia. But while she finds a bit of resistance to her threesome at Ailey, she doesn't think it follows racial lines, perhaps because the school is too small to support large racial factions. The Level VI and VII cliques break down mostly to LaGuardia, PPAS, Manhattan private schools, and suburbanites, and all of the groups except the LaGuardia group are mixed, with a few close interracial friendships. Ailey's faculty is quite varied.

Racial factors are still more important than both the adults and the teens are willing to admit. It is occasionally argued that students of color tend to get into more repertory workshops; that has something to do with which ballets are performed and who is doing the choreography. Performing in a repertory, of course, often leads to getting to know company members, who, not unnaturally, lean toward mentoring students who evoke their own youthful selves. Travis and Charlotte, for example, don't know any company members well. At the same time, both feel they have profited from Ailey's varied training; they chose to come here, and are more comfortable at Ailey than they were in other places. The year that Travis came to Ailey, Deborah Magee remembers coming home one evening to find a roomful of young dancers, most of them African-American. One classmate looked at Deborah, looked at Deborah's son, and exclaimed, "Travis, I thought you said your mother was black!" Travis smiled wickedly and said, "I lied." Thus Ailey students are hardly blind to race. It is simply not their arena.

Their arena is dance. The life they live is fraught with real competition. They do not need to manufacture any.

Five

The Sorcerers' Apprentices

While Beatrice is learning to be the Queen of France, she and Afra, the contestants sponsored by The Ailey School this year, are also rehearsing their entries for the Arts Recognition and Talent Search. ARTS is the most prestigious competition in music, dance, theater, writing, and visual arts for high school seniors across the country. More than 5,000 students—a tenth of them dancers—compete to win cash awards and join the 120 finalists who are invited to Miami for a week of performances, master classes, seminars, and exhibits. Twenty of these winners become Presidential Scholars and spend another glamorous week in Washington, D.C. There are spin-off awards as well as honorable mentions and merit recognition awards in each field, and any favorable placement is influential for college admission. ARTS alumni pervade their fields: a quarter of the dancers in Ailey's First Company won some prize in the competition when they were high school seniors, as did the same percentage of the dancers in the New York City Ballet.

The competition lists its winners according to their high schools. Still, the application asks contestants to report the dance schools they attend. An accumulation of winners among its students over the years adds stature to a dance school. LaGuardia High School has the faculty, studio space, and equipment to sponsor its own students, even the ones who also go to Ailey, but Ailey still feels a proprietary joy when one of its LaGuardia kids wins something in ARTS. Ailey itself sponsors a select few of those who go to PPAS or any school other than LaGuardia. Its sponsorship means that rehearsal space, choreography, and coaching by Ailey teachers are available to a student without charge.

This adds up to an enormous amount of individual attention from a professional dancer the student admires. It is a sort of apprenticeship, during which the master dancer focuses on the details of a student's performance—the strengths and weaknesses, what to play up, what to improve, and what to get around. Seniors with serious ambition for a dance career hope to be sponsored, and those who aren't chosen and have a little spunk will make their own arrangements to compete in ARTS, seeking out a coach among the faculty or in the company and scheduling practice sessions.

To enter the contest, each dancer submits a four-minute tape that fulfills a set of criteria laid out by the National Foundation for Advancement in the Arts. Every year a new panel judges the competition, a feature which school officials sometimes use to explain why their students succeed one year and fail the next.

Two Ailey students had been finalists, one of them a Presidential Scholar, in the 2000 competition, with several more students winning the lesser awards, but the following year—when no one from New York City had gone to Miami—only one Ailey student, sponsored officially by LaGuardia, had won Honorable Mention and another had won a Merit Recognition, the lowest level of award.

There are several different categories for dance contestants to enter, and the Ailey contestants usually do modern. A dancer's audition tape must include two minutes that demonstrate mastery of the technique and two more of solo performance. Earl Mosley of the Horton Department choreographed the girls' technique sections. Right after doing this, he had an out-of-town commitment, and two Horton colleagues took over the rehearsals. Francesca Harper, Jefferson's daughter, recently returned from a stint with the Frankfurt Ballet and a resident choreographer this term, is handling the solo performances.

Preparing an ARTS tape is an experience midway between taking class and participating in a show. It is definitely more exciting than class, but because the dancer just mails off a tape instead of performing before a live audience, it has a bit less of both the electricity and the tension that characterize live performance. After one has mailed in the tape, it is easier to detach from it, and losing the contest is—supposedly—less painful than losing a part in an audition.

Beatrice is Mosley's favorite student. He has known her since she was in the ninth grade and he admires her diligence, her quickness, her versatility, and her quiet firmness. When Mosley is choreographing a dancer's contest tape, as he told me later, he tries to stress what looks best on each individual. He asks a dancer, "What is your best leg that you turn on? If you're going to fall to the left, is it going to be funny looking? Should you fall to the right?" Having earned a sort of familial right to speak bluntly, he had told Beatrice, "Don't put your butt to the audience," and softened it a bit with "Let's show off your legs."

Afra is newer to the school and Mosley knows her less well, but he has a definite take on her. He thinks Afra is statuesque, gorgeous, and insecure, outgoing only outside the studio. "She knows she's beautiful and she knows she's talented, but knowing something and trusting it aren't always the same," Mosley said to me. "Even in her moments of glory, this little voice will say, 'Did I really do that?'" So he wanted to keep Afra moving because he thought she didn't like to stand still and look in the mirror; if she did, she would withdraw.

On this Friday afternoon in October, the dances are almost ready. Afra is out on the floor; Beatrice is sitting in the corner. "That second jump looks good," Harper says. "You should move more, really exaggerate. A huge arabesque, almost *penchée* [leaning forward]. It's all about the arms in position more than the leg high. Make it more luscious! Think of the fire under you, why you dance."

Afra runs through the choreography once again, after being told to "be more sensual" and "think of the whole thing as one continuous thread. Go through every transition so it's all one movement." Harper modifies the transitions she thinks don't work. Jefferson and Person come in and watch Afra, who looks ever more slithery and athletic. Harper puts Afra's disco music on. The dance ends with a big *attitude* in back, and an attitudinous wave good-bye as she exits. Harper's last instruction: "When they see the solo, they want to be taken emotionally. Now that you've got everything technically, I want to get more emotion out of you, the sensuality in the second part. Also a little edge to it, like you're one up on the people watching. There's some of that in your personality. . . ." Everyone laughs.

Beatrice has been warming up in a corner, like the next figure skater in the Winter Olympics. She has got it the way it should be. She looks more sensual and passionate than ever before, and unexpectedly agile and strong. Beatrice has told me the dance is very spiritual, and reminds her of sadness (about her weight problems) and overcoming that sadness. Jefferson and Person applaud, and Beatrice is wreathed in smiles. "A young woman!" Jefferson says, in her best motherly tone. Everyone is excited to see Beatrice cut loose. "You stopped thinking, which is just where it should be," Harper says.

For the taping, Beatrice will wear a grass green unitard that is a gift from Elena Comendador, and which sets her off perfectly. Afra will look snappy in purple.

Of course they will win. I, for one, am sure of it.

But Afra and Beatrice, though they were Ailey's pick, are not the only Ailey seniors competing for ARTS: they are two out of four. As Afra has told me, once the four of them send in their tapes, they are really competing on their own in a large field of dancers across the country, and all of them wish one another well. Conceivably, every one of them could at least get to Florida. Travis, the third contestant, is a good PPAS friend of both girls, especially close to Beatrice.

The fourth contestant is a bit of a loner. Brian Brown, a muscular seventeen-year-old with dark curly hair and glasses, is the only student at the upper levels of Ailey who goes to Professional Children's School, and is thus out of the mainstream public school group. Moreover, he came to Ailey from San Francisco in the summer program before his junior year, went back home for six months, and didn't return to Ailey and settle in New York until last year's spring term. Both of these factors worked against his forming solid friendships with students his own age, and now he is taking most of his classes with the older group.

The Ailey School is filled with kids who see themselves as "different." But Brian is more different still. He is, of course, from the West Coast, which suggests some cultural disparities with most of the other Junior Division students, who grew up here. More important, however, the others all live at home with at least one parent and have no personal financial responsibilities, while Brian, who this year shares an apartment with a roommate from the Professional Division, needs to pay the rent and go to the grocery store. Finally, there is the matter of why he is here, which led directly to how he has entered ARTS.

Like many of the boys—and indeed, many professional male dancers—Brian started dancing late, at the age of twelve. Right away he showed enough talent to enter the regional competitions—the same that Beatrice had competed at in New Jersey—representing the Fabulous Feet Dance Studio in Brentwood, California. But when he was fourteen and studying with the San Francisco Ballet, he experienced a sort of rebirth.

He was flipping TV channels one night and saw dancing and stopped cold. PBS was running "Hymn for Alvin Ailey," a memorial tribute choreographed by Jamison in combination with Anna Deveare Smith's oral history interviews of company members and friends. It was a powerful performance with a highly spiritual tone, including old clips of Ailey himself talking about his "blood memories," and about the social statement implied in

*A thirteen-year-old Brian does an African dance
at Fabulous Feet Dance Studio in Brentwood, California.*
(COURTESY OF BRIDGETTE BROWN)

founding a company of black dancers. There were scenes of Ailey's funeral at the Cathedral of St. John the Divine, and Jamison herself saying—very much in tune with the context of the performance—that she has always felt she "has God in her ear," that she now sensed Ailey was "here—he can't show me physically the steps to do—but he's here," and "I could sit on his wings and fly." Both Jamison and Ailey himself said several times in different ways that dance was a manifestation of spirit, that a dancer must "spiritually go to the wall" and dance from the gut. All the dancers on the show had Ailey's passion. Brian saw, as he said later, that there was "much more to dance than just doing a lot of turns and smiling."

He read up on Ailey—the biography by *New York Times* dance critic Jennifer Dunning and whatever else he could find. Everything new he learned was, you might say, a revelation. Mr. Ailey (as Brian always calls him) had difficulties, and he lived through them honestly as best he could. The fact that Alvin Ailey wasn't comfortable with his sexuality, that he had problems with drugs, these things made him a human being and he used them in his work, and because of that he was a better dancer. Learning this gave Brian the sense that he didn't have to be perfect.

When he had to do a report on something for school, it was always about Alvin Ailey. Then, a year later, the company came to Berkeley and Brian and his mother went to see them perform. On the program were two ballets with religious themes, Ronald K. Brown's *Grace* and the omnipresent *Revelations*. Brian was moved to tears, and Bridgette Brown was herself awestruck. As they were walking out, they saw a poster announcing auditions for The Ailey School the next day. Denise Jefferson was on one of her nationwide forays to spot talent for the school's summer program, to which young dancers pour in from all over the country and the world, while many of the New York kids who study at Ailey through the school year pour out in search of a change of scene. Brian passed the audition, and came to Ailey that summer.

So there was another way in which, from the very start, Brian perceived himself as different from the other Ailey students. They were coming to learn technique. He was here to learn how to put his soul and his faith in his dancing and thus follow what he believed Mr. Ailey had started the school to teach. Brian, who had been raised Catholic and sent to a rigorous parochial school, did not share Alvin Ailey's religious beliefs in the strict sectarian sense, but he felt The Ailey School was neglecting the spiritual side of dance and thus not perpetuating Mr. Ailey's vision. He thought, to be fair, that the school was well run, and Miss Jefferson was turning out dancers with "amazing" technique. He felt more freedom to put himself in his dancing than he had experienced at the San Francisco Ballet. But he needed to impress on Miss Comendador and Mr. Benjamin—who, in addition to running the jazz department, had the role of father figure when boys developed problems—what the school should be about. Convincing the school's administration that he had the inside track on what the late founder intended was a tough and unwelcome sell. Then at the same time Brian was not all religious fervour. It was his first summer in New York City—he wanted to have fun, and he wasn't always as focused on ballet as Miss Comendador thought appropriate. In sum, there were arguments galore.

Despite all this contention, when the summer was over, Brian wanted to stay at Ailey and Bridgette Brown wanted him back in San Francisco. Stephen Brown, his father, who lived in Maryland, was vehemently opposed to his son's staying in New York on his own. Brian was too young for this. Enough was enough, said each parent separately. It was time to return to private school and study hard in the eleventh grade with an eye toward college. He could still dance in San Francisco. And then at some point when Brian was busy fighting this, *Mr. Ailey let him know it was okay to go home.* So Brian went back, but after a while Mr. Ailey said it was time to go "home" again, and this time home meant New York. Brian was not hallucinating, but felt the kind of spiritual connectedness that Jamison had described on the television program. The difference, of course, was that Brian had never actually met Mr. Ailey in person (and thus adults at the school tended to dismiss his feelings). Brian told his parents he wanted to go back to Ailey for the spring term.

How could Bridgette (the custodial parent) say no? His heart was set on it. When he had talent like this, and this determination, how could she not help him? And she couldn't even get off work to get him settled here. Bridgette said Brian could stay with his cousin in Hoboken and go line up a good school—the education side was what worried her the most—and get what financial assistance was necessary. After he did that, he would need to find a place to live.

Within a week and a half of coming east, Brian found, liked, and got into Professional Children's School. PCS is a private school that dates back to 1916 and has a host of famous alumni. It exists to provide a good education for children from the fourth through twelfth grades whose careers make demands that ordinary schools cannot accommodate: the students can go on tour or travel on location or take classes in their specialty in the middle of the day without losing the thread of schoolwork. Very few Ailey students go to PCS, partly because they can't afford it and partly because they feel more comfortable in the arts-based public schools. It is, however, filled with dancers from SAB, with Asian musicians, with equestrians and figure skaters from all over the United States. The criteria for admission are academic, not professional, and the school gives financial aid according to need: Brian and Bridgette put in for aid and got what they needed promptly.

Then Brian found a student dormitory the family could afford in Brooklyn. Bridgette required him to call home at ten o'clock every evening, and she called PCS weekly to make sure he was keeping up with his schoolwork.

This year, since he has left the dormitory, financial responsibilities are even more worrisome. To maintain his fellowship, he works in Ailey's marketing department. He also has a job at the Hetrick-Martin Institute, a social service agency that aids gay and lesbian youth: most of the clients are poor kids who face problems of coming out and homophobia among their families and friends, one issue that Brian, who was comfortably out as soon as he wanted to be, did not experience. He could help these kids while paying his telephone and electric bills. In every way, Brian now feels he has given up his adolescence to dance, and is entitled to full adult treatment and respect—with or without his recent tongue-piercing.

So here is a boy who wants what he wants intensely, and has the competence to go about getting it. One thing he came to want this past summer was to enter ARTS, and another thing he wanted even more was to have Dwana Smallwood choreograph his solo for him.

From the first time he saw her dance, Brian admired Smallwood more than anyone else in the First Company. She could, he felt, pull out all her emotions to tell a story onstage with style, grace, and attitude. He wanted to dance with that same explosion of energy.

When a student wishes to get to know someone in the First Company, summer—that is, sometime between July and the first week of August, before the school closes for vacation—is a good time to do it. The dancers, back from their spring tour, are upstairs rehearsing new dances or generally hanging out; by the time the fall term begins, they are off on tour again. So summer 2001 was when Brian Brown decided to approach Dwana Smallwood. One day during the lunch break when she was alone in the studio, working out some of her own choreographic ideas, Brian walked in and said, "Miss Smallwood, may I talk to you for a second?"

Practicallly no one ever calls her "Miss Smallwood." She is "Dwana" to all the kids. On the rare occasion when one of them addresses her formally, she knows he must be really scared. So this boy she cannot recall ever seeing before asks her if she would choreograph a solo for him in a contest he is planning to enter, saying how much he loves her dancing and how that is the way *he* wants to move. Smallwood, remembering this later, says she was "shocked and honored that he would even think about me choreographing anything" (although this declaration has, at least partly, the flavor of artistic humility that is considered appropriate at Ailey). In truth, while it is a bit unusual for a boy to pick one of the women dancers to model himself after—most of the boys choose, say, Troy Powell, Matthew Rushing, or Anthony Burrell, all of whom are known to be highly approachable—Smallwood, who was on Ailey's fortieth-anniversary poster, wearing her white tiered *Cry* dress and striking a Jamison-like pose—would be one of the first women anyone would choose. Smallwood had done some choreography but not much, and thought it was time for her to do more. Thus she agreed.

First, however, so she could get the measure of him, Smallwood asked Brian to take class with the company for a week. After having watched him in class, she praised his facility and technique, but said it was time for him to know "where his movement is coming from."

The solo, Brian told her, should be two minutes long, in line with the ARTS requirement. (To a nondancer, two minutes sounds like nothing, but in fact, as all the ARTS solos demonstrated, it is a lot of time to fill.) The first thing Smallwood asked Brian was which of the two of them should choose the music. Smallwood said this project should not be just a technical thing. She wanted it to be a growing process that would take Brian to the next level. She thought Brian would feel more ownership of the solo if he himself had chosen the music.

Brian looked for a piece that would evoke what Mr. Ailey had meant about dance being a manifestation of the spirit. He remembered an album called *Innovators,* by Kurt Bestor and Sam Cardon, a sort of New Age CD that he had used in his dance competition days. Each piece on the album had a story behind it, and Brian and Smallwood started with one he knew called "Prayer of the Children" about a child who steps on a land mine. That proved not to work for the choreography he needed, so he found another piece called "Requiem." This had a strange but to him compelling story: it was about a village in Europe at the time of the Black Plague. Everyone in the village has died except a father and son, and when finally the father is stricken, as Brian recounts it, "He decides to bury himself alive rather than have his son face the burden of burying his father. So he does that and it is about giving up his life for his son, giving up what we love for other people and how that affects us." It was hardly a run-of-the-mill choice for a high school student: when necessary, teenagers can discharge grief in their dancing, and this expression does bring relief, but it isn't the sort of thing they seek out. Most of the time they prefer to divert themselves toward fun.

Several times a week, during the company's lunch breaks throughout the summer, Brian worked with Smallwood on the piece. She taped the music and took it home to listen to. She went into the studio alone and danced a bit to the music to figure out what she was feeling and what it would look like. Then Brian would come in and fall into some sort of movement, and she might say, "That's okay—keep it," and suggest some modifications. He was so excited, so anxious, he would do the steps so hard that Smallwood would have to tell him to calm down—you don't have to kill it—the dancing itself would be powerful. "Just do the steps," she would say, a most uncommon instruction for a student at The Ailey School: most of the time, teachers and choreographers were knocking themselves out to get the kids to do *more* than just the steps.

It was Brian's hunger that first impressed Smallwood. Studying hard was the norm among kids at Ailey's upper levels, but there were a few who strived obsessively for excellence, and this obsession gave them the confidence to go up to a dancer in the First Company and say, "I need you to get me to the next level." At the same time, there was a certain cockiness Brian would have to get past. He was gifted, but Smallwood thought he threw it away. He took advantage of his facility, and that irritated her. She saw that things came easily to him, and he'd say, "I know this—I don't need to rehearse it again." "But you do, over and over," Smallwood would answer. "You haven't got it yet. That's why I'm giving you lessons." From Brian's point of view, he was involved with the emotions of the piece and Smallwood was hammering him on technique. And every single moment he felt intimidated.

Sometimes they would rehearse a bit, and Smallwood would lose patience and say, "Okay, enough of me talking and yelling. I'm going to leave. You've got fifteen minutes to work it out and then I'll come back." She would go out and when it was time to return, she'd ask him if he was ready, and he'd say, "No, I'm not ready yet, I need to do more." Later on, after their rehearsals together were over, Brian said that leaving a dancer to work it out himself was the best thing a teacher or choreographer could do: it always brought about improvements. And in fact, he hadn't just sat down in there—he wasn't taking advantage of her—he had been working intensely in her absence: Smallwood knew that because she had peeked in the door and seen him.

Moreover, despite occasional clashes and despite their highly divergent backgrounds, there was a certain affinity between Brian Brown and Dwana Smallwood. When Smallwood, raised in Brooklyn, was ten years old, her family embraced Yoruba religious practices. She went to African-based alternative private schools before her years at LaGuardia; she has been dancing since she was three, but she began in African dance and didn't get into ballet until junior high. She has always believed that when she dances, she is a vessel for communicating with God. She wonders whether her spiritual approach to dance is more suited to the company as it was when Alvin Ailey founded it—less technical and perhaps more authentic. When she runs a workshop, the studio is a "sacred room" which admits no observers so the dancers will feel free to let go, and if she thinks someone is just going through the motions, she may tell them to leave until they're ready to focus, as she did with Brian. Smallwood doesn't recognize ordinary days: she expects unflagging emotional truth.

There is nothing African in Brian's background: his father came here from England as a child, and his mother is Latina. But clearly, their views on the spiritual side of dancing were in tune.

When the 2001 summer program was over, Smallwood went off on vacation and then on tour. Brian's two-minute solo was more or less in shape, and at the beginning of the fall term he approached Denise Jefferson and Tracy Inman for permission to submit the solo to ARTS and secure help for the technique tape that was also required. Both were impressed at how far Brian had come on his own: he was ambitious, he was disciplined, he followed the rules of courtesy by consulting Jefferson, and he was, Inman admitted, actually more efficient in lining up studio space and choreography than the school itself might have been, were it officially sponsoring him. Inman—inundated with work and learning a new job—agreed to help. Since Brian was entering without the official sponsorship granted just to Afra and Beatrice, Inman might have charged Brian for his time—which amounted to two hour-and-a-half sessions a week over three or four weeks—but he didn't. "These kids are trying to go somewhere," he told me, "and you've been there yourself and you don't say, 'You've got to pay me for this.'" Inman personally believed doing this was part of his job. Moreover, the school did have a vested interest in Brian's performing well.

So Inman did for Brian what Mosley had done for Beatrice and Afra: sized up the student's strengths and weaknesses and made a routine that conformed to the requirements for Horton technique. Brian, Inman decided, understood the technique, and had a flexible body with great feet; on the other hand, he hadn't been studying that long and so the technique wasn't as neat and clean as it might have been. Inman himself had started dancing very late—at age twenty—and had worked incredibly hard. He had been taught, nurtured, and pushed by Jamison—in fact, ever afterward, when he was teaching Jamison's choreography, he felt he was "almost her." Not really, he would demur, but all the things she had said to him and to the other dancers working together under her direction he now found himself saying to the kids. So Inman and Brian worked hard together through the early fall.

The meaning of the ballet itself had changed for Brian, who was still polishing it with Inman's help after September 11: from being about dying, it needed to be more about celebrating life in the shadow of death. He finished it and showed it to Jefferson who thought the solo reflected Brian's special physicality and passion but requested cuts in some parts she found melodramatic. He got it taped, and sent it in. On December 1, the results come out.

This year 592 dancers have entered the competition, and because the sponsoring foundation has less money than usual, only fifteen (instead of twenty) have won the top prizes and will go to Miami for ARTS Week. None of them are from New York City. Another ten dancers receive Honorable Mention, a $100 prize. One of them is Brian Brown, who thus might have gone to Miami in a normally expansive year. Neither Afra nor Beatrice nor Travis receives anything. Afra says to me she doesn't mind not winning herself, but Beatrice should have won something. Beatrice went into the office and told Melanie Person she had not placed in the competition. She didn't strike Person as particularly bothered by not winning anything; Person says Beatrice had worked very hard on her entry and "it would have been a nice scoop of ice cream on top of the pie." But Person knows all the things dancers say to themselves in order to tolerate rejection and move on: "It wasn't live," they might say. "If they had really seen *me* and not me on videotape . . ."

After Brian has won Honorable Mention, he becomes more difficult: it is time to tell Inman (who is new in the job) that the school is not fulfilling Mr. Ailey's dream. Inman says, "How do you know what Mr. Ailey's dream was, and how do you know it wouldn't have changed?" They go back and forth, and finally Brian stalks out. Later on, Brian misses a number of classes and they fight again. "He's here in the big city and he's finding himself," Inman tells me. "He's coming of age and he's not going to be bullied."

In the course of the year, The Ailey School puts on two shows for its own community (students, faculty, alumni, and friends) in the upstairs studios—the "January Explosion" and "Global Harmony" in March. They are high points of the year: the audience buys tickets in advance, waits in line with mounting excitement, exchanges multiple hugs and kisses with old friends, and ends up packed inside on folding chairs with a necklace of standees. The music is taped. In their own way, these productions are even more electric than performances at City Center (where student dancers are not the main attraction). Afra, Beatrice, and Brian get to perform their ARTS entries in the January show. Travis will do his in March.

Dwana Smallwood returns from her tour in time to hear of Brian's triumph and work with him on polishing his solo again for the performance. The ballet has evolved further. When Brian went home for Thanksgiving, he learned that a good friend of his had been killed in an automobile accident. He dances the solo to express all his grief: later he says, "Every time I've done that piece, it's been different."

Smallwood is excited and offers to sew him a costume: she has a small business making "Soul Sister Dolls" which she sells on the Internet, and there is some brown Lycra in the house which makes a nice unitard. The dance, she feels, has changed enough to be his more than hers, and all she can do now is sharpen a few things. But some of the same tussle occurs again. They are in the hallway, waiting to go on, and Smallwood has to say, "Brian, you're talking too much; you're moving around too much. Just be still and quiet and that way command silence from everyone around you." She wants him to understand that there will be a difference in the result according to whether he plays cards before he goes on or whether he just meditates or stays still. And she tells him to demand the audience's attention by not pressing the PLAY button until they are absolutely quiet. Then, as Smallwood has said, "The most beautiful performance will come out." In his two-minute solo Brian is, indeed, the personification of grief.

Not only Brian but Beatrice and Afra perform with more feeling and maturity in the January Explosion. Most particularly, when Beatrice made her final tape, Inman got into the act and kept pushing her to be less inhibited in her dancing. He feels it worked. Apparently, Beatrice thrives under pressure, and at last she has learned to let go. From this point on, everyone at Ailey says her dancing is more than just clean technique. In the March show, Travis does his solo to "Sevilla" by Isaac Albeniz and shows a new athleticism and stirring response to the music; he has also used the tape for his college auditions. The Magees and Travis's girlfriend, Nici, an Ailey School alumna on her spring break from college, make an enthusiastic and relieved claque. All this bears out what both Smallwood and Person tell me, that the experience of preparing the ARTS tapes and performing them solo in front of an audience are of great value to a young dancer, whether or not he or she gets to go to Miami.

While the seniors were practicing their ARTS entries, Shamel Pitts had his first taste of performing with the company in *Memoria* during the winter season. Next year he would certainly enter ARTS, but even this year he was able to have somewhat of a similiar experience. He was one of only two dancers from the Junior Division in the group of older Ailey School students who danced briefly at the end of the ballet. He had learned something about professionalism in *Anansi*—just the business of getting ready for a performance, running through it, having lunch, running through it again, then relaxing quietly backstage before it was time to go on. Then in *Memoria* he shared a dressing room with Burrell and a new company member, Abdur-Rahim Jackson, listened to them talk and laugh in their regular unpretentious way—putting on their makeup just casually as they talked, while he struggled to dab his own on and finally had to get help. They were friendly to each other, Shamel saw, but when it was time to work they got serious. So you could do business and also have some kind of pleasure. He had certainly seen plenty of adults who were bored with their jobs. He thought at last he had found a job that he would love to do, that wouldn't just pay the bills . . . and anyway, dancers don't make much, so you have to love it.

Clearly, Shamel and Brian are two very different personalities: Shamel seems to be the ideal future Ailey dancer: hardworking and professional but cool and sociable at the same time, absorbing just what he is supposed to pick up from Burrell and Jackson, taking control of his own personal demons. Brian is talented, eager, and highly competent but can also be difficult and frustrating for adults to deal with. Both of them are fervent about dancing. Throughout my year at Ailey, I am drawn to research on what factors augur well for success in artistic performance, and why some teenagers persist: increasingly this research has a human face that I have come to care about.

For some twenty years, the psychologist Mihaly Csikszentmihalyi, late of the University of Chicago, now of the Claremont School of Management, studied how American teenagers spend their time. He worked largely with beepers, which went off at random in the teenagers' pockets every couple of hours, whereupon his subjects would fill out a page-long questionnaire reporting in detail what they were doing, whom they were with, and how they felt about it. He backed up this work with questionnaires, psychological tests, and interviews with the teenagers, their parents, and their teachers. He has also studied talent and creativity at every stage of life. Csikszentmihalyi works frequently with Howard Gardner of Harvard, and while each of them has his own special interests, their underlying assumption—that talent is a social construction that includes an individual's traits, the cultural domain in which he works, and the social field of experts who evaluate performance—is similar.

The work that is most applicable here is a five-year longitudinal study[1] of more than 200 teenagers chosen by their teachers as exceptionally promising in either art, athletics, mathematics, music, or science. His chief question was the same as Benjamin Bloom's had been a few years earlier: what makes some people pursue their talents while others lose interest? The difference is that Bloom's subjects had already succeeded and were looking back, while Csikszentmihalyi's were, like the Ailey students, in the process of deciding whether to go on.

Pervasively, Csikszentmihalyi and his colleagues found that the measure of a teenager's individual gift was less important than what the subject made of it: while their study of the teenagers' personalities and patterns of living is minute and complex, in general the talented teens, as opposed to their peers, were self-starters, "highly focused on achievement and endurance"[2]—in sum, a lot like Brian and Shamel, as well as most of the other young dancers I got to know.

A chapter in the book appears particularly pertinent to the Ailey students' experiences preparing for ARTS and rehearsing with the company: sometimes, in fact, it seems almost as if Csikszentmihalyi and his colleagues are talking directly about Shamel, Afra, Beatrice, Travis, and Brian. The authors begin by reflecting on the development of talent through apprenticeship which prevailed in preindustrial societies, before modern schools turned the teacher into an "information technician."[3] In the apprenticeship system, the psychologists observe, "The ultimate success of a relationship depended on the fit between two unique and often incompatible individuals." This kind of teaching offered two benefits: it weeded out students without the stamina to survive in their field of talent, and it allowed those with ability to spend some time patterning themselves after a committed master teacher. Italian Renaissance painters and sculptors—the example Csikszentmihalyi cites—had a profound influence on their apprentices: Donatello taught Verrocchio, Verrocchio taught both da Vinci and Perugino, and Perugino taught Raphael. The phrase Csikszentmihalyi uses to describe a master teacher in this system— "a daily model of the deeply interested life"—applied to all the teachers I met at Ailey, and to Smallwood and other company members as well, with every one of them forceful and idiosyncratic, some of them still performing, and others making a life in the dance world after their performing days had finished.

Both Smallwood and Inman thought of themselves as having been apprenticed to Jamison. When Smallwood came to The Ailey School one summer while she was a student at the North Carolina School of the Arts, she saw tapes of Jamison dancing and said, "I want to be where she is." She worked extra hard in order to be noticed by Jamison, and she kept a journal with Jamison's picture plastered all over it. Much later, when Smallwood had been in the company for a while, Jamison said to her, "You've gotten what you need from me, Dwana—stop living in my shadow." Smallwood felt Jamison had pulled the best out of her and taught her to stand on her own feet. Smallwood has worked not only with Brian but with earlier students as well, and has befriended the Supremes; and every now and then Jamison comes over to Dwana's for a visit and a long private talk. Inman experienced the same sort of apprenticeship. Now he feels indebted not only to Jamison but to a group of teachers who helped him in his previous talent field, when, in his teens, he was a violinist.

Evoking Shamel, Csikszentmihalyi notes his earlier findings that "teenagers are singularly uninspired by the lives of most adults they know." Shamel's comment about many adults having boring jobs reflects, according to this psychological research, the fears of most teens. Average teenagers wonder how they can avoid this, but, the psychologist says, "lack the skills and focused motivation to prevent daily life from slipping into similar patterns." The prospect of being as cool as Troy Powell, Anthony Burrell, and Abdur-Rahim Jackson while having fun in midair, hearing the applause, and making even a small living is enough to keep Shamel Pitts stretching at the Ailey barre and spending lunch hours doing back bends on an enormous blue inflatable ball that rolls around on the studio floor at LaGuardia.

Evoking Brian, Csikszentmihalyi describes the tension between two of his teenaged subjects, a singer and a mathematician, and their teachers: "Talented teens," he writes, "are unusually sensitive to the quality of teaching in their talent areas." The two serious students he describes would, he says, "try the patience of any teacher from time to time, with their insatiable curiosity and singleness of purpose that may seem occasionally selfish or arrogant."

Nonetheless, the teachers persist, and so do the students. Alvin Ailey taught Judith Jamison. Judith Jamison taught Dwana Smallwood and Tracy Inman. And Smallwood and Inman, for their part, are passing on their legacy.

PART THREE

WINTER

Six

The Winter of
Our Discontent

S unday, January 6, the day of fellowship auditions for the
spring term, is a bleak, bitter New York winter day, a perfect
objective correlative for the delivery and receipt of dispiriting
news. But the sixty girls who stretch, gossip, and giggle in Studio
3 while they wait for the proceedings to start are bubbling and
perky after the holiday break, not at all like the tense, contained
ensemble that meditated in this room before a similar occasion
last summer. They are, indeed, too perky for Denise Jefferson,
who, after delivering her familiar opening speech on discipline
and excellence, grumbles, "This is an audition, not a party! You
should be warming up! I'm disappointed in you. You're not be-
ginners!"

All schools take stock at midyear. Enough time has passed for both students and teachers to figure out whether progress is being made, and enough remains to pull out of a rut. At a rigorous training academy, students must not be allowed to coast. The faculty panel is mindful of this as it files in. This term's jury includes the head of the ballet department, two Horton teachers, and one Graham teacher. The drill is always the same: the auditioners are divided into two age groups. A couple of Ailey II dancers are here to demonstrate the combinations. As always, the Ailey-trained girls look notably more self-assured and competent than the outsiders. After dancing, the auditioners, wearing their numbers, wait quietly for a few minutes, facing the panel in what looks like a police lineup, then exit to the hall. The panel winnows out the obvious losers, and the survivors undertake the Horton portion.

When the judges deliberate, they admire Beatrice's dancing and worry about her weight problem. Candidates deemed too heavy get screened out of the dance programs at Juilliard and other desirable schools, the teachers say. For this reason, Jefferson says, Ailey tries to warn students to watch their weight. The panelists review the progress of all the girls over the past term. It is Monique's first audition, and everyone agrees that she and the other Supremes have talent, but Monique must build up her strength. Frajan and Laurence need to focus their attention and work harder.

While the Level VI and VII girls maintain their scholarships, they get a severe talking-to for their attendance records. Frajan and Laurence have *twelve* unexcused absences. How could they slip this way? Frajan says, "My mom called when I was absent." Jefferson regards her sternly. "Who's got a scholarship, you or your mom?" she asks. "You're talented, I'm disappointed." Laurence says she has a math tutor who visits after school. "You have to call," Jefferson says. "It's like a job. If you don't come to the job, you get fired." On Saturdays, of course, it is a job: the girls come in at 9:30 to help out with the little kids' classes. Laurence has been late, and she's warned that being caught in traffic is not an excuse. "I've also heard you don't work one hundred percent," Jefferson adds. "You're very talented. You've been with us a long time." Beatrice has missed too many modern classes. She cites ARTS and performance rehearsals, but she hasn't notified the instructors. Afra's multitude of absences—for outside auditions— land her on warning.

All the girls who get a lecture are told how talented they are, how their techniques will fall off if they are absent too often, and how the little girls in the Saturday classes depend on them. After they leave, Jefferson says, "Laurence could be amazing—the facility, the musicality—but she doesn't know that."

After the auditions, January is a quiet month. The fall term is ending and the spring term beginning, but the different groups that make up The Ailey School have staggered calendars, and when I come in, I find the studios not all occupied and the student lounge almost deserted. The Junior Division students have received their evaluations—the second-half-of-the-winter one- two punch—and they come in individually to discuss them with Inman.

Frajan sits in Inman's office, looking at a stack of evaluation sheets with comments ranging from the generally supportive to the minutely corrective. Litvinova, for example, writes that "Frajan has come to this class with a reasonable understanding of technique. She has an excellent ability to apply correction. She made a lot of progress this semester. Improve your performance qualities and dynamic range." This means that like many Level VI and VII students, Frajan needs to add artistic passion to the technical skills she has built up over several years of training. It is the same problem that bedeviled Travis at the beginning of the year, and Ailey teachers are always raising it with one student or another. Before Frajan can bring herself to cut loose, she needs to grow up a bit emotionally.

What should she work on next term? Here the suggestions are actually quite specific and technical. In pointe work, Frajan is progressing, but Litvinova warns her to make sure her feet are not "sickled"—a term for turning the foot in or out at the ankle and thus breaking the perfectly straight leg line, an egregious fault in the ballet world. To avoid this, she must, Litvinova writes, stay correctly on top of the supporting leg when it's in a turned-out position. In Litvinova's class she is very good in appearance, attendance, attitude, and behavior, but for all of this effort she rates only a B-plus grade, defined as "good to excellent."

While the Graham world speaks a different language from that of the ballet world, Kevin Predmore's comments nail down the same flaw: Predmore praises her overall technical progress, but says her artistry needs work. "Artistically, Frajan is developing," he writes. "She is musical. I would like for Frajan to start exploring more musically, using the movement differently at times with the music. For instance, arriving on the music as well as moving on the music." Predmore would like Frajan "to think of the lines that each movement creates, straight, curved, spiral, emanating from her center beyond her body." Emotion, Martha Graham believed, is rooted in the torso and flows outward through the body into space. The arms and legs, therefore, are subordinate to the torso. Graham dancers don't count the beats:

they relate to rhythm in a more visceral way. These are difficult ideas to comprehend. While serious ballet training is meant to begin in childhood, Graham designed her technique for older students. It is the most challenging method to teach children and the last modern technique the students learn. As both Predmore and Denise Jefferson, herself a Graham teacher, have told me, the movement and choreography require physical, emotional, and intellectual maturity.

Predmore is even tougher than Litvinova: he gives Frajan a C-plus. Grade inflation is apparently not an Ailey vice.

Frajan does not seem overjoyed. She tells Inman, in a reticent tone, that she could have got a higher score. Inman asks her how she could have got a higher score—by working harder or by doing something better? Frajan feels her floor work—a basic element of the Graham warm-up, one of Martha's innovations and usually foreign to ballet technique—has not been good. Inman continues to probe, asking her what about it wasn't good: is there something she doesn't understand or something she can't do? Frajan can't seem to express more than vague malaise. "That's something to figure out," Inman says. "If you feel you could get a higher grade or higher level or get more out of it, then you should know what you can do to make that happen. But overall," he sums up, "I think your evaluations were good?"

"Yes," Frajan says, weakly.

Next Inman reminds her what is expected of Van Lier fellows: she must be at Ailey winter, spring, summer, and fall, with no more July diversions to the Dance Theatre of Harlem. When she is obliged to be late or absent, she must call first and fill out a form. Before she got the Van Lier, Frajan tells me later, she could more or less come and go as she pleased: she was then too

young for any sort of fellowship, and when your parents are paying, attendance is their worry, not the school's.

Gloomy as she seems, Frajan tells me this evaluation is actually
better than those she's got in the past, but she's not used to these
conferences. At lower levels, they used to just mail your report to
you. And then having to talk it over with Mr. Inman, whom she
doesn't know very well, was also something new for her.

By the end of the month, classes are in full swing, but winter
doldrums pervade the air. In Litvinova's class the girls are doing
sissonnes and *pas de chats,* tricky jumps. Laurence looks at her performance in the mirror and wrinkles her nose. *Chassé, step, attitude.* Frajan is intently biting her lip. The studio, enveloped in
mirrors, is a panorama of lavender-clad girls finding fault with
their reflections. And to survive in the dance world, they must
learn to manage the lows, which abound, as well as the highs.

For dancers the mirror is both an essential tool and an instrument of self-torture. "It's very important to explain to them how
to work with mirror, with their own body," Litvinova tells me.
The mirror, she says, is an extremely effective feedback device.
Once an instructor has told them what needs to be done, students must keep checking to make sure they are incorporating
the correction. With attention and hard work, Litvinova and all
her colleagues believe, it is possible to change the body, making
it far more flexible and athletic. "The teacher can't stay with you
all the time and push you," she says. Some responsibility lies with
the student.

Fair enough. But when Predmore—the reed-thin young man
with curly brown hair and glasses who still performs—has got the
lavenders in his studio, he calls out, "Be careful, you guys—focus
is part of the *spiral.* If you look in the mirror, you're not fulfill-

Afra, applying makeup, casts a critical eye at the mirror.
(MARY ANNE HOLLIDAY)

ing it, and it's also very vain." The spiral, a precisely descriptive term for an upward rotation of the torso, depicts one of the basic Graham movements, about which every instructor seems endlessly perfectionistic, and the turning of the head toward the mirror—left or right, instead of up—violates this line.

For Laurence, the mirror is addictive: she likes looking at herself, she says. Afra, too, is tempted to look at her reflection more than she should, a habit she considers counterproductive because there is no mirror to guide dancers when they are onstage, and also because it invites an unhealthy type of self-criticism. "I don't like my weight," she says, "so being in front of the mirror all the time is not good." She also repeats the dancers' conviction that every studio has "thin" mirrors and "fat" mirrors, a distinction which is lost on me: I fail to find an Ailey studio that looks like a fun house.

Afra is five feet six and a quarter and weighs a solid 145. She looks handsome, tall, and strapping, and all the teachers say she has a "good body." That means that besides being so naturally flexible that she needn't work quite as hard as some other students, her weight is sufficiently well distributed that she can get away with a few extra pounds. Still, Afra has been told not to gain and was praised for having lost some weight over the summer. Last year she gave up eating meat and now, as 2002 begins, she is laying off milk and cheese, substituting soy products.

Beatrice, however, is three inches shorter than Afra, and tends toward plumpness. The frustrations of trying unsuccessfully to lose weight sometimes put her in a depressed mood, and this mopeyness affects her carriage, making her look heavier than she actually is. Moreover, when depressed, she moves slowly, burning energy at a slower rate. In auditions and performances she needs to be tautly pulled in every minute, whereas a thinner dancer—Frajan or Monique, for example—might relax occasionally without being penalized. How she looks onstage depends on whether the costume flatters her best feature, her long legs, or accentuates the heaviness around her hips. Some teachers think the pounds will drop off naturally in a couple of years. They feel they are in a bind with Beatrice: to achieve her goals in the outside world—to get jobs and be accepted at one of the conservatory colleges—she must lose the weight, but they worry that pushing a student too hard might drive her to anorexia. Like Afra, Beatrice has given up meat, but the beans-and-rice that play a starring role at the Latino family table still entice her.

There is no way around it—dance is a performing art dependent on how the dancer's body looks as it moves, and an athletic art governed by physical prowess in performing steps. At least some of this is, despite hard work and years of training, innate. A positive way of looking at this situation is, as the anthropologist Judith Lynne Hanna points out,[1] to observe that, in many different cultures around the world and throughout history, dance has represented a human triumph over the limitations of the body. Our notions of beauty, however, vary according to our culture and the required athleticism differs with the choreography. Historians trace the ideal of the thin ballerina to the sylph and faerie roles of Romantic Era ballets. In the 1930s George Balanchine established an even more radical aesthetic of thinness for women dancers: he liked them visibly bony and absent the usual adult female curves, with a shape often labeled prepubescent.

"Mr. B.," as Balanchine was called by his ballerinas, was intensely loved and feared in his own company. His dark side was very dark, indeed: cold, relentless, authoritarian, and infantilizing of young women who were compelled to look like children and be treated like them. At the same time, it was exhilarating for a dancer to satisfy his high standards of performance, win his admiration for her beauty, and be part of an elite, world-renowned troupe that had brought a centuries-old art form into the modern era. This mercurial mixture of experiences kept several generations of ambivalent dancers in thrall to Balanchine until his death in 1983. One of them was Linda Hamilton, who went on to become a psychologist specializing in the problems of performing artists, especially dancers.

For the past fifteen years, Hamilton—often in collaboration

with her husband, the orthopedic surgeon William G. Hamilton, and various physical therapists—has probed the ballet culture, studying male and female adult dancers in leading companies both in New York and abroad, their peers in less demanding regional companies, and student dancers at SAB. Throughout their years of training and professional life, ballerinas who do not meet rigid standards of weight and body shape, whatever their talent and technical skill, will find the gates of elite schools and companies barred to them. Since ballet is not aerobic—on the average, a woman burns up only 200 calories in an hour-long ballet class—dancers too often control their weight by starving themselves. Poor nutrition leads to menstrual disorders and inadequate bone density, which then gives rise to stress fractures and scoliosis.

Professional elite ballerinas, Hamilton has found, frequently weigh 15 percent below the medical ideal for their height—a figure that matches the one in the psychiatric criteria for anorexia. Male dancers, while they can't be overweight, are not required to be so dangerously thin: they must, in particular, be strong enough to lift their women partners. Interestingly, actual eating disorders prevail more widely among European, Russian, and Chinese dancers—not the children of Balanchine—than among Americans. Anorexia becomes more pervasive as competitiveness increases: there is more of it among professionals than students, and more among dancers in national than in regional companies.

What Hamilton discovered in her research, however, was not quite as simple as laypeople might believe: eating disorders among ballerinas do not necessarily originate in the failure to satisfy some warped, asexual ideal of beauty. They result from a complicated reciprocal interplay of action and reaction, in which dancers with anatomical weaknesses develop unhealthy eating habits which, in turn, end up exacerbating their physical problems. In particular, she and her colleagues spent four years following forty SAB students[2] who, at the beginning of the study, were at about the age and level of the Supremes; they represented just over half the SAB students their age. The compelling question, of course, is why some ballerinas become anorectic and others don't, and more broadly, who survives the increasing pressures of this arduous regime and who gets weeded out. All of these girls, after all, had been admitted at age eight according to their body features and presumed talent, and had endured both annual screenings and intense training ever afterward. What was different now was the fact that their bodies were changing.

At the start of the study, Hamilton and her colleagues took an exhaustive medical history of the girls, checking for the age at which they reached puberty, whether there was obesity in their families, what injuries they had incurred in the past, and whether they had any of the minute anatomical variations that compromise ballet technique: the researchers looked for bowlegs; knock-knees; asymmetries and other minute technical imperfections in the foot, ankle, knee, hip, and spine; poor range of motion; and something called "left turning preference" (because *right* turning preference is, well, *preferred* by choreographers). At the same time, the students filled out forms querying their eating habits and answered a standard psychological profile developed by Daniel Offer called the Offer Self-Image Questionnaire. A full 15 percent of all the students Hamilton and her colleagues studied met the criteria for a clinical eating disorder, many more than the percentage of anorectics and bulimics in the general population.

Then, over the four-year period, little by little, the girls either dropped out of dancing entirely or found work in other professional companies until, like the Ten Little Indians, none were left at SAB by the end of the study. When the researchers compared the dropouts with the students who got jobs, it turned out that their orthopedic screening exam had predicted with uncanny accuracy who would leave the profession, and that, moreover, the dancers with apparent eating disorders had more anatomical deviations than those with normal eating habits. The dropouts had more deviant eating habits and more injuries, and unlike their more successful late-maturing peers, they tended to reach puberty at an age considered normal, thus losing the preferred ballet shape (late menarche is also apparently conducive to developing a long, linear body). Compared to the successful dancers, they had asymmetries in leg length, flexibility, and turnout, which impinge on technique. Hamilton and her group, pointing out the Darwinian survival nature of the ballet profession, suggest that some ballet dancers might develop eating disorders because of their technical deficiencies. Moreover, the dancers who succeeded in becoming professional tended to be naturally thin and didn't need to starve themselves to fit the ideal.

One of the Ailey Level VI girls, thirteen-year-old Charlotte Kaufman, spent four years at SAB before switching to Ailey. Even as an elementary-school child, she felt conscious of having the wrong sort of body. "I was always taller and more muscular," she says, "and I guess I made myself uncomfortable." Status at SAB accrued, in Charlotte's description, to the little girls who got into the party scenes in *The Nutcracker,* while she, because of her size, had to settle for the less desirable part of a tin soldier. "They like the really little girls," she believes, "because there's a big size difference between the grown-up dancers and the children and that looks better onstage, and the costumes they have fit the small children." Charlotte says she was told she had potential and asked to stay but didn't because she was miserable. A friend of hers remained, and tells Charlotte that now many of those once-favored little girls are being held back or weeded out, and more talented tin soldiers are staying on. Charlotte still has a muscular body and is glad she transferred. She is comfortable at Ailey, and doing well.

As Charlotte discovered, modern dance is more forgiving. Modern dancers need only achieve the ideal weight for their height. They do not need 180-degree turnout and the musculoskeletal characteristics that favor extensive pointe work. At the same time, modern companies endorse a range of different aesthetics, and weight is more important in some than in others.

When Judith Jamison discusses weight, she doesn't mince words. "In the hundred and eighty ballets that I have, there's not one of them that has a very rotund person," she tells me. "I'm not looking for a rotund person, I'm looking for people who have a line that I like. I realize that you can't raise your leg in arabesque if you've got ten pounds of blubber sitting on your hip. You can't function the way I need you to function using the techniques I need you to use." At the same time, she says she isn't an extremist. "I don't want that bone-thin ballet thing," she insists. "I'm looking for healthy people. Alvin loved people that were full-bodied. I have always been a full-bodied person with hips and boobs."

What Jamison ordains must be accepted philosophically by company dancers—or dancers who hope to get into the company—and interpreted by Ailey School officials and faculty from Denise Jefferson on down. In the company, the dancer Bahiyah Sa'eed-Gaines tells me, she thinks Jamison expects African-

American dancers to be built "how we're built," but does some-times require weight loss, saying, "You have to dance in this uni-tard by next spring." It is all, Sa'eed-Gaines explains, "very cut-and-dried and it's up to you: some people can't eat meat and some can't eat chicken and some have to work out every day to keep svelte, and there will always be a person in the company who can eat a slice of cake every night." Sa'eed-Gaines is mature about the ways of the modern dance world. "There will be a lot of instances where someone won't hire you because you're not tall enough or because your hair is not blond or because you're not short enough or dark enough. In a lot of American compa-nies, if a short, dark-skinned woman left the company, they'd try to hire another short, dark-skinned woman."

Another interesting factor helps explain why the plague of eating disorders has mostly passed over the Ailey company. Back in 1986, when Linda Hamilton and her team studied black and white American dancers in nine national and regional compa-nies,[3] they found that despite a dramatically high prevalence of anorexia and bulimia among the white dancers, none of the black dancers had eating disorders at all. This phenomenon the researchers attributed both to the lack of emphasis on thinness in black culture and the fact that black dancers were relative new-comers to the ballet world. Thus Ailey's demographic, plus the more relaxed aesthetic of modern dance, may contribute to its scarcity of eating disorders. The school has had three cases in the Professional Division, all of whom, as far as Jefferson knows, ar-rived with existing problems to which their classmates alerted the administration. The school, after talking with Hamilton, made the students' stay at Ailey contingent on their seeking help. They are no longer at the school.

Still, when it comes to weight questions, Denise Jefferson knows she is walking on eggs. If you tell a high school student, "You need to lose weight," she says, "to them it's like saying, 'You're fat, you're horrible, you're disgusting, you can never dance.'" The college-age students are more objective and businesslike, and will just ask, "How much do you think I should lose?"

This year, Jefferson is dealing with students' weight problems first by hiring a nutritionist, who gave workshops throughout the fall. She and other faculty members try to offer realistic advice about the varied modern dance world to students who are ready to hunt for jobs: she asks them to look at the dancers already in a particular company, and "see if there is anyone there who looks like you." The conclusion becomes fairly obvious.

There are also legal issues to consider, made more urgent a few years ago when a parent lodged a human rights complaint against a West Coast ballet school for rejecting her eight-year-old daughter, an experienced student, allegedly because the girl had a short, muscular body that didn't meet its admissions criteria. It is now verboten to write on evaluations that a student is fat, nor do these forms have a category that says "body type." Weight problems might be subsumed and glossed over under "appearance" (which also covers whether the student is neat or messy-looking). In the Professional Division, Jefferson says, teachers use particular euphemisms: the student "needs to tone her body more," or "work on developing a longer, more slender line."

Most dancers, as Linda Hamilton found in a national study, are dissatisfied with their bodies.[4] Nutritionist Brenda Schwartz tells me one story that drives home the difference between "overconcern" and real anorexia. A girl came up to Schwartz one day, "heavily dressed with layers of clothing so I couldn't see what she was wearing," Schwartz remembers, "and she said to me, 'How can I reduce my stomach?'" Schwartz began to tell her about sit-ups and which particular foods caused bloating, and suddenly thought to ask the student, "Let's just see. Take off that sweatshirt, and the other shirt, and the other shirt." Schwartz saw the girl was, she says, "flat as a board" and told her, "You look just perfect." What might be called the differential diagnosis lay in the student's reaction to what Schwartz said to her. "She was," Schwartz declares, "happy as a clam." An anorectic, of course, will not believe anyone who tells her she looks fine. "There's a big difference between anorexia and being just overconcerned about the way your body looks."

One enemy of good nutrition, the workshops reveal, is the students' frenetic schedules: when school in Manhattan starts at 8:15 in the morning and many of the kids live in Brooklyn and Queens, for example, how do they manage to eat a healthy breakfast? The older students (and Brian Brown, who is mostly self-supporting) add outside jobs to their dance and study obligations, but control their own meals (for better or worse); the younger students, who live at home, eat what their parents are willing to serve. During the day the high school students, in particular, display the standard deplorable eating habits of ordinary American teenagers: junk food abounds, both as the chosen plates on LaGuardia lunch tables and as snacks brought into or bought in the Ailey student lounge, even when nutritious alternatives exist. One day, I go out to lunch at the local Chinese restaurant with Afra and her friends. Afra dutifully orders the entrée with the tofu. Then, on the way back to PPAS, she stops off in a deli and picks up a cinnamon Danish.

Poor nutrition is not, of course, the only way dancers can punish their bodies. The union contract with Ailey directs that a physical therapist travel everywhere with the First Company. On Ailey's upper floor, near the studios where the First Company rehearses and relaxes when it's in town, a clinic is open to students and teachers as well as performers. A small room with the requisite stationary bikes and treadmills and charts of musculature papering the walls, it is a busy place.

The student sitting out a class with an ice pack on her ankle is a familiar Ailey sight, and the prospect of a more serious injury is the sword that hangs over all dancers from the moment they decide to commit body and soul to this art. This, along with the inevitable close of the performing career at an age when artists and writers are just beginning to hit their stride, actors and musicians are looking forward to a lifetime onstage, and even singers will last another couple of decades, adds a special poignancy to the young dancers' passion. All year I watch these kids nervously, never sure they'll be here the following week. The adults in their families and at Ailey are always telling them to have a backup in case they suffer some permanent damage. When I ask the kids about the future, it is difficult to judge an ambivalent answer, to assess vacillation from month to month. Are they reluctant to entrust themselves to the fragile promise that they'll escape with their bodies intact?

Of the students who are my focus this year, only Beatrice has experienced a serious, debilitating injury—the painful shoulder tendinitis that lasted a year and a half and kept her out of repertory workshops—and she is now over it. But when I began to visit Ailey, I met a potential superstar the age of the Supremes who had been sidelined for a year. She never came back afterward. She had, it seems, enjoyed being an ordinary ninth grader, had done a sort of cost/benefit analysis, and had chosen to quit.

Are the dancers' bodies, those gorgeously tuned instruments that move with such suppleness in the studio, doomed to painful, untimely erosion? Early in my days at Ailey, the instructor Robert Atwood told me that while the format of a ballet class is roughly the same as it was two hundred years ago, the knowledge behind it has dramatically changed. The transformation, he said, comes from a better understanding of physiology, which has produced exercises that use the dancer's muscles efficiently to bend, straighten, and rotate the legs. The Atwood classes I watch have a slightly mechanical quality to them, as if the studio were vibrating with a host of different pulley systems. "The leg has to be rotated so you don't get tension in the hip," he might tell the boys. "Turn the heel forward, Jerome! Lift the left side of your back—get tall!"

What happens, I wonder, when things go wrong? What has this better understanding of physiology done to protect dancers? At last, when, fortunately, I have still not had to watch any of my teenage dancers being rehabilitated, I make my way to the clinic upstairs to talk with Shaw Bronner, the physical therapist who operates it.

Bronner herself was a modern dancer who got injured back in the early eighties. In those days, she says, orthopedics simply amounted to telling a dancer who had already been injured to "rest, take drugs, and don't dance. You wouldn't treat a soccer player that way. Dancers are athletes as well as artists," she tells me, "and they have yet to benefit from the great inroads we've made in sports medicine." A modern dance company's injury rate over a thousand hours of dance, Bronner discovered, was substantially higher than that incurred over the same period by figure skaters and soccer players, for whom researchers have carefully studied a host of risk factors in the environment, the training regime, and the athletes'own physiology.

As the Level VIs and VIIs start their careers, they will face a less dangerous environment than Alvin Ailey himself—who developed terrible knee problems—encountered fifty years ago. Dance floors are built of kinder materials, and ballerinas can use the new pointe shoes made of shock-absorbent synthetic fabrics. Physical therapists know the importance of cross-training for dancers as well as athletes, so they don't overuse some muscles and underuse others. At the same time, Bronner points out, audiences demand more pyrotechnics from performers—multiple turns and higher jumps. "Whatever you're doing to prepare them for what they once had to do, now they have to do more and you have to do more to catch up," she says.

In addition to treating injured dancers, Bronner has assembled a program at Ailey that involves screening company members and students at the beginning of the year to assess whether they are vulnerable to various injuries. She also runs workshops on preventive movement and exercise. All of this is paid for by outside funding, which will run out this year in the middle of April. Like the psychologist Linda Hamilton and the nutritionist Brenda Schwartz, she addresses mostly Ailey II dancers and college-age students, whose needs are considered more urgent and take priority, both because they are out in the world as professionals and because they live independently from their families, placing the school to some extent in loco parentis. Bronner does, however, treat a few of the teenagers for characteristic problems.

Adolescents have a lot of knee trouble and shin splints, she tells me, because they are experiencing explosive skeletal growth and their muscles haven't yet caught up to their bones. These injuries are most common among the boys, who are going through the biggest growth spurt, although growing pains underlie some of the current weakness and frequent minor injuries that Monique Massiah is suffering. "It is hard to get them to follow through on extra stretching, which is really boring," Bronner says, "and to say things like, 'Don't jump,' because that's the really fun part of class."

There is a lot of denial going on, Bronner tells me. All dancers ache, she says, just as all athletes do: it's part of the normal training process, and they must learn to differentiate between good and bad pain. Normal pain comes from using new muscles, and it's worse after vacations. "When you haven't been to class for a week and you come back and do the jumps, the next day you walk down the stairs and your calves and thighs are just killing you, but that's normal overuse, not an injury per se. I'm always wishing I could send the kids a letter saying, 'At least ride a bike every day' between the end of school and the beginning of the summer program. Otherwise their bodies freak out, and they come in here in hysterics because everything hurts. I've begged the teachers to have them do fewer jumps the first week, until they're ready."

The teenagers may be as stubborn about seeking and following through on physical therapy as they are about healthy eating. Monique, for example, has back trouble that comes from injured hamstrings and scoliosis, a lateral curvature of the spine. A long time ago, she says, she tore her hamstrings, and apparently they didn't heal properly, "So if I'm not really warmed up, they'll pop," she says. "The muscle tears and you can hear it go pop. Then I have to go through the process of being healed again. It hurts a lot and I can't do some steps. My right hamstring is better than my left, so I can only do a split with my right leg." When it gets to hurting too much, she might sit out part of a class. Monique had physical therapy outside of school last year, before Bronner arrived at Ailey, but stopped going back after the summer—"I didn't have the time"—and just deals with it herself, exercising with weights when the knees get painful.

Exhibiting the stoicism typical among dancers, she has not told Ailey about her scoliosis. "I don't know why but I just haven't," she says. "Because I guess if I tell them, then they'll say you shouldn't do this, you shouldn't do that. So I basically work through my back injury."

Bronner is content to have spent time with the older students and the members of Ailey II—and hopes to have had some kind of influence on them. Even if these dancers don't get into the First Company, she observes, they are feeding into all the modern dance companies and Broadway shows throughout the city. Perhaps good preventive habits will spread. Meanwhile, Bahiyah Sa'eed-Gaines, now twenty-seven, feels fortunate to live in a time when dancers are better informed about taking care of their bodies: artistry, she knows, comes from life experience, and with absolute conviction she says, "I'm going to dance forever."

But winter ends, and as the weather gets warmer and the afternoons lighter, the girls' spirits—as resilient as their bodies at this age—pick up. One April afternoon, Litvinova is teaching the lavenders and the burgundies—Level V—together, because their teacher has had to cancel. There are twenty-five girls and two boys in class today, and Litvinova rolls her eyes and mutters to me, "Tough!" I am not sure whether she feels taxed by the greater number of students—certainly fewer than she finds in the summer session, when classes expand to fifty kids—or by the need to teach two distinctly different levels of skill. But here, when they dance side by side with the burgundies, I can see the progress the lavenders have made, inch by inch, this year. The burgundies are talented students, but they are clearly clunkier, and their legs don't go up as high. They watch as Litvinova demonstrates a combination, and then asks Monique to demonstrate it, too.

After class, despite the challenge of teaching more kids at two levels, Litvinova is excited. "They are working very good, my kids!" she says, and then volunteers; "Suddenly, Monique began to trust me. A few months ago she looked up from a *plié* and had the look of 'I respect you.' Before that, she was going through the motions. I gave up on her. Now it's different. They are no longer fighting their body. They are enjoying it." And Litvinova does a quick arabesque, just to illustrate.

Seven

Where's Shamel?

It is the same chilly January Sunday on which the girls audi-tioned for their fellowships. At three o'clock, after they have gone home, the boys come in. The most striking thing about a gathering of male student dancers, compared to a gathering of female dancers, is how few boys there are; and the odd fact that the demographics become significantly more lopsided in the younger grades. The January auditions assess fifty girls and twenty-eight boys, a contrast that looks overwhelming in the studio where fellowship applicants await their moment to perform. When they are divided by age for the actual auditions, however, an interest-ing difference emerges. The seventeen-and-over boys' group, which includes Travis, Brian, the kids in the Professional Divi-sion, and a few outsiders, numbers twenty-one, as opposed to twenty-six girls—not quite equal but hardly outrageous. But there are only seven boys signed up in the younger high school group, compared to twenty-four girls, and Nigel Campbell, a diminutive Level V who has just turned fifteen and is thus on his first Ailey fellowship audition, is obliged to go across the floor without a partner. He blasts off in an explosion of leaps and turns, clearly reveling in his performance, which receives a big round of applause. "That takes chutzpah," Jefferson whispers.

Moreover, Shamel and Ryan Rankine, a promising Level VI classmate, are at first nowhere to be seen. Finally, they appear, breathing hard and full of apologies. They have been a few blocks up, demonstrating steps for the auditions at LaGuardia.

There are never enough boy dancers. Anywhere. Although untalented boys are not chosen or given scholarships, it is more or less true that while talented girls compete with one another for parts, parts compete with one another for talented boys. And while the girls have the technique but must learn to cut loose, the boys—even if they sometimes bump into one another—have the passion. Comments about "artistry" are less frequently applied to the boys, whereas their technical skills must often be quickly brought up to par.

Then, within a couple of weeks after classes start, Shamel and Ryan go missing. Jerome, another gifted Level VI boy, is hardly ever around.

Late in January, Shamel had told Tracy Inman that LaGuardia hadn't enough boys for its senior concert, and would be dipping into the junior class. He knew this a while ago, but it is only now that he is directly confronting the complications it raises for his life. All the way back in the fall, Michelle Mathesius, chair of LaGuardia's dance department, had asked Shamel to dance in a

piece then being made by an outside choreographer for the concert, with rehearsals to start immediately and continue through
the spring. Shamel—who was then rehearsing for *Anansi* and
Memoria and taking regular classes at Ailey in addition to his La-
Guardia work—signed on. He was sure he could handle it all. In
January, however, Penny Frank invited Shamel to participate in
her repertory piece for the senior concert. There was no way
Shamel would—or could—say no to that, and he still thinks he
can handle it. But rehearsals last till four o'clock three days a
week at LaGuardia, and Shamel's aunt wants him to go to the
school's SAT prep course two days a week. At first, Inman says
there will be no problem with Shamel's going to LaGuardia rehearsals as long as he lets Ailey know the dates. In theory, Shamel
could still get to most of his classes at Ailey and attend rehearsals
for the Ailey spring repertories, all of which start later in the afternoon, but there would be precious little time for schoolwork
and none in which to simply catch his breath.

Then it turns out that the LaGuardia senior concert and The
Ailey School show will take place concurrently. Now Shamel is
really forced to choose. Practically speaking, he has to choose La-
Guardia, because school must take first place in every student's
life. The idea of going to class at Ailey and then sitting around
watching his friends rehearse for a show he can't be in is painful.
He is utterly torn. To make things worse, it is also embarrassing
to let people down, and Shamel dreads telling Inman and Jefferson he has chosen LaGuardia over Ailey. What will they say? The
result is that Shamel doesn't call in, doesn't drop by—just stops
going to Ailey.

After three weeks, Inman calls Michelle Mathesius to find out
how long Shamel will be otherwise engaged. Mathesius tells In-

man that the rehearsals will continue throughout the term, and that school is much more important than Ailey classes. Inman, however, is irritated. He feels that while Ailey is an extracurricular activity, so, too, is the LaGuardia senior concert for a boy who's in the eleventh grade, and it's up to Shamel to decide which show he wants to dance in. Shamel is so responsible, Inman says, and he usually tells Ailey when he has outside obligations. Inman believes Shamel has vanished because LaGuardia must be putting pressure on him. It is true, Inman says, that the boy is at an age when everything has to be "fun" and kids don't like to think about unpleasant things. Inman well remembers feeling that way when he was sixteen, and a student violinist with conflicting commitments to juggle.

There is another complication, however. Shamel has a Van Lier Fellowship, and both Inman and Shamel himself will have to talk to Denise Jefferson about whether he can keep it if he is not coming regularly to Ailey classes.

Shamel is not the only LaGuardia boy in the eleventh grade who is taking the term off from Ailey to be in the senior concert: Ryan Rankine has the same problem. Ryan's dilemma is complicated by academic difficulties: While Shamel has a relatively safe 87 average, Ryan is barely making 80, and has less family support for his dancing than Shamel. One day, he stops by Ailey for a visit and tells me, "I'll be back in the fall. I want to keep my good name in both schools." I am intrigued by the value he is expressing, which sounds unexpectedly mature and mindful of his future in the dance world: Ryan has—from somewhere—absorbed the idea that it's better to take this term off at Ailey than to pile up absences. Another Level VI boy, Jerome

Warren, who doesn't go to LaGuardia, is also performing else-where, and is seldom in class at Ailey. Teachers have told me that teenage boys are more erratic than teenage girls (and the girls are clearly less than perfect). But the boys have learned what they are supposed to do, even though they don't always manage to do it.

This past fall, seven of the forty-four students in Levels V through VII were boys (the audition grouped the boys by age, rather than level in the school, so the cast of characters was slightly different, but the numbers work out the same). They were excit-ing, energetic, and full of talent and enthusiasm. In his boys' bal-let class, De Vita, imbued with the Ailey sense of noblesse oblige, urged them on. "What are you doing with your arms, Serge?" he sang out one day in October. "Don't try to look like a windmill!" A few minutes later he called out, "I don't care to see you next year with your butt completely out! I don't know what is the dis-cipline in LaGuardia but not here! Not because you got a schol-arship, you finish working. You work double, to be fabulous!" The instructor was moving among them, rearranging arms and turning torsos. Suddenly, he came to a stop in front of Ryan Rankine. "Sometimes," he said thoughtfully, "you are very good." And finally, when Jerome Warren seemed to be slacking off, De Vita exploded. "Jé-rrrome! You are seventeen—don't lose time! A dancer retires at thirty-one. . . ."

When the class was over, the boys looked at one another like a chamber group agreeing on its cue, and suddenly all together began a small Charleston riff, ending with their hands crossed on their bent knees. After that, they broke into the customary ap-plause for a good class, and De Vita picked up his bag and left the room. For the next ten minutes the boys continued practicing the combinations he had given them, and calling out to each other in heavy French accents. *"Jé-r-rome!"* Later, Ryan said to me, "He's tough, but if they don't yell at you, they don't care."

Over at LaGuardia, Michelle Mathesius echoes Ailey's enthusiasm for this group of boys. "They feed on each other," she tells me. "They're all going to be dancers. There's no question about it. When they were freshmen, they used to come up all the time to watch the advanced classes. I can't get them to go to the lunchroom—they want to be up here in the studio, dancing. I shoo them out of the building at the end of the day, but they just want to stay and dance and watch everything that's going on."

The scarcity of boys high-school age and younger at The Ailey School, so conspicuous during the auditions, is at the outset a bit puzzling. One of the first things a visitor notices on entering the Ailey studios, particularly in the summer when students are older and the company is in town rehearsing, is a palpable quantity of male energy. The tone of the place is not delicate. The halls bustle with strapping young men in white tank tops or T-shirts, and when they are in class or onstage, there is nothing fragile about their arabesques. In fact, men outnumber women in the First Company by sixteen to fifteen. In Ailey II, the score is even: six men and six women. Within a short time, I figured out what is happening: with the professional dancers and high school graduates, Ailey has skimmed off some of the cream from around the country and the world, but the Junior Division reflects the percentage of boy dancers in the local population, and it is very low, here and everywhere else.

Male dancers have been an embattled minority in Western culture only since the nineteenth century, when new ideas of ap-

propriate male and female behavior began to crystallize, and—
for a variety of reasons now offered by social historians—ballet
was allocated to the feminine sphere. Particularly in London and
Paris, an all-female corps de ballet became fashionable. Older
male dancers moved into character roles, often those that mixed
dance with mime. One historian, Ramsay Burt of De Montfort
University in Leicester, England,[1] suggests that in Copenhagen
and St. Petersburg, where ballet was under royal and aristocratic
patronage, male dancers still flourished. In London and Paris, on
the other hand, the companies needed the support of the bour-
geoisie, and the sight of men dancing evoked either "the degen-
erate style of the old aristocracy" or "the rude prowess of the
working classes." At the same time, to watch a ballerina perform
was thought to be partly an erotic experience, and thus men in
the audience worried that "to enjoy the spectacle of men dancing is to be interested in men." The belief that concert dance was
a domain best populated by women and gay men, according to
Burt, began in the era of Diaghilev and Nijinsky in the early
twentieth century.

This idea has kept a lot of little boys—some of whom, perhaps, might have the athletic and musical talent to realize a satisfying avocation and even a successful career—away from dance
lessons. Some of the boys I met were gay, some straight, and
some ambiguous, but most had encountered either bullying in
school or resistance from their families, or had absorbed the association of dance with gayness in men and felt anxious about it.
"The first time I saw men in tights, when I was a little kid, I
didn't want to wear tights. I thought I would become gay," Serge
Desroches told me. The result of this is that few boys who ex-

hibit an inclination toward dance—at the same early age that girls do, and in the same way, by dancing at family parties or in front of the television—get lessons immediately. Often it is only in middle school, when, perhaps, they see male dancers in a performance by some arts-in-the-schools program, that they decide to pursue their interest. Among the male faculty at Ailey, several began dancing late in life: Inman, Mosley, and Atwood started out at twenty, and Predmore was a high school athlete who began taking ballet to improve his gymnastics, found himself increasingly drawn into the dance world, and ended up, many years later, performing with Martha Graham.

Many male ballet dancers start very late indeed, and whether it is because of the beating they take in the outside world or because of the particular stresses of life in a ballet company, they do not appear to be a happy group. When the psychologist Linda Hamilton and three colleagues at the Miller Health Care Institute for Performing Artists at St. Luke's-Roosevelt Hospital Center studied fourteen women and fifteen men from the New York City Ballet and American Ballet Theater,[2] the researchers learned that on average the women had begun ballet classes four years earlier than the men and entered their companies at age eighteen with eleven years of training. The men came in at age nineteen with only seven years of training. And when the researchers asked these subjects to fill out a host of standard psychological questionnaires, they found that the women were not much different from non-dancing women, except for having more competitive and aesthetic careers. They were, in fact, less troubled by lack of recognition and success, less vulnerable to adjustment and mood problems, and not physically sick as often. They were, however, very different from their male colleagues—"significantly more adjusted, tough-minded, disciplined, and caring than their male counterparts."

As if this weren't indictment enough, the men, while more creative than men in the general population, were less extroverted, adjusted, tough-minded, disciplined, and enterprising, and more withdrawn, submissive, hostile, and rebellious. One possible reason for this, the researchers suggest, is that "male dancers may be reacting to the basic inequalities that exist within the ballet company, since this essentially serves as a showcase for the ballerina, while limiting the male to partnering and occasional moments of technical display."

Apparently, Hamilton and her colleagues report, some research suggests that men who are outperformed at work by women or in professions considered to be "feminine"—male nurses, for example—are more likely than other men to become angry and anxious and develop poor health habits. For both men and women, ballet ranked high in several measures of occupational stress: dancers in these two leading companies had a poor sense of what criteria their superiors used for evaluating them, they were beset by conflicting loyalties and demands, and they suffered from erratic work schedules and isolation. But the men experienced more personal strain, as well as poor health and fatigue, and more of them drank too much. Hamilton and her group, in somewhat ambiguous phrasing, suggest that because ballet is considered to be a "feminine" profession, the men who choose to enter this career may "differ psychologically from the general population," but that only a longitudinal study could answer that question. Male dancers, clearly, have taken a lot of battering. One could construct two hypotheses from this: they might, perhaps, be demoralized by this treatment, but on the other hand, a Darwinian survival mechanism might prevail, and it may require greater strength to last long enough to achieve professional status.

The Alvin Ailey American Dance Theater is not just a showcase for the ballerina, but the boys—gay or straight—who arrive at The Ailey School and enjoy its distinctive mix of cosseting and rigor have been willing to put up with some persecution from nondancers while pursuing their interest. Some of them have managed this because of family support, which is based on a range of values. Travis Magee's family is captivated by performing artists. Nigel Campbell's family also admires art and dance. Brian Brown's parents are comfortable with his sexuality, and his father thinks all kids should have some organized after-school activity. Serge Desroches Sr. believes that a drive toward any artistic expression translates into general success in life and wishes more parents would encourage their sons to develop their talents: Mr. Desroches—who, I am told, varies markedly from the stereotypical Haitian-American father—chauffeurs his son and daughter back and forth from their different dance schools several days a week and says he would like to see Serge Jr. reach the top in dance, with medicine as only a fallback career.

Other boys have faced strong disapproval from one or both parents. One Level VI boy, who swears he has known he was gay since the third grade but never told either of his parents, took up dance in middle school and says he was soon thrown out of the house because his mother, with whom he lived, believed dancing was making him that way. The boy was obliged to camp out on the doorstep of more accepting relatives. He had to take one term off from Ailey because he couldn't come up with the $200 needed to supplement his fellowship. This boy once told Inman he always keeps a suitcase packed in case whichever adult relative he happens to be living with should send him away. He is considered to be very talented.

It seemed amazing to me that any boys get even as far as La-Guardia and Ailey. I asked Michelle Mathesius where they train before she sees them, and she gave credit to particular junior high school teachers and to some after-school programs in the outer boroughs. "These women and men," Mathesius said, "who are middle-aged teachers, they grab these kids and instill a love of dance. Then they put the boys in their station wagons and take them here for the auditions because the boys don't even know how to get here."

Ryan Rankine, Nigel Campbell, and Jerome Warren, among other boys over the years, have all been discovered and developed through an after-school program called Creative Outlet Dance Theatre of Brooklyn, which is managed by the dancer-choreographers Jamel Gaines, Kevin Joseph, and Lakai Worrell. When I visit the program in January, Gaines's wife, the Ailey dancer Bahiyah Sa'eed-Gaines, has just finished performing *Cry* during the First Company's season at City Center. While Creative Outlet is not formally connected to Ailey, throughout its eight-year history it has shared and exchanged some instructors with the school. When the First Company is in town, Sa'eed-Gaines also teaches at the program, which holds most of its classes on Saturdays at a public high school in the East New York section of Brooklyn. These are makeshift quarters: some classes, held in rooms intended for math or social studies instruction, have no barres, and students are obliged to hold on to rearranged desks. Staffing is done by parents and parishioners of St. Paul's Community Baptist Church, a lively institution whose minister, the

Reverend Johnny Ray Youngblood, has received wide press coverage.

Gaines and his partners are members of the church, and often perform there. I ask Kevin Joseph how they get so many boys interested in dancing. He says the boys don't even know they want to dance. Some come in after a performance or when they're walking their sisters to class, and those whose parents don't go to the church and who don't have dancing sisters hear about it from their friends. "It's like we trick them," he tells me. "We don't start them off with extreme ballet or extreme modern. It's just some hip-hop, and then slowly you start converting them over to dancing. You say, 'Let's put some classical music on; let's go on to jazz,' and from the hip-hop to the modern comes a little more line, and then 'Let's start in first position.'"

A by-product of what Creative Outlet does might be called social work with those children who have family problems. "When they first come to us," Joseph says, "they just see some brothers who feel good when they're dancing." Joseph and the boys sometimes play basketball afterward, and then he may bring them back home for dinner. It is, he says, an escape from whatever bad things are going on in their families. The staff hears sad stories from the boys, Joseph says, left and right.

While the group performs in venues all over the city and in public schools, it is not, in The Ailey School sense, a training ground for future dancers. Those students who show talent and inclination to go further, however, are groomed and polished for auditions at LaGuardia and Ailey. The dance vocabulary in an Ailey audition, in particular, would be intimidating to a boy who came in without the proper training. Gaines and his colleagues also try to teach social skills—how the boys present themselves to new people, how to answer the phone correctly, how to speak clearly and grammatically, and even how to put together a press kit if they have performing ambitions. He tells me when a kid gets 80 on a test, he's likely to say, "Great, let's see how you might get a 95."

When I ask the Gaineses how they spot a boy who might go further, Jamel says he picks up a hunger in the eyes, and Bahiyah Sa'eed-Gaines answers just the same way as Michelle Mathesius did at LaGuardia a few weeks earlier. "We have to throw them out of the studio," she says.

Two of the Ailey boys declare to me that they think of Jamel as "like my father." One result of all this, however, is that boys who come to Ailey and LaGuardia don't break their ties with Creative Outlet, and when they are forced to choose one or two places to perform at, they remember their roots and don't disappoint Gaines. After they have vanished from Ailey this term, I see Ryan and Jerome dancing in one of Jamel's performances.

When boys arrive at Ailey, they encounter a set of institutional aesthetic and cultural values. Dance expresses a range of profound human emotions, and one of them, logically enough, is sexuality. The attitudes toward sexuality in the company and the school derive from those of Alvin Ailey himself, who was gay in his personal life but straight (to the point of machismo, some critics observe) onstage. Denise Jefferson explained the Ailey view to me, pointing out that artistic institutions (including Ailey) are a haven of acceptance for gay men and women, and indeed for anyone who is "different." At the same time, she said that "certain behavior is appropriate in one place and totally inappropriate in another," and that flamboyantly gay dress and behavior— which might be fine at a club or party—is not acceptable at Ailey.

Jefferson also said that "Judy's aesthetic is one in which men onstage look very masculine" (although Jamison herself adroitly dodged this question, telling me she wanted dancers who could transform themselves like chameleons onstage, becoming the character that a particular ballet required). Jefferson did call my attention to other dance companies like the Frankfurt Ballet, in which, she says, androgynous dancers look right and do well. Still, she explained, it is not the Ailey aesthetic.

Ailey instructors, like the students, may be gay, straight, or mysterious. The younger African-American gay men, however, feel a duty to help and act as models for boys who resemble their younger selves. They do not take a *position* on embracing one's sexuality at any particular age (clearly a complicated issue, and fraught with potential problems that are beyond the purview of a dance teacher), but they are plainly out and comfortable about it, and they make a living and enjoy perks like foreign travel. Students who are starting to come to terms with their sexuality at the end of high school might look at Powell, Inman, and Mosley and see the possibilities for a comfortable and satisfying life. Moreover, young men beginning their dance careers might discover a certain poetic justice in the rewards that come from perseverance in the face of ridicule. Inman told me that the chance for a boy from a poor family to experience upward mobility as a dancer sometimes tied in with concerns about being gay: that is, they might find that "the other boys made fun of me for being gay, and now I'm dancing all over the world and they haven't left the neighborhood."

In the fall of the year I spent at Ailey, the boy with the always-packed suitcase went through a period of dyeing his hair orange and wearing makeup and ruffled blouses from the misses' department, a style not conducive to finding employment in many places outside Ballets Trockadero, the French transvestite company. Inman handled it lightly:

Inman: Why are you wearing makeup?

Boy: I'm not wearing makeup.

Inman: Look, I was not born yesterday. I *do* makeup. You're wearing it.

Boy: It's who I am.

Inman: It's not who you are—it's who you want to be. And who you are is you without makeup. You can do it if you want, but when you come in the door for an audition with makeup and some pink fur coat on, I don't care how well you dance, even if you dance like a man, the impression is what they see when you first come in.

By the spring term, the boy's hair is its own color again and he's wearing black. Inman is pleased with him because he is dancing at Ailey and not hanging out, as far as Inman can tell, at places where he might get into trouble.

With questions of sexuality roiling around beneath the surface, it is not surprising that the usual teenage romance is minimal around Ailey. I heard that a Level VI boy and a Level VI girl were dating for a while, but without being told about it by other kids, I would not have spotted them: boys and girls are constantly holding hands or walking arm in arm without the gesture having any meaning at all beyond chumminess. Some of the girls have outside boyfriends. There is usually one all-Ailey couple every year. Travis Magee and Nicole Wasserman were last year's couple, who eyed each other for a whole semester, walked to the subway together on an evening they both stayed late, and remembered events in their relationship by auditions and class schedules. This year, because Nici has gone off to Virginia Commonwealth University School of the Arts, they are no longer officially a couple, but they are in touch with each other several times a week and when Nici comes home on her breaks, they seem as tied to each other as ever.

Both Travis and Nici say that Ailey is a place where people's private lives are kept separate. There is, perhaps, an added bit of security for some teenagers to be free of pressure to couple off. The chance to have, as Travis puts it, "an emotionally rich experience" is a tempting distraction from dance, but perhaps the reverse obtains as well. It is possible that postponing romantic relationships is one of the sacrifices some student dancers make to develop their talent, but it may also be likely that developing their talent gets them out of dealing with sex before they're ready. The psychologist Mihaly Csikszentmihalyi and his collaborators, in studying teenagers talented in a wide variety of fields not including dance, administered the Offer Self-Image Questionnaire, the same psychological test that Linda Hamilton's team had posed to their student ballerinas. Hamilton had found the young dancers "compromised in their sexual functioning," a fact she attributes to their having gone through puberty late. But when Csikszentmihalyi and his colleagues studied teenagers talented in fields other than dance, they, too, found that the talented group differed significantly from the norm in only one measure, the Sexual Attitudes Subscale.[3] Talented teens, the researchers found, "are more conservative in their sexual attitudes and less confident of their sexual attractiveness than their same-sex average peers."

Whether the boys were more conservative than the girls depended on the field they were in: did developing talent in that field involve cutting loose from what was considered appropriate behavior for their gender? Some of the girl dancers at The Ailey School—who are, after all, doing what every little girl is supposed to want to do, although doing it more seriously than other girls—express conservative attitudes, and at least pay lip service to the idea of postponing sex until they are out of high school. Other girls have boyfriends, on and off, outside the dance world, but clearly dance is their first interest. Teenage pregnancy is one problem that does not seem to worry officials at The Ailey School.

Whatever difficulties boys may have faced in the outside world, they are warmly welcomed in the world of dance, and in modern dance, unlike ballet, they need not feel subordinate to the girls. I hear occasional grumbling from girls and their parents about the easier time the boys seem to have. One day I say to Mathesius that once boys start dancing, they seem to have very little to push against, while girls, on the other hand, despite the universal pride of their families, face a daunting amount of competition. Mathesius agrees. "The boys have it made," she says. "if they've got the least bit of interest in dance. It's really sad to watch sometimes, because you'll see these wonderful girls who have worked so hard and are often disappointed, and boys who haven't worked at all and just have this raw talent, and they're going to get whatever parts they want."

Ailey adults smile nervously when I ask them whether boy dancers have it easier than their girl classmates, and firmly deny that boys are cut any more slack than girls in following the school's firm rules. After the January audition, Celia Marino, head of the school's ballet department, tells me that in auditions "we are more generous with the boys. We want to have male dancers, and they start late. With them you cannot be expecting as much training as the girls." It is true, however, that the boys come up to speed very quickly, probably, Marino said, "because they want badly to do this and they have been for years trying to dance."

It is hardly news to state that every society lays out different rules for men and women, and that whatever career we choose, our success will be affected by our temperament and what happens in our personal life. As Csikszentmihalyi's work shows, these factors play out differently for athletes, scientists, and musicians. They also operate characteristically for dancers. For a boy to persist in dancing despite roadblocks in the outside world requires relentless commitment, a certain stubbornness, and comfort with his own eccentricity—all qualities that will be useful in surmounting the other difficulties that dancers encounter. The memory of obstacles overcome increases the pleasure of every victory, and that, too, augurs well for a boy's persistence. A girl, on the other hand, may not discover her backbone until a few years later: when young dancers enter the competitive professional world, the women meet a more crowded field, and indeed, backbone may not be enough to assure success. For men who have held out this long, the upward path is clearer.

After several weeks of postponing the difficult moment, Shamel finally goes to see Denise Jefferson. He does not know her very well. She doesn't seem like a mean person, but he has heard she is very strict. To his surprise, Jefferson grants the leave of absence and maintains the Van Lier Fellowship. She tells Shamel to make sure he goes to the SAT class because it would give him career options, opening the door to more than just dance. Dance, she reminds him, is not forever. Inman is there, too, and Shamel looks at him mischievously and says, "When I stop dancing, I can take your job."

From Jefferson's point of view, the conflict with LaGuardia is a delicate but not unfamiliar problem. She has been facing it since the school's scholarship program began in the seventies. She asks Inman to work out a schedule so that if Shamel is free one or two days a week or if LaGuardia cancels a rehearsal, he could still come over to Ailey and take class. Shamel would be responsible for staying in touch with Inman to keep him posted on the LaGuardia timetable. "I feel we should not put up roadblocks for the students," she tells me a few months later, "because they need to meet the requirements in both places. They've got to graduate. They're going to get a diploma from that place—they're not going to get a diploma from here." This solution applies because Shamel has had a good attendance record up to now, and the school's generosity also depends somewhat on the student's degree of talent.

The problem of how to be everywhere at once continues to plague the teenage students at LaGuardia throughout the year, but the boys' attendance is spottier than that of the girls. One day De Vita shows me his roll book, throwing up his hands in frustration. This, too, does not surprise Jefferson. "They're teenagers, and they're pulled in so many different directions."

Jefferson gives out a deep sigh. "Good heavens," she says. "We're asking a lot of them. Which is why I believe that when they need a little flexibility and we can give it to them, we need to do that."

But as April begins, De Vita, too, is in an expansive mood. There are seven boys in class today, and he is liberal with praise.

Beautiful! Good boy! Travis is having a fine day, demonstrating double pirouettes. When the class is nearly over, De Vita says, "The studio is free. We can go another half hour. You need to work on *double tours en l'air.* You are not twelve any more. Don't say in modern dance you don't need it—you do! Did you see the Ailey II three weeks ago?" The *tour en l'air,* which Travis has demonstrated, is a high turning jump from *demi-plié* with tricky footwork in the landing, and De Vita thinks the class needs more practice doing two of them successively. The boys are up for it.

And as the term goes on, there seems to be a certain fluidity between LaGuardia and Ailey. Some of the boys who are not in class turn up in the Ailey corridor from time to time. And it turns out that as auditions and rehearsals progress for the Ailey shows, Shamel will not stop feeling their powerful attraction.

PART FOUR

SPRING

Eight

College Time

April is a tense month for high school seniors and their families all over the country. Throughout the year, they have been worrying about college—taking SATs, figuring out where to apply, wondering whether they will measure up. It is a time that tests the relations within a family: how far do the parents really trust the child to put the application together and make decisions? How much independence does the child dare to assert? College application, moreover, makes a handy arena for all the other dramas in the family to play out: where does this child stand out in comparison to sisters and brothers? Which of the parents' dreams—reliving their own college days, being the first in the family to move up—is the child responsible for fulfilling? For Beatrice, Afra, Travis, and Brian, these questions have been playing out all year, and each family has dealt with them in its own way. Now they are about to learn the results.

While students in ballet academies are usually encouraged to start professional careers right after high school—and while many of the instructors at The Ailey School have done just that—these days the school tries to persuade its pupils to go to college first. The modern dance world tends to believe—going back to Martha Graham—that well-rounded individuals make better dancers. And the notion of having a professional alternative is pragmatically consistent with the less competitive admissions policies at Ailey: when students are not weeded out every year, who knows whether their hopes will come true, or indeed whether a life in professional dance is really what they are hoping for?

For the past several years, The Ailey School has had a cooperative Bachelor of Fine Arts program with Fordham University. It looks impressive, particularly in the seriousness of the Fordham side of the curriculum (the Ailey part is by now familiar), which, according to the brochure, is "rooted in the Jesuit tradition of academic excellence": the dancers have to take such courses as English Composition and the West from the Enlightenment to the Present, suggesting that they will come out literate and fairly rounded. Nor is it very easy to get into: however well applicants dance, they must have competitive SAT scores and good enough high school grades to suggest they can handle the academic side of the program. Fordham students are a visible presence in the school's Professional Division, and since the seniors take class with them, they can find out the unofficial story as well as the authorized one. Most of the seniors do apply to Ailey/Fordham, but it is seldom their first choice.

It is no surprise that despite the quality of the Fordham program, by the time they get to the twelfth grade most of the Ailey kids are itching for something new in their lives. Thus they submit to some of what other seniors go through, visiting schools (if they can afford it) and composing a number of applications. At the same time they seem to me a bit less tense than other high school seniors I have met, because in the unhappy event that they get in nowhere, there is still an attractive alternative: to take classes somewhere in the city and go to auditions, to start testing the professional life a little earlier than they'd planned. And while they have taken in the idea that a solid academic education is a worthy insurance policy, it is not where their passion lies.

Last year, one of The Ailey School's star performers went to Brown, but in general Ailey kids do not seek admission to the Ivy League. Their Harvard is the Juilliard School, and besides Juilliard there are a handful of other hot conservatories that everyone applies to. In sum, it is the same situation that prevails among seniors who don't dance, but the dancers have their own separate world.

Juilliard offers a BFA program similar to Fordham's, with an undeniable fifty-year-old cachet: both José Limón and Martha Graham have been on its faculty, and its noted alumni include Lar Lubovitch and Paul Taylor, as well as several members of Ailey's First Company. It is less academically demanding than Fordham: Juilliard doesn't consider College Board scores for admission, and high school transcripts serve only to weed out failing or D-level performance. What counts the most is a strenuous 2½-hour audition in ballet and modern dance and a short tape that applicants submit. Juilliard students tend to be more interested in modern dance careers than in ballet, although the school—not unlike Ailey—aims to produce a "fusion dancer," versed in both techniques. It wants students who are likely to stay the full four years, rather than going off earlier to join a dance company. It does eliminate candidates with a history of injuries or certain physical characteristics that are conducive to injury— admittedly, according to a Juilliard official, "a long shot because most dancers end up injured at some time in their life."

Beyond upholding the special characteristics of this school, it seems that audition judges at all levels are moved by the same fundamentally subjective criteria. The Juilliard official talks of "physicality" and "expression" and exhibiting "the joy of dancing as opposed to just having phenomenal technique." The "phenomenal technique" is, of course, a given, but beyond that she doesn't sound much different from LaGuardia's Michelle Mathesius, who favors the eighth-grade applicants that "move with wild abandon." And Juilliard, at a more advanced level, has the freedom to choose what it considers "top of the crop" nationally, not just locally. What that means is that some four hundred students apply, and only twelve girls and twelve boys get in. Unfortunately, this year none of these successful candidates turn out to be from Ailey, or indeed from New York City. They come from Texas and Florida.

The individual college dramas the kids have been experiencing jibe with what I know about the values and history of their families. Travis's application process somewhat resembled the familiar frenzy endured by nondancers, beginning with a Stanley Kaplan SAT prep class (spottily attended), buttressed by Deborah Magee's flash-card vocabulary drills and, as she describes it, "the arguing and the rolling of the eyes and the 'leave-me-alone's,' and 'whatever I get, I don't care,'" which she considered "torture" but "typical stuff." Then Travis, an A-B-plus student, came back with 1290 (a B-plus sort of score), more than adequate to get him into any good BFA dance program. He had discharged his responsibility. Perhaps Travis, given his diverse abilities, might have achieved an even higher score, but he cares more about dance than academics.

The Magees were demon researchers with fresh and extensive experience in applying to college. From the small town in upstate New York where they were living four years earlier, Travis's older brother had got into Stanford. The guidance available was minimal, and they had been required to do it all themselves. They had books and charts and files on every college that might satisfy Josh Magee's particular requirements. A few years later, when Deborah's cousin in Texas hired a private college counselor for her kids, the private counselor did exactly what Fred and Deborah had figured out for themselves. This year, they knew what they wanted the guidance counselors at PPAS to do for Travis, and the school was happy to give them what they asked for. Once again, they were exhibiting what researchers like Howard Gardner and Mihaly Csikszentmihalyi call "cultural capital." They had learned how to work the system, and they found the school "very responsive, though not proactive." They were satisfied.

Ailey has sent many graduates to the dance program at SUNY Purchase, which is one of their highly recommended schools. Travis applied, but he and his parents found the campus rather prisonlike. NYU, on the other hand, seemed an inviting place, but, as Travis told me in the fall, some people at Ailey were unenthusiastic about its dance program. Travis still applied there. With these and Juilliard, his other choices, rounding out the applications to six in all, were the hot schools: Boston Conservatory (considered about as desirable as Juilliard), the Philadelphia College of the Arts, and the North Carolina School of the Arts. When I see Travis the first week in April, he has got in everywhere but Juilliard, and is excited to be going to Boston Conservatory. He is, he tells me, laying on a wardrobe of funky dance wear that Boston allows but isn't permitted at Ailey.

Afra and her mother took a totally opposite path from that followed by the Magees. Mary Anne Holliday, who graduated from Reading University in England, has no personal experience with the American college admissions system, and what she knows of it by hearsay she doesn't like much. At the beginning of the year, Mary Anne considered it prudent to ask Robert Atwood his candid opinion of Afra's prospects for a dance career. Atwood told Mary Anne he thought Afra was company material. What she needed most, he said sternly, was to clean up her technique, which he thought had suffered from her scattered approach to attending class.

Throughout the year, Afra was turning over in her mind whether she really wanted to go to college. Would going help her dance career? She asked her mother repeatedly, "Should I go? Shouldn't I go? What do *you* think, Mom?" Mary Anne made it clear that if Afra wanted to live at home and do what she pleased—that is, go to auditions for shows, videos, films, and commercials and take dance classes anywhere in the city—and not go to college, that was perfectly fine with her. Afra could get some little job if she wanted, but there would be no pressure to contribute to their expenses. Mary Anne would be glad to have her. Mary Anne felt Afra was so clear about what she wanted in life, and so capable about going after it, that the right thing for a mother to do was just stand back and let her at it.

Outside of the conversation that Mary Anne had initiated with Atwood, she and Afra did not discuss her future plans with any school officials. They weren't obliged to undergo any college counseling at PPAS. Afra had grades similar to those of Travis, above 85 and on the school's honor roll, and Mary Anne could not even remember Afra's SAT scores.

High-school guidance counselors in most schools were sitting down with juniors and seniors and their parents, assessing the students' records, and suggesting which colleges were realistic choices and which were "reach schools." PPAS, however, had a new counselor who was busy bringing herself up to date, and its procedures were in flux. This senior class found itself in a transitional year. Mary Anne and Afra were not required to have a meeting with the school, and this, by Mary Anne's lights, was all to the good: she thought the impetus for counseling should come from the students and their parents. The traditional school system, she felt, squelches students' dreams. "What counselors tend to do," she told me, "is give you all these statistics about how many people want to make it and how few do, and they have nothing to show you but doom and despair." Mary Anne herself had started dancing only in college, and had managed to join a small performance-art group right at her university. She had gone on tour with it all over the continent for a couple of years, had had the time of her life, and had then come to the United States and found work here as a dancer. She had made a small career even after starting late, and Afra, in contrast, had real talent and years of training. Afra should set her goals and follow her dreams and she would succeed, and when she no longer wanted to be a dancer, there was time enough to go to college and find another profession.

Afra has, therefore, applied to Juilliard and Fordham, which were convenient to her objectives; she hasn't bothered to audition for SUNY Purchase, because it is geographically a bit removed from the hub of the dance world, where she and her mother agree she needs to be. When April comes, she gets into Fordham, and after thinking about it for a few weeks, she decides to wait a year before starting college. She feels she's ready for a break. She and Mary Anne are driving home from Ailey one day. Afra says, "Mom, I've decided I'm not going to college next year." "Fine," says Mary Anne. And then, the tension broken, they both burst out laughing "because," Mary Anne tells me, "it was such an atypical parental response."

The elaborate procedures for applying to selective colleges were new also to Beatrice Capote and her family. Barbara and Julio Santiago had both emigrated to the United States when they were children, but while each had gone to college, neither had experienced the stressful procedures of applying to a group of competitive schools. Over the years they had become increasingly savvy about dance, but once dance intersected with academics they found themselves in uncharted territory. And there was no formal mechanism at PPAS that year to clue them in.

Beatrice was a strong dancer: her technique had continued to improve over the years, and in the fall, partly just because she was maturing and partly because she had special training and had put effort into her ARTS entry, she was blooming artistically. She had a B average in school, which was good enough for any BFA program. At the same time, she had not conquered her weight problem, and at certain angles, in certain costumes, or if there was any slack in her leg for a minute, she could look heavy. She had a history of injury. For a highly competitive conservatory school, these flaws could count. As a sophomore, Beatrice had taken the PSAT and had not done badly. PPAS offered juniors an SAT prep course, but neither Barbara nor Beatrice herself thought she needed it. Then she took the SATs twice, in October and December of this year, and both times her score was disastrously low.

Beatrice was becoming friends with Melanie Person, who had taught ballet courses to the PPAS students before becoming codirector of the Junior Division. Person, thirty-nine, had been something of a prodigy in her early youth: she had been discovered by Arthur Mitchell and had joined Dance Theatre of Harlem on graduation from Professional Children's School at age sixteen. She had danced professionally for ten years and retired from the stage at twenty-six. Despite this super-achieving history (or perhaps because of it: Person had never had to push or struggle), she was a gentle, approachable woman the kids always described as "nice," and perhaps the only teacher at the school who never intimidated anybody. At first, Person found Beatrice quiet and diligent, but not particularly expressive or forthcoming. But a few weeks into this year, Beatrice began sitting down next to Person on the bench in the studio during class breaks. Person would say, "What do you want?" and Beatrice would say, "I'm just sitting here."

Person thought there was probably something more. Beatrice, she knew, must be thinking hard about colleges and ARTS and whether she would find a place in the dance world, and also about her relations with her family: the family was known to be close-knit. She started talking with Beatrice about colleges. Beatrice, like everyone else, wanted to apply to the hot schools, to Juilliard, Boston Conservatory, Purchase, North Carolina, and Philadelphia. Person said she supported these choices, but that also, with so many students going for the same big-name schools, it was possible not to get in, and that this wouldn't mean she was not a good dancer. Person wanted, in her own supremely tactful way, to prepare Beatrice for what might be the reality. There were, Beatrice should know, some colleges that weren't quite so famous that had great dance programs: Florida State, Marymount right here in New York City, and a couple of schools on the West Coast that might be excellent if Beatrice was willing to go far away. Person did not foresee academic problems. Beatrice's grades were okay, though not high. There was just the weight question.

It was Person's perception that Beatrice was choosing not just hot schools, but mostly hot schools close to home, and she didn't know whether this was Beatrice's preference or Barbara's. She herself would like to see the girl spread her wings. So Person called Barbara to discuss college plans. Barbara said she thought Beatrice was definitely mature enough to go out of town, and whatever decision her daughter made Barbara would support. She did believe that Beatrice might want to be close to home. Person thought it would be hard for this mother and daughter to be far from each other, and having planted the idea of choosing a distant school, she had done all she could. It was now up to them.

Every college with a dance program requires an audition. Beatrice and Barbara thought seven auditions were enough to go to. Their minds were fixed on the auditioning, which was what

Beatrice does best, rather than the academics, which were her weak point. Back in February, despite what Person had said to them, both Beatrice and Barbara thought she was bound to get into one or two out of seven. "Even though I had low SATs, I think I deserved to get into a college," Beatrice said to me. "I did not think it was so hard," added Barbara.

Beatrice enjoyed the auditions, and didn't find them difficult. Although no one but Ailey/Fordham asked for a sample of Horton technique (in which Beatrice was well prepared to shine), she had had some Limón (which they did ask for) and was challenged, not intimidated, by the requirement to show some Merce Cunningham technique, which she had never had. In any new situation, Beatrice just watches very carefully what the teacher does with the arms and the upper body and tries to copy it. Her auditions went well. She especially liked Purchase. It was a snowy day, and both Barbara and Julio Santiago came with her. After the audition they had lunch in the student cafeteria, and Beatrice had this funny premonition that she was already there, surrounded by a crowd she fit in with, and her parents were just visiting her. She felt that this was the place for her.

The first letter Beatrice got—after the universal "no" sent out by Juilliard—was from NYU. It said she had passed the audition but had not been accepted by the academic program. Fordham/Ailey, which spoke with one voice, also said no, as did the Philadelphia College of the Arts. When Barbara called these schools, they told her, she says, "that it wasn't the talent, that she was a beautiful dancer, but they have a rigorous program and they didn't think she had the academic skills." Barbara didn't call Juilliard, which told me it doesn't look at SATs. But in an arena as

Beatrice, looking "fierce"
(COURTESY THE SANTIAGO FAMILY)

competitive as Juilliard's, no matter what officials might say, I suspect the weight problem is bound to kick in, and Beatrice's history of injury would not have helped her.

There remained Purchase and North Carolina. In mid-April, Barbara starts calling Purchase and gets bounced back and forth between the dance department and the admissions office. They ask Beatrice to reaudition, and after she does, they bounce her around some more. After several weeks of this, Purchase says no. North Carolina says it is reviewing Beatrice's application and will let her know on May 15. It is her last hope.

When they hear all this, Atwood and Comendador call the

director of the dance program at Marymount (Comendador teaches there also) to see if they will have a look at this very strong dancer they have here at Ailey, and the director says the school is not allowed to look at any student with SATs below a certain score. Beatrice's are below that score.

Atwood is gloomy, not surprised at what has happened to Beatrice, depressed and irritated by her unwillingness to follow Person's suggestions and apply to some less celebrated schools. This is, he believes, yet another disheartening trend among the current generation: "They don't come to us for advice," he says. "We always tell the kids, 'If you have a question, come to us. Stop thinking like *kids*—start thinking like *dancers.*' A dancer sees the teacher as a resource; a kid sees us as *the other.* We had to track Beatrice down! Melanie Person tried to *hint* to her to apply to other schools!" It seems that Ailey officials are in a bind. They balk at seeming overbearing, and worry about undermining a student's self-esteem, but "hinting" is sometimes not enough. Beatrice and her family understood the hint, but didn't feel the need to act upon it.

But as Beatrice and Barbara wait to hear from their last choice, they are determined to make a plan for college and further dance training. There are community colleges to go to, and open classes at dance schools all over the city. If she is not part of a dance program, she will have to draw up her own schedule for instruction. She can prove her ability to do college work, and then apply to other BFA schools in January or next year. They are still not resigned to the notion of an SAT prep course, which is expensive. But Beatrice seems dauntless. Whatever tendencies she has shown toward sadness and depression are balanced by an unrelenting determination not to lose hope, and it seems that

Barbara shores her up. Meanwhile, there is the senior prom to think about. Beatrice doesn't have a date, but a dressmaker Barbara knows is busy sewing up a yellow silk fishtail dress with a slit in the front and a train in the back, and Beatrice will rent a limo and go to the prom. Afterward, everyone goes out to a club together, so a date isn't really necessary.

As the school year moves into its last month, I am gripped by the puzzle of what will happen to the seniors. It seems that the futures of Afra and Travis are partly within their control: Travis must decide whether he really wants to dance, Afra must decide what kind of dancer she wants to be, and when they have figured out their goals, they will act accordingly. The rest is a matter of blind chance, the same blind chance that affects all of us. It is Beatrice's fate that remains poignantly mysterious. She could or could not get into North Carolina, but either way, it is the weight problem—and the way she deals with it—that will determine her future. Several Ailey teachers have suggested to me that "the minute she gets out of here, the weight will drop off." On the other hand, my experience in life suggests that most college students tend to gain weight, not lose it. Academic pressures, campus activities, and the need to fill the stomach cheaply and quickly do not favor healthy nutrition, whether one lives at home or away. What if the weight doesn't drop off? There are heavier professional dancers than Beatrice, and if she is as enterprising as she is resolute, she might cobble together a life in dance. (I am putting aside the question of how she would support herself, which draws in a host of other issues: how much money an individual requires to live contentedly, what skills she has to find a backup career, how much rejection and penury she is able to tolerate before she "makes it," how she defines "making it." All of these things will also affect Travis and Afra, but not quite yet.) Is talent enough for a woman dancer? Where will her temperament take her?

But as I look at these seniors, it is also clear to me how each has benefitted from strong family support, and how difficult it would be for any of them to go far without it (difficult, not impossible). The type of support the families offer is idiosyncratic and widely varied, and seems, somehow, to fit what each particular child needs: the Magees mix in, Mary Anne Holliday stands back, and the Santiagos have a pride and belief in their daughter that keeps her going, whatever the obstacles.

There is one more senior I need to check.

Nine

Where's Brian?

There is a fourth senior—Brian Brown—whose future plans I haven't yet heard. I know he was planning to apply to Ailey's Fordham program and probably nowhere else, and I know he had good grades at Professional Children's School. But when I set out to catch up with Brian, he's nowhere to be found. He's not in class, he's not around the halls, he's not in the back office where he has a part-time job in the marketing department. Ana Marie Forsythe, the Horton instructor who heads the Fordham program, tells me she never received his transcript. Nobody seems to know where Brian is.

Finally, I try Inman, who reports that Brian has dropped out of Ailey. I am shocked. If there was one student who seemed to have put down roots here, it was Brian. *I want to be here until Miss Jamison says, Will you come to the Alvin Ailey American Dance Theater,* he had said back in January. "Why?" I ask Inman.

"He will have to tell you why himself," Inman says.

I have no success reaching Brian on the phone, and so I write him a letter, which Inman agrees to give to Brian's roommate, a student in the Professional Division.

The letter reviews our past conversations, tells him how impressed I am with his honorable mention in the ARTS competition and the appealing story behind it, and says that "I feel as if I have been watching a very suspenseful movie and the TV breaks down just before the ending." It tells Brian I will need a wrap for the year.

I suspect, the letter says, that Brian's reason for dropping out would be either the loss of financial support or burnout from the stressful life he has been leading. Perhaps there might be some third cause I haven't guessed, but whatever the reason, it doesn't undo his successes and I would like to be able to write about it. It is, I tell him, an important part of the story of a young dancer's life. I ask him once again to please give me a wrap.

So Brian calls, and agrees to talk with me one day after work. He is working in a shop that sells edgy menswear in Chelsea. I pick him up late one afternoon and we camp out in a nearby Starbuck's, where he tells me the second half of his story.

He is trying, he says, to decide what to do with his life. He feels being at Ailey limited his knowledge of the New York City dance world, that he was constricted and needed to go off and learn what else is out there and what he is capable of. He feels that he has grown in artistry and technique at Ailey, but has

nothing to show for it. Brian did not get into the Spring Performance, in which upper-level students from The Ailey School
will be dancing an excerpt from *Revelations.*

In general, Brian tells me, he doesn't let auditions get him
down. "There's always going to be the next one," he says. He is
aware, he adds—repeating the consolation that dancers always
use when they don't get a callback—that sometimes you aren't
the type for the part. (This could or could not be a meditation on
skin color. I was at the audition. Travis, the other Caucasian in
my group of students, didn't make this repertory, either, but tried
out for and got into other ballets. But Afra got in, and onstage
she doesn't look any darker than Brian.) Still, Brian says, "I'm
dancing at Ailey to be an Ailey dancer, and if I'm not right for
the part in an Ailey piece, I've got to question what I'm doing
here. Though I know that piece isn't the *whole* company."

Then Brian says, "A part of me thinks it's my personality
that's making me feel this way. Maybe I don't have concrete
things to show, but that doesn't mean I haven't made progress."

I tell Brian I heard his attendance hasn't been great.

The whole semester, he says, has been a big juggling act, between school and Ailey and the marketing job and the internship
at Hetrick-Martin, the social services agency. Then, he tells me,
he has been going to therapy for a shopping addiction, which
first appeared in the ninth grade, but was supposed to be finished
when he came to New York. And until this year it was.

It had started when Brian went to a private high school where
all the kids came from families richer than his. Brian's parents
have been divorced since he was five, and while they provided for
basic needs, there was no money for the luxuries his schoolmates
had. He was the only dancer in an all-boys Catholic school. He

was different in several ways, and he wanted to be popular and fit in. So Brian binged on an Armani jacket and other expensive clothing. His mother, while "shocked," Brian says, sent him for just a few months of therapy and after that, "it was something we never talked about again, but it was a lot harder for me to move here because I had to win back that trust from my mother." Besides having to face the expected challenges of living independently from the age of sixteen, it appears that Brian and his family had a load of unfinished business.

This fall, Brian binged again, to the tune of $6,000. It was, he says, different from the first time, because he did it "consciously as a way of getting attention." It was Brian's perception—and still is, it seems—that his family is only aware of him when he does something wrong. When he gets "amazing grades," Brian tells me, no one says anything, but when he gets an F on a test, everyone calls. No one cares about his accomplishments, like ARTS. This is, perhaps, a more extreme expression of a ubiquitous teenage complaint. Ever since I first talked with Brian, he has shown ambivalence about the life he is leading: he is proud to be an adult who works and pays the rent and has nothing in common with ordinary teenagers who go to the mall and live with Mom and Dad; and he feels he has lost his childhood, and that sometimes he wishes he could just be a kid.

Brian has had enough sense to go promptly to his employers at Hetrick-Martin and get them to arrange and pay for therapy (which, of course, is one more time-consuming obligation). He has also been going to his first outside auditions and doing rather well, getting some callbacks from *Aida* and a national tour of *Rent*. Last week, he went down to Philadelphia to audition for Philadanco, the small, well-respected modern dance troupe which both entertains a spirit of rivalry with Ailey and is one of the groups that feed dancers to Ailey's First Company. The director, Joan Myers Brown, later confirms to me that she was ready to hire Brian until she heard he is not yet eighteen, and thus below the ordained minimum age for employment in her company. She has suggested he come down for the summer and take class with Philadanco, and if all goes well, he could join after his birthday in January.

The result of Brian's relapse and his decision not to go to college, however, is the loss of support from both his mother on the West Coast and his father on the East Coast. Both Browns want him to return to San Francisco and continue with his schooling, and they have let him know that their financial assistance will end in August. That is another reason he dropped out of Ailey: he is still going to PCS and wants to graduate, so he needs to spend the rest of his time earning some money for next fall.

A few days ago, Brian went back and had a talk with Denise Jefferson. Like Shamel, he was pleasantly surprised. Jefferson told Brian she understood his decision to leave and go off on his own. While Jefferson said (once again) that she found his style of dancing melodramatic, Brian felt that was his artistic identity, which some choreographers would like and others not like. She thought he had indeed come a long way in technique and artistry but still lacked self-discipline, and offered him the opportunity to come back on a revised schedule for the last two weeks of school. The time he missed would be counted as a "leave of absence." This would be an opportunity, Jefferson said, for Brian to work on his self-discipline.

Brian has decided to take the opportunity. Whatever he does once the two weeks are over, he says, Ailey is a home he will always come back to, and in that sense it is easy to leave. In the

*Brian dances at the Professional Children's
School commencement.*
(PETER GORMAN)

course of our conversation, I point out that his work on ARTS and the fact that he kept his grades up suggest he can get it together when he needs to. Brian says this has always been true: "If there's something I want bad enough, I'm going to find a way to do it—that's the bottom line."

On the way home, I mull over the strange combination of qualities that Brian presents. Some of his outbursts are pure teenage rebellion and will diminish as he grows up, but in part these eruptions seem built in to his personality and view of the world: they are exhibits of what is widely known as the "artistic temperament." Most of the instructors at Ailey would say "non-sense" (or something stronger) to this label, considering "tempera-ment" a monumental self-indulgence, although Ailey, Graham, and Balanchine all had their temper fits at different times. How much temperament you can afford, of course, depends on how talented you are, and Brian, who is clearly intelligent, will soon discover exactly how much he can get away with and continue both to perform and pay the rent.

While Brian definitely wants to be a dancer and simply needs to show his independence, some teenagers decide, by the time they reach the upper levels, that they've had enough. This sort of burnout has been threatening the Supremes—especially Frajan—all year. Frajan has been dancing since she was three years old. This is her second year at LaGuardia, where everyone around her is focused on dance. It is more serious, more strenuous than she had expected as a child (if she thought about it at all), and she is realizing this is not what she wants. But Frajan is not the sort of girl who rushes into things, and she is afraid that if she actually leaves, she will regret it. If she left Ailey, she would, of course, still be at LaGuardia. But dance has given her an identity for all these years, a place in a particular world. What would it be like to cut herself loose from it?

She has talked to her mother. Yvonne Payne says she can't leave Ailey now, she has put all this time into it, and being a dancer could help her get a college scholarship. It is a cutting

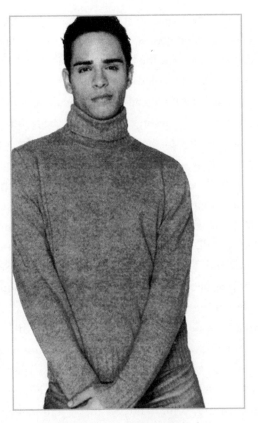

Brian's picture in the PCS yearbook.
(COURTESY OF PCS)

loose for parents as well: family life has revolved around dancing school—in the case of the Paynes, Frajan's younger brother is equally smitten with football, and with catering to the two of them, the adults have hardly time for any separate life at all. Yvonne remembers Frajan at three, singing and dancing and clapping and waving scarves around till Yvonne thought, Wow, there might be a dancer in our life. Then at the neighborhood dancing school, little Frajan would be doing ballet, tap, and modern dance with the preteens. The teachers said she was good enough for that, and then she became *too* good, and Yvonne was advised to send her to Ailey. It is hard for a family not to be caught up in the glamor of all this, particularly when they remember the Supremes' moment of glory at the Kennedy Center.

Frajan has always said she doesn't want to make a living as a dancer, just to do it on the side. She talks firmly about wanting to be a lawyer. "It gets really tiring sometimes," she tells me. "I feel like I can't do it anymore. But I guess I just have to live with it." When I talk with Yvonne, she says, "It's so funny because now she'll say, 'Oh, I need a break from school.' But in the summer she says she's bored. Will she want a break in September? She'll be bored, because she'll be coming straight home instead of doing something after school."

I suspect Yvonne is right to keep Frajan from making a precipitous change now, because Frajan seems still unformed to me. As the year draws to a close, I think the seniors—Travis, Beatrice, Afra, and Brian—have acquired a more mature sense of themselves and what they want in life. Shamel, a junior, seems halfway there, focused and disciplined toward clear goals. But the Supremes are still becalmed. I would not hazard a guess as to which—if any—of these three girls will pursue a career in dance. It is quite possible that something will catalyze Frajan next year.

Monique wants to continue dancing now, but says she doesn't want a dance career, for the familiar practical reasons of low pay, potential injuries, and the brevity of it: she is, indeed, the most pragmatic of the three girls. Sometimes, she tells me, questions about staying with it pop into her head: she does dance "also" for a possible college scholarship. But, she says, "I don't want my dancing career to just *end,* so if I get a chance to teach at a dance school when I'm in college, I can do that. There are so many doors opened because I've danced so long. I still have the joy of dancing onstage, but I just feel I can do something better." Monique plans to go to college before starting a career, and when she's finished with college, she says, it may be too late.

The one Supreme who still wants to be a professional dancer is Laurence. "I'd like to become a dancer just for a little while," she says, "to be in the company and see what it's like." She talks of getting a good education but mainly as a backup. At the same time, she has occasionally had the same burnout feelings that Frajan is experiencing, and has discussed them with her mother. "My mother," Laurence says, "likes the fact that I'm dancing because she used to dance also. I think my mom likes it more than I do. Because sometimes you know you get a little sick and tired of dancing and you just want to take a little break." Laurence says her mom hates it when Laurence doesn't dance during the summer, because she thinks Laurence will just lie around the house, doing nothing. Guilaine has found a summer program she thinks Laurence might like, and got her to audition for it: clearly this is mostly Guilaine's idea, because Laurence doesn't know much about it. The alternatives would be the summer at Ailey or the Dance Theatre of Harlem, both of which she has done before.

Laurence and her mother each tell a slightly different story: Laurence says she started at Ailey three weeks late this year because she needed a break; Guilaine says she kept her daughter out at the beginning of the year in order to see how Laurence would adjust to her schoolwork, and every day Laurence would plead to go back. Perhaps both of these things are true at different times of the day. When I listen to the Supremes, I remember hearing a student voice the same objections—and more—to a dance career shortly after I arrived at Ailey: you can't make a living, you might get hurt, it's too competitive. "They all say that," Elena Comendador told me, and Denise Jefferson said, "When you're very young, and you realize you're very talented, it's absolutely terrifying to own that talent. I remember being in the same place. The basic question is, 'Am I talented enough to make it?'" Inman, on the other hand, believes that most teenagers by the end of high school want to reinvent themselves, and that may be what the Supremes are moving toward. In high school, Inman was as serious a violinist as these kids are as dancers; then he took up dance to lose weight, and ended up dropping the violin and becoming a dancer.

The parents are equally torn by the same questions, and by the responsibility of guiding a young person's life. It seems to me right that they support their children's continuing, because if a contemporary American child in late adolescence really does not want to do something, no power on earth can force her to do it. When and if the Supremes are ready to stop dancing, they will stop.

Brian dropped out because of a desire for independence; the Supremes are having a sort of identity crisis which may end in their dropping out; and there is a third kind of dropping out that is fairly familiar in the Ailey world. It is simply a matter of having too much work and choosing what's important. Last summer and in the fall, the flavor of the season among the female dancers was a new girl from LaGuardia, an eleventh grader named Alanna Morris, considered to be brilliant, hard-working, and generally star material. Alanna did not come back for the spring term.

*Alanna, Monique, and Shamel at LaGuardia High School
for the performing arts in New York City*
(MAGALIE HOO-CHONG MASSIAH)

When I saw her at LaGuardia in the spring, I asked her what had happened.

Alanna told me she didn't want to stop but it was getting too hard to keep up with her schoolwork: her average dropped from 93 in her sophomore year to 87 when she was going to Ailey as a junior. She was coming home at eight o'clock in the evening, never getting more than six hours of sleep a night, and feeling physically worn out from all that dancing. In addition to two sets of dance classes, there were repertory rehearsals.

Alanna lives with her mother and grandmother, both of whom supported her getting the most dance training possible, but when Alanna's average dropped, both she and her mother got frightened. It was important to get into a good college. "They never told me you have to quit Ailey because I'm sensible," she said, "and I care more about my grades than my parents do, so I just decided I couldn't do it—it was too hard."

I asked Alanna if she felt pulled apart by the two schools. "Yes," she said. "At Ailey they asked me where I was going to dance, and I was like, 'I *go* to LaGuardia.'"

The best dancers, boys and girls, are in demand everywhere, partly because of that same sense of responsibility and passion to do good work that often leads them to choose one place or another. There are experiences at Ailey—performing at City Center with the First Company, for example—that students who dance only at LaGuardia will miss. At the same time, they feel they cannot spread themselves too thin, nor can they choose Ailey over LaGuardia. In that contest among high school students, LaGuardia will always win.

Ten

Revelations

R*evelations,* first performed in 1960 and gradually modified over the next four years, is the core ballet of the Alvin Ailey American Dance Theater. Ailey made it to evoke the religious music and devotion he experienced as a child in black churches in Texas in the 1930s. In the service of this theme, the movement deploys both Horton and Graham techniques in Ailey's own choreographic voice; the costumes are both stark and appealing, suggesting the time and place of the action in a manner that is also contemporary. It has always remained in the repertory, and in performances around the world it has never failed to electrify an audience. Like any classic, *Rev* (as it's familiarly known in the Ailey world) has had its critical ups and downs, but the version in the recent City Center season earned lavish praise.

It is Ailey's acknowledged masterpiece, and the yardstick by which he was measured, to his irritation, ever afterward.[1]

Accordingly, to dance in *Revelations* is a rite of passage for students, who are from time to time allowed to perform sections of the ballet in school shows. A sense of the company's lineage does not usually preoccupy teenagers (one reason why Brian Brown's obsession with it stands out), but dancing *Rev* is different. It is, in more ways than one, holy.

That is why, on the early April afternoon when students in Levels V, VI, and VII are invited to audition for the performances of an excerpt from *Revelations* at the Gala (the annual benefit the school gives for major donors) and again ten days later at the Spring Performance that will wrap up the year, forty-two of them show up. Shamel Pitts is there, even though he is technically on leave of absence and will not be able to dance in the Spring Performance because it conflicts with LaGuardia's Senior Concert. He looks sad and yearny not to be part of the final show, but is hoping to persuade Inman to let him dance at the Gala. Monique, who has a minor injury, is sitting on the side, also looking forlorn, but she will get a chance to audition when her knee is better in a few days.

The section usually chosen for student performance is the baptism scene, danced to the spiritual "Wade in the Water." Though challenging for young dancers, it is manageable to stage: it is neither a solo nor a piece for an entire congregation. There will be two performances of the Gala show, which will also include repertories presented by the Professional Division and Ailey II. The first performance—the one I will be invited to—will be done for the Ailey community (school faculty and families and friends of the performers), and the second for the benefit audience, all of whom have paid a fat fee for their tickets. The school's own Spring Performance (to include repertories by all the lower-level classes but not by the Professional Division or Ailey II) will have three shows. By using alternate casts, the school will give more kids an opportunity to perform.

At audition time, Inman has not yet been told how extensive the portion of "Wade" will be and how many performers he will need. The basic cast would be one, two, or three couples in a performance. In addition, the full "Wade" section of *Rev* includes "the umbrella woman" (once danced by Jamison herself), a sort of priestess figure who weaves in and out among the couples, and three parts for male performers who dance with props and are thus known internally as "Twiggy" and "the pole boys."

While the kids are wearing the usual numbers, an audition for a performance is otherwise different from the fellowship auditions I'm used to seeing, because the dancers are competing with one another. It shows what factors will prevail in performance auditions for the rest of the dancers' careers.

"Come forward, don't be afraid," Inman says (perhaps for the benefit of the Level Vs, who haven't performed at the Gala before). "Ladies, you'll have a long white skirt. Hands up, take the left foot back. Gentlemen, the right." He recites the words to the spiritual in rhythm and demonstrates the step the couples will use for moving in the water. "Let's put on the music," he says next, playing a tape. "You're walking beside the lake, scooping the water up. When your arm goes forward, your knees stay bent, the whole time. Release, back, release, deep, deep *plié.*" Then there's an *attitude turn,* a pivot on one leg while the other leg is raised and bent behind the dancer. All the kids try it together. Their arms do a snaky, ripply undulation suggesting the water while they walk in *plié.* "You all swam around the lake in sixteen counts—hello-o?" calls Inman. "It's not the Olympics! Here's where you should be on each count. Can I see Numbers One through Ten?"

Comendador is here to help judge the candidates. Inman addresses the kids by number as if he'd never met them before, divides them into smaller groups, has each group do the steps, and then lines them up numerically while he takes notes. Before he does the first weeding out he says, "I'm going to make a decision now about the people I want to see again. It's not personal. We haven't got a full cast of *Wade.* We could have only two or three people onstage for this."

Frajan and Laurence, Brian, Roger (a long and lithe eleventh grader from LaGuardia), Serge, Nigel, Beatrice, Afra, Travis, Jerome, Joi, and a few Level Vs make the first cut, and will audition again. The others, Inman says, should go home and do some homework. They shoulder their backpacks and shuffle off gloomily.

Now, Inman is preoccupied with matching the girls and boys into couples. While height has something to do with it, it is not all: he seems to be considering general *essence.* Brian with Afra, Nigel (short and forceful) with low-key Frajan, Serge with Beatrice (both of them dark and intense), Travis with Joi, other pairings. A soprano sings operatically in the adjoining studio, breaking the mood. The couples dance, and Inman reshuffles them a few times and whispers to Comendador. Comendador then whispers to me, pointing out a Level V named Nirine Brown who looks good because she seems to "feel" it. By contrast, Laurence is dancing well but looks as if she's "putting it on" from the outside: it occurs to me that Laurence is a Haitian Catholic, not an

African-American Baptist, so she has an artistic stretch to make for *Wade*. This is not a concern: dancers in the First Company come from a variety of backgrounds, and once one has achieved a professional level, it doesn't matter. Nor will it matter here, after many rehearsals.

"Can you guys wait outside?" Inman says. "Even me?" asks Shamel, trying to have it both ways, to be at once performer and observer, adult and youth. "You, too, Shim-sham," Comendador insists in a stern voice. Person comes in, and the three discuss the performers. They are looking for ways to use as many kids as possible. Beatrice and Afra, who are undulating beautifully but look too mature for the boys and overpower them, could alternate as the umbrella woman. Beatrice, it again occurs to me, is also not an African-American Baptist, but as Comendador observes, "Something in her gut makes her feel it." At the same time, Frajan, ethnically correct and technically proficient, has a blank face. The best Level Vs, Nirine Brown and a boy named Kai Braithwaite, have a little less training than the others but are, the teachers agree, "very instinctive when they get the vocabulary." Nigel Campbell, another outstanding Level V, is an extroverted performer. It is hard for me to apportion the components of bodily kinesthetic intelligence as described by Howard Gardner, some sort of spiritual affinity, ethnic background, and artistic development that affect these dancers' efforts to learn a particular new ballet. I am, of course, the only one in the room who is thinking about this: everyone else is choosing a cast. The dancers are all basically at the same level, and who will get the parts ultimately has a lot to do with which kids look well together.

Comendador wants to burnish the Junior Division's reputation at the Gala, and presses to do *all* the parts. Inman says Brian would be wonderful as Twiggy. In addition to showcasing the couples, he will ask Jamison's permission to use two umbrella women, a boy and girl as alternate Twiggies, and two pole boys. "If we do the whole thing, though," he says, "the couples will be *fried* when they get to class after rehearsal. This is *so hard* on the thighs."

A few days later, after Monique has had her audition, after Shamel has tried working on Inman, after Inman has appealed to Jamison for a larger cast and decided on the couples, the word is out. No Twiggy, no pole boys. Yes to two umbrella women, Beatrice and Afra. For couples: Frajan and Serge. Nirine and Nigel. Roger and Monique. Laurence and Kai. While Shamel, because he's on leave, is not allowed to be in the first cast, Inman will let him understudy. The other boys know if they miss too many rehearsals, Shamel is lurking there, waiting to pounce. Perhaps this serves Inman's purposes, too.

At the first rehearsal, there's an air of high excitement. The kids fool around pirouetting while they wait for Inman; they are never still. When Inman enters, he is wheeling a TV with a VCR, so the kids can watch the company's tape of *Wade*. He also has an enormous black umbrella, which gets passed back and forth between Afra and Beatrice as Inman works with each. He demonstrates the steps, singing "God's gon-na trou-ble the wa-a-ter" in a near monotone while the video plays. The kids assume a Groucho Marx–like walking step, but they don't go down far enough. "That's not *plié*—that's bent knees!" Inman yells. He bends further, way down. He's an old man of forty-one and still looks good. "In *Revelations this* is *plié!* Umbrella girls, you've got to be much more proud and bigger! How are your arms—tired? Good!"

Serge is absent today, and Shamel is beaming as he dances with Frajan. Inman works alternately with the couples and the umbrella women, each group getting a break while the other is on, but Shamel never takes a break. When Beatrice and Afra are working, Shamel is off in the corner, practicing. Inman's way of delivering a correction is demonstrating or describing an extreme version of the wrong way, so everyone laughs. Nervously. The constant *plié* is very taxing, and the kids are worn out.

At the next rehearsal, Serge is back, and Shamel is working with him, bringing him up to date on what he missed: friendship is once again the flip side of competition. Today the couples are rehearsing a section which requires rolling on the floor—how do the arms go?—then kneeling opposite each other, holding hands and undulating. Then the boy has to lift the girl. "Listen up, this is important. The guy's going to pull you to him—step, step, drop. He's gonna lift you up." Lifts are relatively new and difficult for Junior Division kids, and Nigel strives valiantly to raise Frajan while *plié*-ing. Inman demonstrates on Monique. There is a general giddiness in the group, which may come from the difficulty of the movements. "You guys, listen! We've got three rehearsals. You've got to get more serious about this. Stay in *plié*, Roger!" Inman is moving Kai's pelvis, trying to get him to undulate properly. Spacing themselves on the stage is also a problem for the couples.

Now Inman demonstrates the shoulder isolations and slithery, tight walk of the umbrella woman. "Small steps, big torso! Afra, take your time, use your back. Run in *plié*, nothing moves on top." Afra has to wind through the rows of dancers without dislodging them. Beatrice, her alter ego, is now looking good, and Inman shouts, "Yes!"

The next two rehearsals continue in this vein. Everything is difficult: the *pliés,* the undulations, the *attitude* turns, the spacing, the lifts. Inman says to me, "It's not in their bodies yet—they're just doing steps." He says to the kids, "You've got to be able to pull it off like the company. Just because you're a student, they're not gonna say, 'How nice—they're students!'" From time to time he invokes Judith Jamison, and at the next rehearsal he shouts, "This CANNOT go out here. It's a mess!" He works with them one by one, and they do look better and better.

At the last rehearsal before two full dress run-throughs at John Jay College Theater, the costumes are here, and they take getting used to. The long, tiered white skirts are hard for the girls to manage, and the idea of going out onstage bare chested consumes these fifteen- and sixteen-year-old boys with embarrassment. Inman is fighting with Nigel about this: "You want to do it—you take your top off!" he orders.

Then Troy Powell walks in, looking cool as usual, dressed in white with a big newsboy cap and sunglasses. He stands, watching, and Inman says, "Mr. Powell, what's the most important thing in this piece?" *"Plié!"* shouts Powell. Inman says, "Hear that? He's done it a lot more than I have. We both did Twiggy." Then Troy speaks to the group. He says, "Try not to overinterpret the steps. Try to get an image of what a baptism is about. If you haven't been baptized, look in the Bible to see what it's about. It's real simple. He's saying, *'Plié.'* When you go down to a river, you test the water. The umbrella woman is like a priestess. You guys look great. It's always a pleasure to see you do the professional rep. If you haven't been baptized, know what it's about." And with that, the good cop exits.

By now, an important choice has been made: the first-night

dancers will be Serge and Frajan, Roger and Monique, with Afra as the umbrella woman. The dancers on the more prestigious Gala night will be Kai and Laurence, Nigel and Nirine, and Beatrice as the umbrella woman. At the last minute, Afra goes away on a family vacation and Beatrice gets to dance both nights. Shamel, who has thrown himself into every rehearsal, will not get to dance at all unless someone comes down with the flu.

This is not the only repertory for which the kids are rehearsing. On Friday nights, a large cast of Level VIs and VIIs are rehearsing Fred Benjamin's spirited jazz rep. They are just as giddy here. During one of the breaks, Travis clowns for Afra and both go into gales of laughter. Both *Wade* and Benjamin himself are in for a bout of serious parody.

Later, Benjamin tells me he always tries to size up the social relationships among dancers, which ones like to be together: knowing this has always proved to help his choreography. He also sees the seniors—Beatrice, Afra, and Travis—as far ahead of the younger students, and puts Serge Desroches, whom he finds an exciting dancer, in the older group. This is interesting because in ballet classes Serge is not considered to have an "easy body." In general, Benjamin tells me he's frustrated with the kids' reserved demeanor. "Their bodies can do tremendous things," he says. "But their faces are to die over. During the breaks, when the choreography ends and the music is still playing, they do the steps in the style of social dancing, and they laugh and fool around, imitating me. I tell them, 'That's what I want to see onstage, that kind of enjoyment!' Then it comes time to go back and do the same steps in the choreography and they get a stone face." Now it's Benjamin's turn to mimic the kids, tightening his face into impassivity.

The Level Vs also have more performing to rehearse other than *Revelations:* there's a ballet rep with Comendador and a Limón modern repertory to bossa nova music. The Levels VI and VII have a ballet rep with Atwood. Then there is a PPAS advanced-class ballet repertory. Everyone is working hard for the spring show.

Besides the rehearsals, other things are coming together. One afternoon late in the term, Atwood and Travis are sitting in the library, discussing how to shape a ballet class. Travis is interested in teaching and has asked to be allowed to try it. There is a question about whether Travis's teaching PPAS peers would present discipline problems. Nonetheless, Atwood is working with Travis to map out a class, even if the use of the final product is still uncertain. There is an innate affinity between Travis and Atwood, who are probably the two most cerebral people at The Ailey School this year. Last summer, Travis had said he admired Atwood for his thoughtful structuring of ballet classes and for having "an intelligent way about him"; they had also talked a bit about politics together as Travis was becoming interested in the subject. Then they fell out when Travis was rejected as an ARTS candidate and failed to achieve the advanced placement he was seeking. Travis, saying Atwood had not gone beyond the school's "corporate" position, felt disillusioned and angry. Atwood, who had represented the school in dealing with Travis and his parents, was sorry for Travis's feelings, but that was how things were. Now, however, this bad period is behind them, and they are enjoying their natural rapport.

A class has the teacher's stamp, Travis tells me. If the teacher is prone to work your mind, he will give more confusing combinations. There are some teachers whose heart isn't in it. Students can see how much the teacher wants to give. When De Vita, for example, is giving his all, Travis feels he has to match it. The worst thing a teacher can say is, "You guys must be tired today." It gives you a reason to slack off. The best teachers don't have to talk much: let the dance do the work, Travis says—teach through the choice of combinations.

They are doing some deconstruction: deconstructing Tuesday's class and deconstructing pirouettes. "Are you going to try the same basic material?" Atwood asks. "Sometimes I feel," he points out, "because of the rhythm of the class or the way people have responded to things, that I'll need to change it a little bit." They are swapping ideas for different sequences of small steps that students could do at the barre, how each of these make the standing leg feel, and then how all that is reflected in the turns they do afterward in the center and going across the floor. It is an excited conversation with ideas coming thick and fast. Atwood wants Travis to put together a whole class. As they have discussed before, "Every accent trains the muscles in a different way," the instructor says, "and so by using different accents in consecutive exercises all the time, you're getting the body ready for different types of movement. . . ." Travis says, "I was trying to find different dynamics and different patterns, and finally I came to that stuff that you did." There are, Atwood tells Travis, many different ways to structure a class, and he is to think about that for the next few days. "Cool," says Travis, and goes off.

Atwood is pleased, and tells me Travis now has "a manly energy. As opposed to a boyish quality." At the beginning of the year, he says, Travis went after what he wanted too aggressively, and then, after having been taken down a few notches, "he overreacted by being, I felt, too obsequious. Now," Atwood says, "I think he's reaching a good balance. He's able to come to you and say straightforwardly, 'This is what I would like to do.' Without being pushy, without being apologetic. You want to develop an adult energy that other people respect in the outside world.

"And along with that," Atwood goes on, "is more decisiveness in his dancing. I really see it! He's absorbing corrections, he's making use of them, he's dancing very well, he's making significant changes. It's been a great, great year for him."

I ask Atwood if getting into two good colleges, Boston Conservatory and NYU, is what affected Travis, and Atwood says, "It was before that. That was a culmination of the changes he'd been making, and when he told us he'd been accepted, it was no surprise to me. I thought, 'Oh, yes, he's a great candidate.'"

The only major place that didn't accept Travis was Juilliard, which Atwood says he also understands, because the competition there is so intense that the people who get in are on the verge of being professional dancers even as freshmen. "And Travis has come a tremendous way," says Atwood. "But he still isn't someone you're going to hire right now for the First Company." There is a long road to being a first-rate professional dancer: Travis is moving ahead, but he is not there yet.

As the year draws to a close, the Supremes, still in the thick of high school and its torments, still way short of artistic maturity, must look outside Ailey for some marker of growth. They find it in the extravaganza that will be Frajan's Sweet Sixteen party. Seven years ago, when Frajan's older sister was turning sixteen, the Payne family (particularly the girls' mother, Yvonne), was inspired by the Quinceanera, the party that Dominicans and other Latinos give when their daughters turn fifteen. Some friends had invited Yvonne to theirs, and she studied how they did it. It was like a mini-wedding. The participants and the guests wore gowns and tuxedos. There were professional photographers with videocameras. In the Paynes' neighborhood these days, while some girls just have plain Sweet Sixteen parties where everyone goes to a catering hall and has dinner, others add a church ceremony with blessings.

Yvonne thinks she was the trailblazer for this ceremony in her community. She worked with the minister at her church in the Bushwick section of Brooklyn to design the ceremony, which by now has caught on among other parishioners. The ceremony involves blessing several items that symbolize womanhood. Frajan will come into the church in flat shoes and leave in a pair of high heels which have been blessed in the ceremony; the minister will also bless a tiara, a Bible, and a diamond ring given to her by her father. There will be a procession with eight girls and eight boys as attendants, and there will be a hundred guests and a full meal at the catering hall. The girls will wear identical light blue dresses and matching shoes, and elaborate hairstyles, makeup, and manicures will be centrally provided. As both Yvonne and Frajan describe it, they will have "everything but a groom."

This is a big expense for Frajan's father, a bus driver, and her mother, an office worker. But Yvonne has always tried to give her three kids things she never had when she and her five sisters were growing up. All three are excellent students, she says, and they deserve some luxuries. They are a reward for ability and hard work. Perhaps this feeling is also behind the Paynes' willingness to make Frajan's dance and her brother's sports the center of their lives. And getting focused, deciding what she wants to do in life, sticking up for herself, and not getting trampled are the most urgent concerns for Frajan now, Yvonne says. Her only worry is that her daughter is too laid-back. This is not some slow-paced southern town. It is the Big Apple, and time waits for no one. Frajan is growing up.

So throughout the spring, Yvonne is stage-managing the rehearsals for the Sweet Sixteen, and the Supremes—cast, as it were, in yet another repertory—sometimes have to miss Litvinova's Wednesday class. Laurence's own Sweet Sixteen will be in August, but it will not be this lavish. For Frajan's party, Laurence has figured out a way to look special, a unique hairstyle with a flat twist in front and a sculptured ponytail in back, to be executed by the Paynes' stylist. Monique's mother, a bit feminist, is rather grouchy about the whole affair, but is trying to keep quiet and let Monique—who won't be sixteen till next winter and will celebrate in a more restrained style—have fun. After a short break in June, all the girls will be dancing in various summer programs.

The Gala performance begins with an upbeat fund-raising speech by Jefferson, describing the year's successes. Most notably, Inman has been running a program called Ailey Athletic Boys Dance, which offers thirty-two boys, aged seven to fifteen, a class in Horton and another in Afro-Brazilian Capoeira—an explosive, athletic mode of dance guaranteed to hook them—every Saturday (some of the Level VI boys are helping out). The students were recruited in the public schools. Because two foundations are backing the project, the school is able to provide these classes free. The school, it is clear, must endlessly shake the bushes for the next batch of Troy Powells—indeed, the next batch of Shamels. Without them, there will be no more *Revelations.*

The Junior Division's performance goes well: the kids lift and *plié* and undulate and space themselves properly, and show a level of passion and spirit beyond that exhibited at rehearsal; I, too, am proud of them. At the same time, when the Professional Division

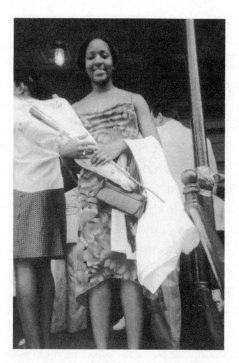

Beatrice at the Professional Performing
Arts School graduation
(COURTESY THE SANTIAGO FAMILY)

and Ailey II come on, it is easy to see that the high school students have further to go: the older dancers can perform more demanding lifts and other athletic feats, and dance with more individual style and character. The Graham-based choreographer Pascal Rioult has made a ballet for the Professional Division to songs of Edith Piaf: the college-age dancers, decked out in berets in a café setting, give *La Vie en Rose* a witty, contemporary spin. Francesca Harper, who coached Afra and Beatrice for their ARTS entries, has made the older students a long, solemn ballet inspired by 9/11. Other parts of *Rev* and Ailey's 1958 *Blues Suite* are danced by Ailey II, showing what the high-school-age dancers might aspire to.

The teachers are here in the audience tonight, and they are pleased. But when I chat for a minute with Litvinova, she says, "It is too bad no one will see their classical work." There is a touch of poignancy to the role of ballet instructor at Ailey: however central ballet may be to the students' daily life, in the eyes of the world the Ailey is a modern-dance institution.

Ballet is much in evidence at the school's own performance later on. Here the Level VIs and VIIs are at the top of the heap, and one can see how far they have come. The younger students are cute and well-behaved, but the advanced students are technically adept and beginning to be artists. I go backstage at John Jay for two out of three shows. The atmosphere of each is very different: Friday evening, the first, is a madhouse, with the kids' own cameras popping; Saturday morning, before the noon performance, is almost tomblike, with a bit of card playing, reading, napping, and homework, accompanied by boom boxes that do not boom.

The first person I meet is a smiling Beatrice. The cavalry has come over the mountains. She has just got into the North Carolina School of the Arts. She is excited about the adventure of it. What she will need to get used to, she says, is the slower pace: she's a New Yorker, accustomed to hurrying. Neither Barbara nor Julio had gone away from home to college, and her mom is very emotional, Beatrice says. She seems newly self-confident. She is listed on the program as "assistant to the choreographer" in Benjamin's repertory. What that means is that she helped him teach the ballet to the other students.

Monique and Laurence with Monique's grandfather, Pierre Hoo-Chong,
after the show at John Jay College in New York City, June 2002
(MAGALIE HOO-CHONG MASSIAH)

Nigel and Serge are hanging out in the corridor outside the dressing room. Serge complains that he didn't make the better cast at the Gala. Nigel, who did, first tells Serge, "You're fierce" but then begins to pump up the volume, telling me how Troy and Bahiyah and other dancers from the first and second companies had complimented his Gala performance. Serge sits silently.

When Jefferson gives her introductory speech on Friday night, she thanks the parents for "keeping your children with us." She is alluding to the event that started the year, the in-spite-of-which event that faintly tinged but did not quite color 2001–2002.

Perhaps because I have already seen *Rev,* I am now taken with Benjamin's repertory. Chaotic in rehearsal, it is performed darkly lit with the dancers swooping across the stage in bright, acid-colored leotard dresses and trousers, the girls with their hair loose and pretty and a feeling of exuberance and joy. The audience is filled with families clutching flowers to present to their children after the show. Next to me is a slightly built man clutching a bouquet, who manages to applaud the Benjamin rep wildly at every opportunity and cheer loudly when it's finished.

"Which one is your child?" I ask him.

"The one in the green dress," he says. "I must give her mother credit for keeping her dancing."

It is Laurence's father.

Eleven

In Conclusion

This book is a snapshot of a group of teenagers and their life together in the same world at a certain time. They are en route to becoming what they will be. Often during the year I spent at Ailey, I tried to remember myself at the age of sixteen. I did not wonder what I had had in common with other adolescents; instead I was curious about what I had had in common with my adult self. How well could my present friends and family recognize me? I rather wished I could have such a snapshot. When we look at sixteen-year-olds with the benefit of hindsight, it may be possible to say, "Of course, you could see what they were even then." But we don't know in advance.

At the same time, I am better equipped to answer some of the questions I came in with. Since we have no idea what twists of fate will shape these students' lives, the idea of picking out which ones are destined to be stars is, as the teachers warned me, pointless. I did gain some understanding of what is required to make a successful career in the field of dance in the early twenty-first century (which is probably what was required throughout the twentieth century, but not necessarily before that).

One afternoon at the end of the year, as the Level VIs were leaving ballet class, I cornered Tatiana Litvinova to talk about their development. She described a dressing-down she'd given Monique during the winter: Litvinova had been very upset and angry, and she had simply laid it on the line, that Monique had better start listening and taking corrections or she would never get anywhere. It was the girl's rebelliousness, not lack of skill, Litvinova believed. And now Monique was making very good progress, and her technique was excellent. Frajan, too, was applying corrections very well. With some people, Litvinova said, you could say the same thing a hundred times and still there would be little improvement.

So I asked Litvinova how she defined talent, and she said it was "incredible desire. You want to accomplish so badly that you can breathe it. You have to. When you have pain, you don't feel that pain." She told me that Serge Desroches—a tenth grader whose ability Fred Benjamin, the jazz teacher, had also praised highly—had been so awkward at the beginning of the year that she had said to herself, "Oh, my God, I can't do it." She didn't see how she could make a ballet dancer out of him, but now Serge's improvement was absolutely remarkable. She could hardly believe how far he had come. Tremendous desire, she said, could overcome a lot of things. She knew this because she herself had not been as good as her classmates at first, and had simply told herself she needed to work ten times as hard just to reach the same level. "As long as you want it so badly," she said to me, "I can't see the limits."

Passion and perseverance may matter more than what is labeled raw talent. But when I ran "desire" past Harvard's Howard Gardner, he brought me down to earth, writing, "The statement about desire is true but not helpful. I would like very much to conduct the BSO or play with the Knicks, but that hardly qualifies as talent per se."

Some middle ground applies. Throughout the year I heard stories similar to Litvinova's about Serge and about herself, and absorbed the difference that hard work, the product of tremendous desire, could make. Moreover, once the dancers had gone through training, had done the utmost to improve their natural endowment, they would need to audition, and would have to keep at it through innumerable rejections, through exhausting nights as waiters and numbing days as receptionists, with no more money than dancers make and a lack of compensatory joy. How long would it take them to pack it in? What then do we say about the dancers with easy bodies—or perhaps more of that elusive quality, raw talent—like Melanie Person, who told me she had never had to test her persistence and couldn't guess what the result would have been had she been forced to do so. So to some extent "incredible desire" begs the question. Besides talent and hard work, luck, of course, is in there, too—the "twists of fate" I mentioned earlier.

As the weeks of classes, auditions and rehearsals passed, I found myself drawn repeatedly to the work of Mihaly Csikszentmihalyi, the psychologist who (with his team of researchers) has studied talented teenagers in fields other than dance. Most compellingly, he and his colleagues suggest[1]

> "We believe the main psychological process that leads from personal skills to the mastering of a talent is not specific to domains, such as music or mathematics; rather it is a mind-set necessary for the acquisition of talent in general . . . the development of complex attentional structures, or the ability to approach tasks with curiosity and concentration; the achievement of emotional autonomy, so that teenagers will tolerate the solitude necessary to cultivate their talent; and the ability to enjoy the activities relevant to their talent, so that intrinsic as well as extrinsic rewards will motivate teenagers to continue on their difficult quest."

Throughout the year and as it ended, I asked myself what was special about this group of teenagers. Clearly, the teenage students at Ailey were endowed with a particular set of talents, or, as Gardner prefers to call them, intelligences, that I knew I, for one, did not have. Most human beings have some combination of innate abilities. But these kids have been able to set goals according to their talents and give up some immediate pleasures in order to achieve these goals. They are not absolutely consistent: they do occasionally cut class, they might oversleep and miss an evaluation conference, they can be late, and they don't always call in. In other words, they are not paragons or prodigies. But they are fairly mature and very disciplined for their age. To an unusual degree, they are motivated to develop their talents. Why? What are the forces that drive them on?

There are some individuals with natural temperamental tendencies to be active, focused, and persistent: this is the sort of fact most of us know from life but don't treat seriously until credentialed researchers tell us about it. Indeed, "activity level" and "attention span and persistence" are two of the nine temperamental markers evident from infancy throughout the life span, as outlined by the psychiatrists Stella Chess and Alexander Thomas in their landmark New York Longitudinal Study, which observed 133 children from shortly after birth to early adulthood.[2] One day I asked Afra to imagine what it would be like not to be a dancer, just to go to an ordinary urban high school. "I would probably be doing something else," she said. "I don't think I could just not be doing anything. I would be doing gymnastics or basketball. I can't picture myself without a job or something. I couldn't just go to school and go home."

At the same time, these children—granted their inherent inclination to be busy—have chosen dance over other activities that tempt modern teenagers and at which they might also shine. Most of them bring home grades that are good but not excellent from schools that are good but not ultrarigorous because academics are not the kids' first priority. Something or someone has pointed them in the direction of dance, and everything else they do seems to serve the goal of being dancers.

As Atwood said to me one day, life skills are important: "The fact is, and this has always been a problem for many artist types, it doesn't make any difference if you're an artist, you still have to figure out what that life insurance policy says, you have to read the small print on the government forms, you have to know how to add up your checks, and unless you've got an awful lot of money you can't get someone else to do it for you." The students at Ailey appeared to have soaked this up, and the importance of getting schoolwork done is a value emphasized by the faculty for this and other reasons that by now we know. But I didn't hear anyone, student or teacher, talk about the satisfaction of proving theorems or reading *Moby Dick*. Moreover, throughout the year I tried to find out whether the set of Gardnerian intelligences with which the kids were equipped—bodily kinesthetic, musical, and perhaps spatial relations—affected the way they approached learning subjects outside dance. I drew a blank. Some said they were good at math; some seemed to be more verbal than others; these skills were, so far as I could see, unrelated to their abilities in dance.

At some point early in the kids' experience, they had been spotted and encouraged by teachers. The Supremes were always the ones selected for performances and workshops. Some of the boys, as eighth graders who had just begun dancing, had been driven into Manhattan by some neighborhood dance teacher and deposited at LaGuardia to audition for entrance. Beatrice had a history of being chosen from the time she went to the local dance school to her stint at Ailey Camp—which resulted in funding to attend The Ailey School to finally receiving a Van Lier Fellowship as a teenager. It's noteworthy that these kids were not ensconced in some feel-good environment in which *everybody's* dancing skills received some praise. They were repeatedly told they were better than others. And it is an unfortunate (or fortunate, depending on how you look at it) truth that being better than others makes most human beings feel good.

Once kids have been told they have a skill, putting it on display by performing makes them feel even better. In the course of my research I encountered a book edited by Shirley Brice Heath and Milbrey W. McLaughlin, two Stanford professors who, with various colleagues, studied community organizations that had worked effectively with inner city teenagers.[3] In particular, Heath, an anthropologist, and Arnetha Ball, then a postdoctoral fellow, had studied several neighborhood performing arts groups. In the sixties and seventies, Heath and Ball observed, neighborhood organizations had focused on ethnic pride. In the eighties and nineties, the inner-city neighborhoods had become much less homogeneous and were beset with more serious problems; supporting ethnic pride was no longer the modish approach to urban revitalization in schools, government, and the media, and didn't seem to galvanize the teenagers. At the same time, performers who had grown up in the neighborhoods and become successful in the outside world were returning to help children "at risk." They found that music and dance were like sports— that is, joint efforts that brought people with "diverse talents and interest" together in rehearsing, planning, and performing. Heath and Ball observe that dance provides young people with "structure and release, creative outlet and consistency of routine, and hard work along with expressive play." While none of the eight main characters in this book could be called "at risk" since all of them had strong, vigilant families, I did meet other Ailey students for whom dance was a haven from great difficulties at home. Three of my eight protagonists, however attentive their families, lived in inner-city neighborhoods where more than ordinary dangers and temptations exist.

To the extent that teenagers think reflectively—and I sometimes had to push the kids to do that—most of them told me that performing fulfills a need to express their feelings. The teachers constantly pressed them to dance more expressively. I saw the kids exhilarated at rehearsals. When a performance required them to exceed the skills they had shown rehearsing and in class, they rose (sometimes literally) to the occasion. Heath and Ball are not the only anthropologists to describe the way dance has met the expressive needs of many cultures around the world and throughout history.[4]

For the most part, these are children who feel different from the mainstream (whatever that might be), particularly but not exclusively the boys. It is, of course, a fortunate fact for students at the performing-arts high schools that this difference can generate its own mainstream. The girls who went to other types of schools—Joi Favor, for example, who attended a public high school in the suburbs, and Charlotte Kaufman, who went to a rigorous private school—felt different from (and a bit superior to) their classmates, Joi for her discipline and Charlotte for her worldliness.

Wherever they went to school, the kids were able to make "being different" a positive thing because, first, they derive an identity from being dancers (and identity is, of course, crucial to adolescents), which would be very difficult to give up; and second, because they are part of a like-minded community. By nature, dance is the performing art which despite its competitive aspects most encourages ensemble spirit. On the other hand, dancers do not really need the capacity to tolerate long periods of solitude, as musicians and artists do.

Some kids see dance as a means of upward mobility, an idea which they only grudgingly admit having: it makes them uncomfortable. Late in the year, I sat in an empty LaGuardia classroom, talking with Shamel Pitts, to the accompaniment of faint music that wafted in over the transom, as it does almost wherever you go in that school. "I swore I wasn't going to be changed when I came to LaGuardia," he said, "but I've changed so much."

"How?" I asked.

"I definitely talk better," he said. "I definitely dress more conservatively—in terms of, my clothes aren't that big anymore. I associate with different people now. Everyone doesn't have to be from Brooklyn, or the same thing as me now. I'm taking everything I can from LaGuardia because no one is the same in this school. No one is the same race. No one is the same culture. No one is the same major. I have vocal major friends, art majors, drama majors."

"Let's assume," I asked, "that Shamel becomes what he dreams of becoming. Is there a question of then being somewhat different from the world you came from?"

Shamel spoke slowly and shifted around in his seat as he talked. "Yes," he said. "I feel it already. I think it's happening already. The path I'm going on now, I'm going to continue down that path. I grew up in a not-so-great area. It was kind of ghetto. I'm not trying to make myself better than the people there, but I'm trying to make myself better than what they have to offer there, which is like nothing, really. Now I feel myself getting somewhere in my life. I feel like, 'Wow! I can go to college!' I have the options now, rather than saying, 'I just want to make it through high school.'"

While Shamel mentioned the desire "to better myself" several times, he wanted to make sure I understood that he was not, he said, "an angel child." He told me, "I have a steady head, but I do have some fun and do some crazy stuff sometimes."

What, I asked him, was crazy stuff?

"I do live a kind of good life," he said. "Last weekend, me and my friends went to Broadway Dance Studio and we took a class there, and then we went to the movies, and we just act crazy and loud and stuff."

Fair enough, I thought.

While, in a few cases, dance teachers have been able (in part) to fill the roles of missing parents, most of the more successful teenage dancers at Ailey have families who are willing to go to a lot of trouble to support them. Still, I was impressed by how different the families were in their styles of child rearing. Occasionally, I wondered what would happen if you shuffled up the kids and their families: put Shamel, for example, under the soft, sheltering wing of Beatrice's mother, and dropped Beatrice into the orbit of Shamel's firm-but-jolly aunt. When Chess and Thomas, the New York psychiatric researchers, parsed their child subjects according to temperament, a quality called "goodness of fit" with the children's parents was in their estimation a crucial ingredient of successful parent-child relations.

The difference between families is not just a matter of financial or cultural capital, and it appears as if the temperaments of these adults and their children were, most of the time, reasonably matched. Even the families in which parents were in conflict with both their children and each other had somewhat similar values for their offspring. Brian's mother and father, for example, both admired his talent, both strongly preferred that he go to college rather than enter the professional dance world immediately, and both were hesitant about his early independence in New York. Brian had, at least, only one set of requirements to satisfy.

What did the families have in common with one another? Csikszentmihalyi notes the current psychological thinking that teenagers—if they want to mature into competent adults—need to renegotiate their parental ties, not cut them off. "Studies are beginning to show," he points out, "that disengagement from family too early leaves teenagers more susceptible to negative peer influence and may lead to lower academic achievement."[5] The context most favorable to talent development, he and his colleagues discovered, was one which balanced the forces of interdependence and autonomy: "supportive families that encourage the pursuit of difficult challenges . . ."

Traditional or modern, strict or permissive, this balance is what characterized these children's families. Perhaps my strongest impression is of hearing Linda Taylor, Shamel's mother, say several months before her death, "I want my kids right here with me. And I know at the same time there's things he [Shamel] wants to do, and sometimes they might take him out of town. And being a mother, I worry. I know he has a good head on his shoulders, but things happen." There was no question in Linda's mind, she told me, that he was strong enough to deal with the pressures of school and dance. She wanted him to be "the best dancer he wants to be and to enjoy dancing."

The kids' motivation, then, resulted from the intrinsic pleasure they found in dancing, from teachers' praise, from identity as dancers and community with their peers, and from encouragement by their families. The most significant aspect of this motivation is that it comes from within the kids, and that the carrot is more important than the stick: it is, indeed, a big bunch of carrots that allow them to tolerate the occasional stick. What that stick was was a clear message from teachers and parents that without doing what they were supposed to do, they would not get what they wanted. I did hear teachers criticize students in class. Occasionally, I could tell that even the best teacher was in a thoroughly cranky mood, and I did learn once or twice that a particular student found a particular teacher unduly harsh. I heard one teacher hassle a student repeatedly throughout a class because the student had forgotten her shoes, and by the end of the class I was spent myself and thought once would have been enough. But I did not ever hear a teacher say to a student, "You are untalented," or "You will never be a dancer." What I heard—in all sorts of variations—was "You will never be a dancer *unless . . .*" which was a different story entirely. When criticism got tough, it was usually leveled at a group of students as a whole, rather than at a particular individual.

Can we expect to see many of these children as company members in the Alvin Ailey American Dance Theater's winter season in, say, 2007, or indeed in any other major dance venue? When Linda Hamilton and several colleagues studied forty teenage students at the SAB, they reported that more than half of their sample group dropped out of the profession during adolescence and only 15 percent were ultimately accepted into a national ballet company.[6] The Ailey School's Junior Division does not do follow-up studies on its alumni. When I asked Troy Powell, now in his early thirties, how many of his classmates at LaGuardia and Ailey had continued as dancers, he laughed and said, "One percent." Statistically speaking, the prospects would not be good for high-school-age dancers, not because they lack talent but because life interferes. But even if they don't make a career as dancers, these students have acquired a set of values—diligence, professionalism, cooperation—which will stand them in good stead, whatever they do. Do they adhere to them perfectly? Not always, but they know what they should be doing and why.

It is fair to ask to what extent the kids were telling me the truth when I interviewed them: it is a question I certainly asked myself from time to time. While some teenagers were more reflective or verbal than others, when my year at Ailey ended, I felt they had been as honest and candid as the adult subjects I have interviewed over a long career in journalism. Dancers—whatever their age—are not used to being asked their opinions or why they do things, and this was both a plus and a minus for me. They seemed to enjoy and be flattered by the novelty of this experience, and I was clearly asking things they had not considered before. They were thinking, as it were, on their feet. I didn't move in with them, as some reporters do with their subjects. I took them aside in some quiet place at Ailey, and in a couple of cases visited students at home or met them elsewhere. They didn't cry or vent anger or do anything dramatic in my presence. But when I asked a question, I generally got a credible answer. Occasionally, they sounded a bit too virtuous to be real, but at those times they were—as Melanie Person had suggested to me when the Supremes discussed the possibilities of competition with one another—describing an ideal reaction to a situation they had not yet encountered.

Many journalists have talked of the inherent conflict between the reporter—who tries to get subjects to let down their guard and say something juicy—and the subjects, who may be moved by the blandishments of the journalist to speak injudiciously, but who try, on the other hand, to present themselves in the best possible light. While this conflict will never quite go away, it was no more present when I talked with Ailey students than when I talked with Ailey teachers. The kids, it seemed, knew how to take care of themselves. I was particularly impressed by a seventeen-year-old Ailey student I met when I began my research (she went off to college as the book year began). She said she'd be glad to spend some time with me, because she expected to be interviewed many times in her dance career and she thought she ought to get some practice.

What really stood out for me was the Ailey adults (the La-Guardia dance teachers I met seemed every bit as good, and certainly touched their students, but I spent less time with them).

As we have seen, the adults at Ailey—both teachers and company members—knowingly served as models for the students: not only through things they said in class but through conversations with kids who sought them out, they evoked their own experiences in the dance world. In class, they taught from a deep practical knowledge of their subject and their own convictions about what was important (high school teachers of academic subjects, of course, may be at a disadvantage relative to teachers in the arts for not having *performed* in the same way, and thus are models only for future high school teachers). In each different technique a dance class covers the same territory as have similar classes for many years, but each teacher also puts his or her own distinctive stamp on it. This sustains interest among the students, and gives them a sense that they may do the same in their turn. Instruction by the best dance teachers (like that by the best violin or voice teachers) is not canned. It is emphatically personal, and I agree with Csikszentmihalyi that this is one thing that hooks the kids.

They cared about the kids. They felt rewarded when students did well and frustrated when they didn't. This emotion was in their voices when we talked. I once asked an accompanist, David Finkelstein, who has played in schools all over the city for the past twenty-odd years, what impressed him about Ailey, and he said that teachers in the lounge talked among one another about the kids. At the same time, except for those teachers who were administratively engaged and had met the parents, they tended to know less about the kids' outside lives than I did, because it was my job to learn about them and not part of the teachers' jobs; a sense of boundaries, it seems, is necessary to go on as a successful teacher without being overwhelmed by individual students' life stories. In the field of performing arts this is particularly important, because none of the choreographers for whom the students will audition will care about the dancers' personal discomforts or tragedies; within reason it is realistic to encourage students toward stoicism. Litvinova once told me she always kept it in mind that the teenagers had outside lives which might be affecting their behavior on a given day, and other teachers were conscious of that, too. But it was not their turf.

What did I learn during the year about the training of dancers—and of talented students in general—that might have broader application to the way we educate and socialize all teenagers? I came to the same conclusions as Csikszentmihalyi and his colleagues, who observe that adults "commonly fault adolescents for what they perceive as laziness, lack of discipline, and a counterproductive defiance of authority. But what came through clearly in our study was an avid willingness to accept challenges and overcome obstacles when the problems were interesting and the necessary skills were within the individual's reach."[7]

Given a sense of ownership for the activity, it's amazing how hard kids will work.

There are, surely, many downsides to a life in the performing arts, with which readers are presumably familiar; I have touched on some of them in other chapters, and to examine them all would be beyond the scope of this book. It is relevant, however, to point out the risks that stood out clearly to me as I came to know a group of teenagers training to be dancers.

The first, clearly, is a necessary preoccupation with the look of one's body, and the depression that can result when one thinks the look doesn't measure up. At the same time, vanity among these dancers was different from the kind I would see in the Sunday style pages of local papers and in articles about ordinary teenagers concerned about buying the coolest expensive clothes. Among these teenagers there was very little consumer vanity, and classmates who couldn't afford fancy leotards or other clothing were not ostracized. The clothes the kids wore were fairly simple.

The second is the probable exposure to constant rejection, should one pursue a career in this field. In all the arts, thick skins are needed—and not always adequately developed.

Teenagers who build their lives around their artistic talent tend not to be doing what are commonly called the tasks of adolescence—testing authority, experimenting with different identities and interests, exploring their sexuality: instead they may be trying to please authority, locking themselves into one identity, and avoiding their sexuality. Provided they do some of these things a few years later, none of this may be a bad thing (it certainly pleases their parents): they will approach youthful experimenting with a bit more maturity. In some ways, these teens grow up faster than their peers, learning to take responsibility, defer gratification, and make adult-level decisions about how to spend their time. In other ways, they mature rather slowly.

Having once been a parent of teenagers myself, I wished the kids would get more sleep, not on the benches in the corridor at Ailey or in the sofas in the student lounge, but in their own beds.

Those are the negatives.

One Saturday afternoon, shortly before *Revelations,* I sat with Magalie and Mike Massiah, wrapping things up. How did they summarize the year, and what did they especially want me to know? At the end of our conversation, Mike said, "I talk to other parents and when they tell me about their teenage kids, I basically say I'm blessed, because [the kids at Ailey] have this as an important part of their lives. They have a social environment that's healthy and creative—it occupies a great deal of their time. They don't get a chance to get into mischief, so from a parent's point of view it's been a blessing to have dance in [Monique's] life and I only see good things about it. Given everything that goes on in our lives today, these kids have a touchstone. They see accomplishment and they see a sense of progress. They have a support system from the teachers that give them the extra skills. They get it from each other—they get the team concepts worked out. It's really a luxury for a parent to have kids involved in a focused activity."

In the end, I, too, think the dancers and their parents are lucky. Obviously, to be aware of having a talent reinforces self-respect. But a cozy experience does not in itself shape character. What does is the knowledge that having a talent is the beginning, not the end, of being an impressive human being. What matters is the hard work one pursues to develop that talent, and therefore, the opportunity one is given to continue working hard.

Epilogue

Summer/Fall 2003

All of last year's seniors are pursuing their dance careers. Brian Brown, the first to join a professional company, will soon go off on a European tour with Gus Giordano Jazz Dance Chicago. The newest and youngest member of this forty-year-old troupe, he performs under his new name, Bryant Williams, which he adopted during the past year to celebrate going into the professional world full-time. He had never liked his old name, he says, and so he modified it, adding a "t" to his first name and an "s" to his middle name and dropping off the last name entirely. Under his old name, Brian was profiled last February in *Dance Spirit* magazine, in a column that introduces young dancers starting their careers.

Last fall, Brian wanted to stay in New York and continue

studying at Ailey, but couldn't afford it. He spent the fall shuttling between San Francisco (where he danced briefly with a small ballet company), Maryland, and New York, and in January settled down in a small town in Maryland where he lived with his father and sister and taught dance to teenagers slightly younger than himself at a school operated by a friend. He became closer to his family there. Despite a persistent belief that college would be beneficial to his son, Stephen Brown expresses respect for Brian's achievements in dance and his efforts to make a life in a city as economically demanding as New York. In the spring, Brian learned about Giordano, which was holding auditions in Chicago. His father financed the plane ticket, and Brian competed with 150 women and 14 other men. He was the only one hired for Giordano's first company, and felt particularly bolstered by the strong references he then received from Jefferson and Inman.

When he taught young dancers, Brian says, he adopted Dwana Smallwood's tactic of sometimes leaving the room to let them figure out combinations on their own. "The dancers work much better when I'm not watching," he says. While he finds it counterproductive to think too much about places where he can't be, he admits he misses Ailey and believes it shaped him as a dancer and a person.

Afra Hines has decided, for now, to take her dancing in commercial directions. She felt ambivalent all year, and as late as June seriously considered sending in her deposit to enroll in the Ailey-Fordham BFA program. But now she has given up her Fordham spot.

All through the year, Afra had got small commercial gigs—not quite as much as she'd hoped for, but still, she says, "something," and worth continuing further. In March she was one of two dancers surrounded by actors in the cast of an Equity showcase production that ran six nights a week for three weeks and was reviewed online and in *TimeOut New York*. She says it was exciting to be onstage throughout the play.

Afra's goal has always been to earn a living as a dancer, and in pursuing that goal she has been willing to work everywhere, including sports events and children's parties. A dance career "takes perseverance as much as talent," she says.

Her current commercial bent seems more a thing-of-the-moment, however. She would still like to be in Ailey II some day. At graduation she had been eager to go off on her own, but by midyear found herself missing the old place, and took some classes there. The showcase rehearsals made independent study difficult, however, and soon Afra vanished from the Ailey studios. "Afra has always been a free spirit," Comendador told me.

Afra lives with her mother—who took the pictures of her that appear in this book—and has made peace with her father.

Travis Magee has gone in an entirely opposite direction. He is happily settled at the Boston Conservatory, where he danced in productions in the fall and in the spring. The first was pure classical, a Bournonville ballet in which he danced a solo ("the hardest thing I've ever had to do," he says), and received a mention in the *Boston Herald*'s review of the ballet. Then he got into a modern piece in the spring.

Travis feels his dancing has improved tremendously. Ailey, he says, gave him great technique, and now the Boston Conservatory is helping him use it. The environment has offered him a fresh start. Travis recognized rather quickly, he reports, that he wasn't going to be the best male dancer in the class: there was one boy he knew was better. But Travis didn't want to be passed over, so he "worked twice as hard, came in early, and never goofed off." His success in school auditions proved that hard work pays. In retrospect, Travis says, "I didn't work that hard in high school." He is grateful for the time he spent at Ailey, and still goes back to visit four of his teachers. The setbacks he encountered during his senior year, he now understands, helped him grow. He feels he can do just about anything.

This year, Travis has been dedicated to dance and has had very little time for photography.

Beatrice Capote has also had new adventures in college. At the North Carolina School of the Arts, she said, the dance is loose and cool, not fast like Ailey's: this is making her more versatile. "They are very grounded in pure modern dance—Limón and Graham," she says, "where Ailey was a mix of ballet and modern." She has also experimented with choreography and liked it.

The atmosphere in North Carolina is more slow paced, Beatrice says. Social adjustment was not hard, because "everyone is very polite—they all introduced themselves to me—and my friends are dancers like the kids at Ailey." She did feel hemmed in by the triple dorm room she had been assigned, and switched to a single. After a bit of coaching, she learned to handle the academics.

Weight has continued to be a problem for Beatrice. During this first year of managing her own nutrition, she put on what is known outside the dance world as "the freshman fifteen." She says it was horrible for her whole family to see her that way; it came, she says, from "adjusting to being independent, and going from being a little girl to being a woman." Now she has lost the weight and is less dependent on her mother.

She has thought about Ailey and how much she misses it, despite the fun she's having. She misses her Horton technique, and the comfortable feeling that the teachers know her and are "like family." Here, she says, they're just getting to know her.

Beatrice wants a dance career, doing choreography and teaching. And she believes that "if one door closes, another will always open."

This fall Shamel Pitts is a freshman with a scholarship at Juilliard, after an exceptional senior year in high school. During the first term he was back at Ailey, and once again he danced with the First Company in *Memoria* ("with a better part," he says). In the fall, he sent in his ARTS tape and, along with Roger Prince, the long and lithe classmate who had danced in *Revelations* the previous spring, and Alanna Morris, the girl who had left Ailey to maintain her academic grades, was one of six LaGuardia students to go down to Florida; an Ailey-sponsored PPAS boy who wasn't in the group during my time at Ailey also won, and while the LaGuardia dancers had not been directly sponsored by Ailey, some of Shamel's and Roger's glory rubbed off on the school. In Florida, Shamel especially enjoyed meeting dancers from around the country and artists in other fields, all of them bound together, he says, "by a common love for art." He and Alanna won Level I awards and were semifinalists for the Presidential Scholarship.

During the spring term, Shamel once again had to leave Ailey because of conflicts with the LaGuardia senior concert. He appeared at the studios on many Saturdays, however, dropping off his little sister, who now studies there.

Four LaGuardia dancers—Shamel, Roger, Alanna, and Adam Barruch, another promising student who had left Ailey because of the pressure—are starting Juilliard this year: Shamel and Adam are rooming together. Although Shamel is a New Yorker, he is still having new experiences through Juilliard, he says: he has seen *The Lion King* and is going to the Metropolitan Museum. He cannot quite believe all this—that after the grief of his junior year so many good things have happened to him.

While Shamel and Roger had regarded Ailey as a second home, the rest of that group of mostly LaGuardia boys who electrified the school *en masse* during the year I spent there never felt the same bond, and did not return: seeking to sample more of the city's diverse riches, they went to different after-school dance programs. Serge Desroches, Ryan Rankine, and Nigel Campbell were all gone. I saw Ryan and Nigel dance at a Creative Outlet concert over the summer. They were as explosive as ever, and more grown-up.

The Supremes are not quite as tight a threesome as they used to be. Monique has done particularly well, dancing along with Shamel in the First Company's production of *Memoria* and winning featured parts in other repertories during the year. But Monique pulled a ligament and was benched for more than a month. Still, she has decided she can't give up dance for accounting and finance, and is looking at universities that offer both business school and dance programs. She likes to be onstage. At the same time, Monique says she is too fearful of rejection to try for ARTS next year (a statement we might take with a little skepticism). She, too, will have conflicting obligations to LaGuardia and Ailey next year but reports that Inman is helping her set up a schedule that will get around them.

Laurence found this past year rather slow. She didn't do any repertories and, like Monique, was sidelined for a month with an ankle injury. While she definitely wants to be a dancer, Laurence is more concerned than before about injury and is thinking about a backup major in business. She says she has become more focused and hardworking in both dance and academics, with better grades and a more ready acceptance of corrections. But Ailey, she says, was "funner" last year, with all the boys lending their energy to the scene; this year there were "too many females."

She says it takes "determination and patience" to make it as a dancer. If some good professional opportunity turned up, she would probably take it and go to school later. She says she doesn't want to go to Fordham. She's been at Ailey a long time, and needs a change.

Only two Supremes remain at Ailey. Late in the school year, Frajan left after an argument with a guest choreographer which, in its final stage, brought in her mother. Frajan had a part in a repertory workshop but had developed shin splints. She missed several days of rehearsals and could not go *en pointe* when she came back. The choreographer, she says, insisted that she mark— that is, walk through the steps—instead of sitting on the side-lines. Frajan felt he had embarrassed her in front of the class. Yvonne Payne came in and told Inman, forcefully, that the choreographer should not have spoken so sharply to Frajan. Inman had a talk with Frajan, during which time she told him she wanted to be a lawyer, not a dancer. Frajan says Inman "tried," but felt in general that the faculty had not taken her part. "Mr. Inman didn't tell the choreographer not to talk to me that way," she says.

At the same time, Frajan says being at Ailey has been a good experience and that going there for extra training has given her an advantage over others. She is still dancing at LaGuardia, and wants to compete in ARTS. But she has had enough of Ailey and doesn't plan to go back. Certainly, it had been clear during the previous year that Frajan was ready to leave, and perhaps this incident gave her a good opportunity.

At the end of the 2002 school year, after months and months of deliberation, Franco De Vita finally decided to accept a most attractive offer from a friend who runs the Boston Ballet School. He has been teaching there for a year, but returned to Ailey for two weeks during the summer (during another three weeks in the summer season, he taught a class at Boston Ballet which Travis attended). He also held some classes for Ailey's First Company when it visited Boston in the spring.

He considers his time at The Ailey School one of the highlights of his career, citing the "discipline, professionalism, and most important, the great atmosphere." He says, "If things work out, I hope to return there."

The rest of Ailey's faculty is still on the job. During the summer session I stopped by. The scene looked just the same, but when I checked out the group of students, I could not find a familiar face.

As for my friend Genie, the violin prodigy who, at least partly, inspired this book, when she got to Juilliard so many years ago, she fell in love with the sound of the oboe and changed instruments. She also fell in love with a French horn player, and after graduation the two of them got jobs in a symphony orchestra in Canada. But some fifteen years later, they lost these jobs in a labor dispute and Genie, who by then had four children, gave up being a professional musician. Now a Canadian citizen, she occasionally visits New York and walks wistfully around Lincoln Center. She may, perhaps, pick up the violin again, as an amateur. Or she may not.

In December 2003, as this book was going to press, Tatiana Litvinova died of cancer. I learned that during the year I spent at Ailey she had been undergoing chemotherapy. To this outsider who sat watching her classes once or twice a week, there was no indication of this: what I saw was her vigor, her joy in dancing, and her passion for transmitting her knowledge to the students she cared so much about. The school will feel her loss.

Notes

CHAPTER ONE: THE AILEY WORLD

1. Abby Goodnough, "Post 9/11 Pain Found to Linger in Young Minds," *The New York Times,* May 2, 2002, pp. A1, B4.

CHAPTER TWO: STARTING THE YEAR

1. I have drawn on two books for this description: V. Kostrovitskaya and A. Pisarev. *School of Classical Dance* (textbook of the Vaganova Choreographic School, Leningrad), trans. John Barker. Moscow: Progress, 1978, and Leo Kersley, and Janet Sinclair. *A Dictionary of Ballet Terms,* 3rd rev. ed. New York: Da Capo Press, 1979, p. 87.

2. Kersley and Sinclair, p. 87.

3. Marjorie B. Perces, Ana Marie Forsythe, and Cheryl Bell. *The Dance Technique of Lester Horton.* Pennington, N.J.: Princeton Book Co., 1992.

4. Howard Gardner. *Frames of Mind: The Theory of Multiple Intelligences.* Tenth anniversary edition. New York: Basic Books, 1993. p. x.

5. Ibid., p. xx.

6. Trevor Hugh James Marchand. *Minaret Building and Apprenticeship in Yemen.* Richmond, England: Curzon Press, 2001, p. 74.

7. Ibid., p. 157.

8. Ibid., p. 236 (italics are Marchand's).

9. Joseph Walters and Howard Gardner, "The crystallizing experience: discovering an intellectual gift," in Robert J. Sternberg and Janet L. Davidson (eds.), *Conceptions of Giftedness.* Cambridge: Cambridge University Press, 1986, pp. 306–331.

10. Ibid., p. 326.

CHAPTER THREE: FAMILIES

1. Benjamin S. Bloom, ed., *Developing Talent in Young People,* New York: Ballantine Books, 1985.

2. Bloom, p. 3

CHAPTER FOUR: BUILDING AN ENSEMBLE

1. For example, in *The New York Times Magazine,* February 24, 2002, Margaret Talbot wrote a cover story profiling the psychologist Rosalind Wiseman: "Girls Just Want to Be Mean." Besides Wiseman's then forthcoming book, the article mentioned three others on cruelty among girls. Soon afterward, *Nightline* host Ted Koppel

devoted a program to interviewing a group of teenage girls on the subject.

2. The population of New York City is 35 percent white and 24.5 percent non-Hispanic black. In both the city and the public school system (though not in LaGuardia), Hispanics outnumber blacks. My terminology is that of both the New York City Department of City Planning and the New York City Board of Education.

CHAPTER FIVE: THE SORCERERS' APPRENTICES

1. Mihaly Csikszentmihalyi, Kevin Rathunde, and Samuel Whalen. *Talented Teenagers: The Roots of Success & Failure* (Cambridge: Cambridge University Press, 1993).
2. Ibid., p. 84.
3. Ibid., p. 177ff.

CHAPTER SIX: THE WINTER OF OUR DISCONTENT

1. Judith Lynne Hanna. *To Dance Is Human* (Chicago and London: The University of Chicago Press, 1987), pp 132–33.
2. Linda H. Hamilton, Ph. D., William G., Hamilton, M.D., Michelle P. Warren, M.D., Katy Keller, P.T., and Marika Molnar, P.T., "Factors Contributing to the Attrition Rate in Elite Ballet Students,"*Journal of Dance Medicine & Science,* 1, no. 4 (1997), pp. 134–38.
3. Linda H. Hamilton, J. Brooks-Gunn, Ph.D., Michelle P. Warren, M.D., and William G. Hamilton, M.D., "The Impact of Thinness and Dieting on the Professional Ballet Dancer," *The Journal of the Canadian Association for Health, Physical Education and Recreation,* 52, no. 4 (1986), pp. 117–22.

4. In a national study Hamilton found that only 23 percent of female dancers and 33 percent of male dancers were happy with their bodies: Linda Hamilton, Ph.D., "A Psychological Profile of the Adolescent Dancer," *Journal of Dance Medicine & Science,* 3, no. 2 (1999).

CHAPTER SEVEN: WHERE'S SHAMEL?

1. Ramsay Burt, "The Trouble with the Male Dancer," in Dils and Albright, *Moving History/Dancing Cultures* (Middletown, Conn.: Wesleyan University Press, 2001), p. 50.

2. Linda H. Hamilton, William G. Hamilton, M.D., James D. Meltzer, Ph.D, Peter Marshall, and Marika Molnar, "Personality, Stress, and Injuries in Professional Ballet Dancers," *The American Journal of Sports Medicine,* 17, no. 2, (1989), pp. 263–67.

3. Csikszentmihalyi, Rathunde, and Whalen, *Talented Teenagers,* p. 74.

CHAPTER TEN: *REVELATIONS*

1. Jennifer Dunning, "The House that Alvin, of All People, Built," *The New York Times,* April 6, 2003.

CHAPTER ELEVEN: IN CONCLUSION

1. Csikszentmihalyi, Rathunde, and Whalen, *Talented Teenagers* pp. 32–3.

2. Stella Chess and Alexander Thomas, *Origins and Evolution of Behavior Disorders: From Infancy to Early Adult Life* (Cambridge, Mass.: Harvard University Press, 1988). I also described the study in an earlier book: Katharine Davis Fishman, *Behind the One-Way Mirror: Psychotherapy and Children* (New York: Bantam, 1995).

3. Shirley Brice Heath and Milbrey W. McLaughlin, eds., *Identity and Inner-City Youth: Beyond Ethnicity and Gender* (New York: Teachers College Press, 1993), pp. 69–91.

4. See also Judith Lynne Hanna, *To Dance Is Human* (Chicago: University of Chicago Press, 1987), *passim.*

5. Ibid., p. 154.

6. Linda Hamilton, et. al., "Factors Contributing to the Attrition Rate in Elite Ballet Students," *Journal of Dance Medicine & Science,* 1, no. 4 (1997).

7. Ibid., pp. 186–87.

Bibliography

DANCE

Books

de Mille, Agnes. *Martha: The Life and Work of Martha Graham.* New York: Vintage Books, 1992.

Dils, Ann, and Ann Cooper Albright, eds. *Moving History/Dancing Cultures: A Dance History Reader.* Middletown, Conn.: Wesleyan University Press, 2001. The following articles were particularly helpful:

Ann Cooper Albright. "Embodying History: Epic Narrative and Cultural Identity in African American Dance."

Kariamu Welsh Asante. "Commonalties in African Dance: An Aesthetic Foundation."

Ramsay Burt. "The Trouble with the Male Dancer . . ."

Thomas DeFrantz. "Simmering Passivity: The Black Male Body in Concert Dance."

Lynn Garafola. "The Travesty Dancer in Nineteenth-Century Ballet."

Marcia B. Siegel. "The Harsh and Splendid Heroines of Martha Graham."

Dunning, Jennifer. *Alvin Ailey: A Life in Dance.* New York: Da Capo Press, 1998.

Graham, Martha. *Blood Memory: An Autobiography.* New York: Washington Square Press, 1992.

Grant, Gail. *Technical Manual and Dictionary of Classical Ballet,* 3rd rev. ed. New York: Dover Publications, 1982.

Hanna, Judith Lynne. *To Dance Is Human: A Theory of Nonverbal Communication.* Chicago: The University of Chicago Press, 1987.

Jamison, Judith, with Howard Kaplan. *Dancing Spirit: An Autobiography.* New York: Doubleday, 1993.

Kersley, Leo, and Janet Sinclair. *A Dictionary of Ballet Terms,* 3rd rev. ed. New York: Da Capo Press, 1979.

Kostrovitskaya, V,. and A. Pisarev. *School of Classical Dance* (textbook of the Vaganova Choreographic School, Leningrad), trans. John Barker. Moscow: Progress, 1978.

Perces, Marjorie B., Ana Marie Forsythe, and Cheryl Bell. *The Dance Technique of Lester Horton.* Pennington, N.J.: Princeton Book Co., 1992.

Videos

Four by Ailey: An Evening with the Alvin Ailey American Dance Theatre. RM Arts, 1986.

Great Performances: Dance in America: Free to Dance. Programs 1–3. Thirteen/WNET, New York, 2001.

A Hymn for Alvin Ailey. (*Great Performances*). Produced and directed by

Orlando Bagwell; choreographed by Judith Jamison; text conceived, written, and performed by Anna Deveare Smith. Channel Thirteen/WNET, New York, 1999.

PSYCHOLOGY, SOCIOLOGY, AND ANTHROPOLOGY

Books

Bloom, Benjamin, ed., and Lauren A. Sosniak, Kathryn D. Sloane, Anthony G. Kalinowski, William C. Gustin, and Judith A. Monsaas, contributors. *Developing Talent in Young People.* New York, Ballantine, 1985.

Csikszentmihalyi, Mihaly, and Reed Larson. *Being Adolescent.* New York: Basic Books, 1984.

Csikszentmihalyi, Mihaly, Kevin Rathunde, and Samuel Whalen, with contributions by Maria Wong. *Talented Teenagers: The Roots of Success and Failure.* New York, Cambridge University Press, 1993.

Csikszentmihalyi, Mihaly, and Barbara Schneider. *Becoming Adult.* New York: Basic Books, 2000.

Feldman, David Henry, with Lynn Goldsmith. *Nature's Gambit: Child Prodigies and the Development of Human Potential.* New York: Basic Books, 1986.

Fishman, Katharine Davis. *Behind the One-Way Mirror: Psychotherapy and Children.* New York: Bantam, 1995.

Gardner, Howard. *Creating Minds: An Anatomy of Creativity Seen Through the Lives of Freud, Einstein, Picasso, Stravinsky, Eliot, Graham, and Gandhi.* New York: Basic Books, 1993.

———. *Frames of Mind: The Theory of Multiple Intelligences.* Tenth anniversary edition. New York: Basic Books, 1993.

Hamilton, Linda H. *The Person Behind The Mask: A Guide to Performing Arts Psychology.* Greenwich, Conn.: Ablex, 1997.

Heath, Shirley Brice, and Milbrey W. McLaughlin, eds. *Identity and Inner-City Youth.* New York: Teachers College Press, 1993.

Leadbeater, Bonnie J. Ross, and Niobe Way, eds. *Urban Girls: Resisting Stereotypes, Creating Identities.* New York: New York University Press, 1996.

Marchand, Trevor Hugh James. *Minaret Building and Apprenticeship in Yemen.* Richmond, England: Curzon Press, 2001.

Radford, John. *Child Prodigies and Exceptional Early Achievers.* New York: The Free Press, 1990.

MAGAZINE AND NEWSPAPER ARTICLES

Anderson, Jack. "Upward, Downward, and Upward Again: The Ailey Toasts a New Season." *The New York Times,* December 1, 2000.

Bloom, Marc. "Among Runners, Elite Girls Face Burnout and Injury." *The New York Times,* April 20, 2003.

Dunning, Jennifer. "The House That Alvin, of All People, Built." *The New York Times,* April 6, 2003.

―――. "Measuring Up for Ballet Class." Dance Notes, *The New York Times,* January 13, 2001.

―――. "Saluting the Ailey Junior Troupe." *The New York Times,"* December 9, 2000.

Gardner, Howard. "Test for Aptitude, Not for Speed." *The New York Times,* July 18, 2002.

Gladstone, Valerie. "The Long Shadow of Ailey's Great 'Cry.'" *The New York Times,* November 26, 2000.

Gladwell, Malcolm. "The Physical Genius." *The New Yorker,* August 2, 1999.

Gold, Sylviane. "Poise, Power, Passion." *Newsday,* December 1, 2000.

―――. "Rocking the Soul." *Newsday,* November 30, 2001.

Goodnough, Abby. "Post 9/11 Pain Found to Linger in Young Minds." *The New York Times,* May 2, 2002.

Gross, Jane. "Getting In: Preparing Applications, Fine-Tuning Applicants." *The New York Times,* May 6, 2002.

Gross, Jane, "Getting In: At Last, Colleges Answer, and New Questions Arise." *The New York Times,* May 7, 2002.

Hamilton, Linda H., Ph.D. "A Psychological Profile of the Adolescent Dancer." *Journal of Dance Medicine & Science,* 3, no. 2 (1999).

Hamilton, Linda H., J. Brooks-Gunn, Ph.D., Michelle P. Warren, M.D., and William G. Hamilton, M.D., "The Impact of Thinness and Dieting on the Professional Ballet Dancer." *The Journal of the Canadian Association for Health, Physical Education and Recreation,* 52, vol. 4 (1986).

Hamilton, Linda H., Ph.D., and William G. Hamilton, M.D. "Classical Ballet: Balancing the Costs of Artistry and Athleticism." *Medical Problems of Performing Artists,* 6 (June 1991).

Hamilton, Linda H., Ph.D., and William G. Hamilton, M.D., "Occupational Stress in Classical Ballet: The Impact in Different Cultures." *Medical Problems of Performing Artists,* June 1994.

Hamilton, Linda H., William G. Hamilton, M.D., James D. Meltzer, Ph.D., Peter Marshall, and Marika Molnar. "Personality, Stress and Injuries in Professional Ballet Dancers." *The American Journal of Sports Medicine,* 17, no. 2 (1989).

Hamilton, Linda H., Ph.D., William G. Hamilton, M.D., Michelle P. Warren, M.D., Katy Keller, and Marika Molnar. "Factors Contributing to the Attrition Rate in Elite Ballet Students." *Journal of Dance Medicine and Science,* 1, no. 4 (1997).

Hamilton, Linda H., Ph.D. and George Stricker, Ph.D., "Balanchine's Children." *Medical Problems of Performing Artists,* 4 (December 1989).

Hamilton, William G., M.D., Linda H. Hamilton, Ph.D., Peter Marshall, and Marika Molnar. "A Profile of the Musculoskeletal Characteristics of Elite Professional Ballet Dancers." *The American Journal of Sports Medicine,* 20, no. 3 (1992).

Hartocollis, Anemona. "Clinton Fulfills a Request at Graduation." *The New York Times,* June 27, 2001.

Homans, Jennifer. "The Day Is Past and Gone." *The New Republic,* April 22, 2002.

Leivick, Laura. "Their Future in the Balance, They Dance for High Stakes." *The New York Times,* May 27, 2001.

Ojofeitimi, Sheyi, and Shaw Bronner. "The State of Research in Dance Medicine," from Soar Research, Long Island University, Brooklyn, N.Y.

Powers, Ron. "The Apocalypse of Adolescence." *The Atlantic Monthly,* March 2002.

Solomon, Becca, and Howard Gardner. "Getting Kids, Parents, and Coaches on the Same Page." Good Work Project Report Series, no. 15, Project Zero, Harvard University, 2001.

"Stars of Stage, Screen . . . and Social Studies Class." *The New York Times,* January 1, 1999.

Talbot, Margaret. "Girls Just Want to Be Mean." *The New York Times Magazine,* February 24, 2002.

"Ten Hot High Schools." *New York,* April 13, 1998.

Yaqub, Reshma Memon. "Getting Inside the Ivy Gates." *Worth,* September 2002.

Acknowledgments

Without the willingness of Brian Brown, Beatrice Capote, Afra Hines, Laurence Jacques, Travis Magee, Monique Massiah, Frajan Payne, and Shamel Pitts and their families to make time and space for me in their crowded and hectic lives, this book would not exist, and they have my deepest gratitude—for the enlightenment, the intellectual challenge, and the fun of getting to know them. I am similarly grateful, in almost equal measure, to the administration, faculty, and staff of The Ailey School and various members of its parent organization, the Alvin Ailey American Dance Theater, for letting me in, for generously granting me a portion of their scarce and precious time and space, and for providing me with an immensely pleasurable education.

Many other Ailey students took time to talk with me, and their experiences have also contributed to the book. Linda Hamilton, the psychologist at Ailey, Brenda Schwartz, the nutritionist, and Shaw Bronner, the physical therapist, supplied helpful insights into their specialties.

The faculty and administration of the Fiorello H. LaGuardia High School of Music and Art and Performing Arts—particularly the dance department—have also been generous and helpful, sitting for interviews and letting me watch classes and talk with students during school hours. I am grateful to the Professional Performing Arts School and the Professional Children's School for interviews. Howard Gardner and his colleagues at Harvard Project Zero shared research and answered questions; Trevor H.J. Marchand took time from an active schedule of academics and fieldwork to reply to several long e-mail questions.

Many of the scholarly books and papers I have discussed here were the work of several authors, and they are all credited in the Bibliography and Notes. In the text, however, to avoid unwieldiness, I have tended to cite one author, either the best-known member of the group or the one whose specialty is most relevant to a given topic. I do want to acknowledge and highlight the important though sometimes unsung contributions of able, hardworking coauthors.

I am grateful to Arthur Abelman, Elena Comendador, Penny Frank, and Genevieve Young for miscellaneous favors. Barbara Frank supplied skillful and dependable tape transcription, as she has in the past.

At Jeremy P. Tarcher/Penguin, my editor, Sara Carder, made intelligent suggestions, and her assistant, Ashley Shelby, gave administrative help. Jill Newman was a sharp and knowledgeable copy editor. I am also grateful to Wendy Hubbert, who first signed up the book for Tarcher.

Immeasurable thanks go to Paul Cirone, the agent every writer dreams of: smart, energetic, enthusiastic, supportive, and eminently sensible—a man for all seasons. His colleagues, Molly Friedrich and Frances Jalet Miller, also provided good advice.

Finally, as always, I am grateful to Joe, Maggie, and Nancy Fishman and Yiftach Resheff, for the good cheer, love, support, wisdom, accommodation, and diversion that the best of families provide.

Index

Italics indicate illustrations.

About the Author

Katharine Davis Fishman is the author of two previous books, *Behind the One-Way Mirror: Psychotherapy and Children,* and *The Computer Establishment.* She has written for *The Atlantic Monthly, New York, Town & Country, Lingua Franca,* and numerous other magazines. A member of PEN and a past president of the American Society of Journalists and Authors, Fishman lives in Brooklyn, New York.